Top Class Competitors

Top Class Competitors

How nations, firms, and individuals succeed in the new world of competitiveness

Stephane Garelli

John Wiley & Sons, Ltd

Other Wiley Editorial Offices

John Wiley & Sons Inc., 111 River Street, Hoboken, NJ 07030, USA

Jossey-Bass, 989 Market Street, San Francisco, CA 94103-1741, USA

Wiley-VCH Verlag GmbH, Boschstr. 12, D-69469 Weinheim, Germany

John Wiley & Sons Australia Ltd, 42 McDougall Street, Milton, Queensland 4064, Australia

John Wiley & Sons (Asia) Pte Ltd, 2 Clementi Loop #02–01, Jin Xing Distripark, Singapore 129809

John Wiley & Sons Canada Ltd, 22 Worcester Road, Etobicoke, Ontario, Canada M9W 1L1

Wiley also publishes its books in a variety of electronic formats. Some content that appears in print may not be available in electronic books.

Library of Congress Cataloging-in-Publication Data

Garelli, Stéphane.
    Top class competitors : how nations, firms, and individuals succeed in the new world of competitiveness / Stéphane Garelli.
      p. cm.
    Includes bibliographical references and index.
    ISBN-13: 978-0-470-02569-7 (cloth : alk. paper)
    ISBN-10: 0-470-02569-7 (cloth : alk. paper)
  1. Competition. 2. Work. 3. Values. 4. Performance. 5. Economic development. I. Title.
    HD41.G37 2006
    302′.14 – dc22

                                  2005034529

British Library Cataloguing in Publication Data

A catalogue record for this book is available from the British Library

ISBN 13 978-0-470-02569-7 (HB)
ISBN 10 0-470-02569-7 (HB)

Typeset in 10/12pt Garamond by SNP Best-set Typesetter Ltd., Hong Kong
Printed and bound in Great Britain by TJ International Ltd, Padstow, Cornwall, UK
This book is printed on acid-free paper responsibly manufactured from sustainable forestry in which at least two trees are planted for each one used for paper production.

To my son Stéphane:
he makes me set ambitious goals . . .

Contents

Acknowledgements

I have been studying, researching, and teaching competitiveness in one way or another for more than twenty-five years now. The decision to write a book seemed like a logical progression on my journey through competitiveness. Yet, undertaking this work was a daunting task. There have been moments of doubt and solitude, but also moments of intense intellectual satisfaction and excitement as writing progressed.

During my voyage, I have been able to count on the support of many friends and colleagues, on the insights of students, and on the encounters with entrepreneurs and managers that so often reveal the secrets of competitiveness. Where possible, I have endeavoured to acknowledge my sources of inspiration throughout the book. However, I would like to offer particular thanks to:

- IMD (The International Institute of Management Development), where I have performed most of my research into competitiveness. Professor Peter Lorange has been a very supportive President, and I am very grateful to him. The faculty and staff of the business school have all given me concrete and moral support during the writing of the book; their advice and continuous enthusiasm have kept me going!
- My particular gratitude goes to my colleagues at the IMD World Competitiveness Center, with whom I have developed and tested many of the ideas expressed in this book over the past fifteen years. Without their extraordinary enthusiasm and commitment to developing international awareness on the subject of competitiveness, this work would never have happened.
- I would also like to thank the University of Lausanne – UNIL, who allowed me to teach a new generation of students about competitiveness, and my colleagues at the Ecole des Hautes Etudes Commerciales – HEC for their support.
- During the final stages of writing, I have been able to count on the support of two Research Associates at IMD: Albert Diverse and Mope

Ogunsulire have improved this work significantly, and I have appreciated working with them.

Finally, the support of my family has been essential. I wish to thank:

- My parents, for their love, for the education they gave me, and, in particular, my mother, for her absolute confidence in her son.
- My brother Christian, who has shared his international business experiences with me throughout his career, and my nephew Christian-Stéphane, whose example of resilience and energy in adversity forced me to persist in this project.
- My wife, Josephine, who has believed in me since the day we met. Her presence at my side every step of the way has been invaluable. She read and re-read the manuscript at the different stages of development: her intuitive understanding of what I want to say after 25 years of "talking competitiveness" helped to make some of my more complicated writings understandable.
- My son, Stéphane, who has put up with an "absent Dad" for much of the last three years. He also has supported my work fully, and has provided a couple of provocative ideas of his own, including: "Competitiveness: it is not as bad as it sounds" after reading Mark Twain's remark about the opera of Wagner . . .

To all, profound thanks!

Credits

Prologue

It's hard to believe that the term "competitiveness" was barely recognised only three decades ago! Today, it is one of the most profusely used – and abused – economic terms. Typing *competitiveness* in the Google search engine produces more than 35 000 000 entries. So, although the concept is publicised widely, its definition remains vague. *The New Shorter Oxford English Dictionary on Historical Principles* describes a competitive person as one "with a strong urge to compete . . ." [1]. The verb *compete* implies to "be a rival" or to "bear comparison (*with* another or *in* a quality)", and ultimately to "strive for superiority."

Today, the existence of the term *competitiveness* is generally widely acknowledged, but rarely defined. In this book we will consider competitiveness as a multifaceted concept: touching not only upon quantifiable, economic issues, such as growth rates, but also upon softer, more qualitative considerations, such as the impact of education and value systems.

The ultimate goal of competitiveness is to raise the overall level of prosperity of a nation and its people. Clearly, a nation's primary source of competitiveness is to be found in its enterprises, since that is where economic added value takes place. In turn, the role of government is to ensure a smooth and sustainable flow of economic wealth from enterprises – creation of added value – to citizens, who receive direct revenues or benefit from State services and infrastructure. A nation's overall level of prosperity, as shown in Figure 1, results from the interaction of three forces:

- competitiveness of firms: focused on profitability;
- competitiveness of people: focused on personal wellbeing;
- competitiveness of nations: focused on sustainable prosperity.

The model is systemic – the relationships between the parts of the model are just as important as the parts themselves. When enterprises change

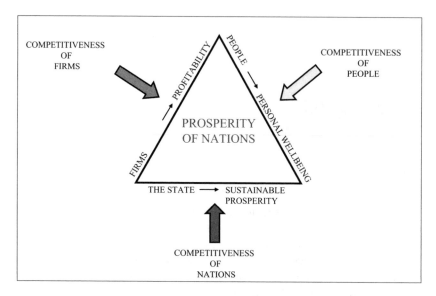

Figure 1 – Competitiveness drives prosperity.

their business models, for example through outsourcing or globalisation, or when people modify their value systems, for example to include greater environmental or ethical sensitivity, the consequences of these actions have an impact throughout the entire system.

At IMD, the World Competitiveness Centre has, for the past two decades, pioneered the study of competitiveness, monitoring developments in the field closely. The Centre publishes the *World Competitiveness Yearbook* [2], a comprehensive analysis, more than 700 pages long, that reports on developments relating to competitiveness in more than 60 nations and economic regions of the world (Figure 2). Some of the findings of the research undertaken by the Centre have shaped the views exposed in this book. My teaching at the University of Lausanne, focused, in particular, on the relationship between the competitiveness of firms and that of nations, has complemented this research significantly.

This book is composed of four sections:

- The first two chapters – *Competitiveness: Changing the Mindset* and *The Long and Winding Road to Competitiveness* – define the concept, and retrace its origins in economic history.
- The next chapter – *Working out National Competitiveness: the Cube Theory* – addresses the notion of competitiveness of nations in particular, and how national competitiveness strategies are designed.

Figure 2 – IMD's *World Competitiveness Yearbook* profiles and ranks the competitiveness of some 60 countries and regions around the world, using more than 300 criteria. The data are accumulated by a worldwide network of 58 partner institutes. The Yearbook has become the most often quoted authoritative source on competitiveness. (Reproduced by permission of IMD.)

- Chapters 4 and 5 – *The Extended Enterprise* and *Competitiveness and Work: A Love–Hate Relationship* – concentrate on the firm at the core of competitiveness, the new business model, and its consequences for company structures.

- Finally, Chapters 6 and 7 – *Competitiveness and Value Systems* and *Competent People and Competitive People: They Are Not The Same* – focus on the competitiveness of individuals.

A very simple observation is at the origin of this book: today, we live in a world where there is ever greater pressure to be competitive. Globalisation and an open world mean that nations, firms, and people confront more competitors than ever before. In addition, technology has redefined the meaning of speed – we now all operate in a real time world.

Competitiveness, like gravity, affects everybody and everything. Some are more affected than others because of their size or position, but competitiveness cannot be avoided – there is no place to hide in this brave new world. Thus, the only alternative is to understand and adapt to competitiveness: what does it mean, how does it work, how does it affect nations, companies, and people? In short, how does competitiveness define the rules for success? The purpose of this book is to address these questions and to provide some answers.

Competitiveness: Changing the Mindset

1

The winter of 1619 was indeed very cold in Bavaria. On November 10th, a young French soldier serving in the army of the Dutch Prince Maurice of Nassau sought refuge in a house that had a large stove, and stayed there meditating all day. René Descartes claimed that when he came out of that house, he had developed half of his philosophical theory. In 1637, Descartes published his *Discourse on Method*, whose second principle reads: "The second [principle] was to divide up each of the difficulties which I examined into as many parts as possible, and as seemed requisite in order that it might be resolved in the best manner possible." [1]

The Cartesian method – splitting mind and matter, subject and object, observer and observed – has become, at least in the West, integral to the way we look at the world. Most of the time we are not even aware of how much the Cartesian method still drives our current modes of thinking. Since Descartes, the fundamental approach employed in understanding any problem relies on one operation: *division.*

Economics and management follow the same logic of dividing things up. Economics itself, as a field of knowledge, is divided into macroeconomics – national income, employment, inflation, money, and trade; microeconomics – the behaviour and decision-making processes of households and firms; and econometrics – measuring economic phenomena. Economists also distinguish between what they can quantify exactly, such as GDP, and what they can only assess, such as the probability of a decision.

Management of a firm follows the same principle of division; a firm can be divided in many ways: business units, functions, and, yes, even divisions. Groups of countries are categorised into divisions of the world called "regions": the Americas, Europe, Middle East, Africa, and Asia.

Markets are split into segments: old and young, rich and poor, status conscious, environmentally concerned, etc. Employees are also divided into groups: line managers, with profit and loss responsibilities, and staff managers, with supporting responsibilities. Finally, strategies also have their own divisions, such as cost leadership, and differentiation. Dividing things up seems to be the preferred pastime in a firm.

The Cartesian method of dividing everything up has thus permeated every field of knowledge, ultimately producing that marvel of modern societies: the expert!

Dividing an issue into smaller parts can be a very effective tool to advance knowledge. However, action requires, at some point, the reconciliation of objectives into a cohesive strategy. This task is mainly the responsibility of senior management in firms, and government leaders in nations. Yet, most of the time, these individuals lack the experience to do so. During a large part of their professional careers, they have been conditioned to succeed in a paradigm of division – not one of integration. For those who find themselves in a position of leadership, the biggest challenge is to integrate multiple layers of objectives into a coherent strategy.

1.1   Managing the totality of competencies

A collection of seemingly divided units and people cannot be managed as a firm. Thus, a firm must build alignment through a shared purpose and value system. The situation with nations is analogous – a nation cannot be run as a simple collection of citizens and institutions. National leadership must convince individuals to join, and rally around, a common cause: the old Roman *res publica* – the public thing.

Prior to the rise of prosperity as a common goal for a nation, leaders were the only unifying factor. These leaders were more inclined to focus on the conquest of lands, the development of power, the increase of their personal wealth, or simply survival, than on the overall prosperity and welfare of all individuals. When the common purpose became *increasing* overall national "prosperity," a new era began. Leaders realised they needed to know which forces were driving the prosperity of their country, and also of their businesses. Those scholars who took it upon themselves to analyse prosperity, determine its drivers, and articulate policies, were thus the original founders of economics – slightly more than two centuries ago.

Economics relies on Cartesian logic. Since its creation, it has remained focused on how a nation develops prosperity by separately analysing trade flows, monetary, fiscal, and budget policies, as well as the decisions made by households and firms. Within their management, firms have adopted a slightly more comprehensive approach to understanding the mechanisms of prosperity. While firms focus on measuring things like market share and financial objectives, management has not been reluctant to include "soft" areas, such as human resources, corporate culture, or patterns in consumer behaviour.

Competitiveness is thus a field of economics that *reconciles* and *integrates* several concepts and theories from economics and management into a series of guiding principles driving the prosperity of a nation or an enterprise. However, the models provided by either economics or management theories rarely touch upon many of the factors that influence prosperity. Such theories often fail to link various elements – such as education, infrastructure, or value systems – with prosperity, even in the presence of evidence that they do make a difference.

The following definition underlines the importance of integrating all the drivers of prosperity, and can thus provide a good starting point for a preliminary understanding of competitiveness:

> *Competitiveness analyses how nations and firms manage the* totality of their competencies *to achieve prosperity or profit.*

In competitiveness, firms play the central role – they generate economic added value. Nations provide the appropriate framework to maximise economic added value. Their responsibility is also to ensure that the results of firms' activities are transformed into tangible signs of prosperity for people. The fate of firms, nations, and people is thus intertwined, and cannot be managed separately.

Competitiveness takes an integrative, holistic approach. Holism is the tendency in nature to produce organised wholes, which are more than the mere sum of the component units. Thus, understanding a firm's, or a nation's, competitiveness requires one to move above and beyond some misconceptions.

1.1.1 Competitiveness is more than productivity

For a firm, productivity is the amount of good produced, or service rendered, divided by a unit of input – money, raw material, or labour – used. The ratio between the sales – or even better, added value – of a firm, and the number of employees is a common approximation of its productivity. For a firm, an increase in productivity is perceived as a sign of increased competitiveness, as it shows that the company has become more efficient. In the case of nations, the indicators used are different, but the measurement of productivity is similar. Economists generally use the ratio of GDP to the number of people employed to track productivity, and refine it by incorporating hours worked per year. Labour-hour productivity serves as a proxy for evaluating the overall efficiency of a nation.

The question arises as to whether competitiveness can be reduced merely to the management of productivity across firms or within a country. Paul Krugman, Professor of Economics at Princeton, expressed that viewpoint in a 1994 *Foreign Affairs* article [2]. Krugman argued: "the doctrine of competitiveness [of nations] is flatly wrong." He stressed that focusing on the competitiveness of a nation could lead to misallocation of resources, trade frictions, and even poor domestic economic policies. He then proceeded to develop the position that competitiveness is just another name for national productivity.

Nobody questions the fact that productivity is a key determinant in competitiveness. Productivity is especially important at the level of the firm. Since the firm is at the core of our description of competitiveness, the overall productivity of a nation's firms greatly determines competitiveness. And, while a government can set its own productivity objectives, such as increasing the efficiency of its administration or public spending, their overall impact on national economic output is rather limited. Some scholars, taking the argument one step further, have even denied the existence of such a concept as national competitiveness. In their view, nations do not compete with one another, only firms do!

Statements that attempt to deny competition between nations over-simplify reality. In fact, both firms and nations compete in international markets. Nations compete in attracting investments or highly skilled labour, in scientific research, and even in educational standards. A highly productive firm operating in a highly inefficient, or even hostile, national business environment cannot be expected to sustain its competitive edge easily.

Productivity is thus a key aspect of competitiveness, because it is an indicator of efficiency: it conveys how much firms or nations produce with limited resources – the more produced with less, the better. Yet, there is a lot more to competitiveness than just productivity.

1.1.2 Competitiveness is more than what you can measure

Competitiveness thrives increasingly on intangible assets that are difficult to value, to account for, to create, and to recover. A nation's economic success depends more and more on the excellence of its education system, the quality of infrastructure, the dynamism of research, and even the quality of its administration. Although these factors have a huge impact on competitiveness, they are not measured easily, and, of course, are not included in the national accounts. Such omission can have pernicious effects.

A country can let its education or research system deteriorate for years before observing an impact on its competitiveness. By the time the problem becomes evident, leaders are confronted with a long uphill battle – sometimes lasting a generation – to correct these wrongs. Economic data produced by governments does not account for the depreciation in the intangible assets of a nation, thus failing to provide an early warning system of national competitiveness deterioration.

The time it takes to reverse trends is a very important consequence of the shift from tangible to increasingly intangible assets as key drivers of competitiveness. In Figure 1.1, it takes a nation one to five years to address a "standard" economic challenge, such as a surge in inflation. A thornier political issue, such as the reform of the pension system, might take longer – perhaps five to ten years. However, deteriorating trends, such as falling standards in education or research, might take significantly longer to be reversed – 10 to 30 years!

The more an issue relates to intangibles, the more time it will take to alter its course – both for governments and companies. Challenges in

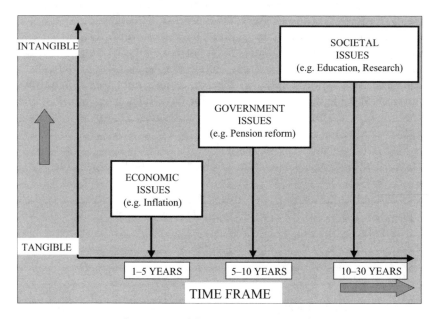

Figure 1.1 – Time to reverse trends.

brand recognition, customer loyalty, innovation, or people skills take much longer to reverse than a problem of excessive costs. The lesson to be learned: pay careful attention to the less tangible factors of competitiveness. In general, by the time the problem becomes apparent, it is too late for a quick fix.

The competitiveness of firms is highly dependent on intangible assets, such as brands, customer loyalty, image, skills, and processes, which are generally not accounted for in the firm's books. The value of brands and other market assets are only accounted for under "goodwill" if there has been a transaction – merger, sale, or acquisition – through which these intangible assets can be valued. Increasingly, companies attempt to incorporate the value of their intangible assets in their annual reporting. For example, Philip Morris (today, Altria), was one of the first companies to list the value of its many brands in its accounts.

Nations also have a "brand" – the image of the country abroad, and all the preconceptions going with it. For a nation, brand management is crucial to its competitiveness. Ireland enjoys an image of attractiveness for foreign investments; Singapore of efficiency in the administration. Other perceptions can be negative: Colombia for insecurity, Italy for strikes, The Philippines for poor infrastructure, the former Soviet Union for corruption. All of these perceptions – whether based on actual facts or not – strongly influence business and competitiveness. Perceptions are powerful, but also highly emotional, from a competitiveness point of view; they should never be overlooked.

If the value of brands (see Table 1.1 for the world's biggest) is still elusive in accounting standards, the financial value of a customer base, or of the competence of a firm's employees, is even more difficult to calculate. Accounting standards state that assets cannot appear in a firm's financial statements if the firm does not have full ownership of them. Obviously, no firms fully "own" their customers, and even less their employees.

Peter Drucker rightly underlined that "the purpose of a company is to create a customer" [4] and, one could add, to retain them. Managers know a loyal customer base is one of the most important assets of a company, and that it deserves utmost attention. For example, Rolex or Apple customers display impressive loyalty. Rolex customers are willing to wait many months for the delivery of a watch worth several thousand dollars – time and cost do not discourage such motivated clients. Apple customers wait stoically for the launch of breakthrough products, stubbornly refusing to switch to Windows, even when the competing machines are at a lower cost and of equal, or better, quality. Steve Jobs capitalised on such loyalty when he took over the reins of the company, and relaunched Apple's fortunes with the iPod series. It seems obvious

Table 1.1 – The world's most valuable brands

RANK 2005	RANK 2004		BRAND VALUE 2005 $MN	BRAND VALUE 2004 $MN
1	1	COCA-COLA	67 525	67 394
2	2	MICROSOFT	59 941	61 372
3	3	IBM	53 376	53 791
4	4	GE	46 996	44 111
5	5	INTEL	35 588	33 499
6	8	NOKIA	26 452	24 041
7	6	DISNEY	26 441	27 113
8	7	McDONALD'S	26 041	25 001
9	9	TOYOTA	24 837	22 673
10	10	MARLBORO	21 189	22 128
11	11	MERCEDES-BENZ	20 006	21 331
12	13	CITI	19 967	19 971
13	12	HEWLETT-PACKARD	18 886	20 978
14	14	AMERICAN EXPRESS	18 559	17 683
15	15	GILLETTE	17 534	16 723

Source: [3]

that such unique customer dedication has a value – yet it is not accounted for anywhere.

A similar argument can be made for employees: they are the cornerstones of any firm. It is a well-known fact that many CEOs end their speeches to the troops by reiterating the cliché: "In our company, people are our most important asset." The problem is that this "most important asset" is accounted as a "cost." Whether a firm employs 1000 geniuses, or 1000 "idiots," their value basically appears to be the same – the cost of their salaries. A firm that invests significantly in the training and education of its workforce does not see an increase in its accounting value. No trace will be kept of this laudable effort of training and education, except, of course, as a line item cost in the books – despite the fact that the *competitiveness* of the firm is certainly improved.

Although accounting standards don't allow a valuation of intangible assets, financial markets are bolder in their valuations and do include figures for the intangibles. Stock markets reflect intuitively how companies such as Microsoft and Nokia are also valuable because of the quality of their intangible assets: brand, customer loyalty, innovation, intellectual property, and even the skills of their staff. The staggering market capitalisation of Microsoft and Nokia (share price multiplied by the number of outstanding shares) demonstrates the importance financial markets attach to intangible assets. The ratio between market capitalisation and revenues illustrates this point. On average, in 2004, Microsoft displayed a ratio between market capitalisation and revenues in the order of 10 to 1 (i.e. $30 bn in revenues for an average market capitalisation of $300 bn). In the case of General Motors, the ratio was exactly the inverse – 1 to 10 – revenues being ten times larger than market capitalisation.

Financial markets have stepped in and are compensating actively for the shortcomings of accounting standards. The valuations they give to a firm include an approximation of the value of the intangible assets. This role has, however, been assumed by default, and the "standards" used by financial markets to assess the intangibles are sometimes questionable. Thus, in the absence of reliable valuation methodologies, financial markets develop a tendency to become easily exuberant. The so-called Internet bubble between 1998 and 2001 and, more recently, the Google IPO, serve to illustrate how financial markets' valuation of companies can sometimes defy gravity.

As we shall see later, key determinants for competitiveness can be intangible assets like science, technology, education, skills, infrastructure, brand, and even image. Competitiveness draws attention to intangible assets in a firm's or country's strategy, even if they are difficult to value.

1.1.3   Competitiveness is more than wealth

Although the purpose of competitiveness remains prosperity, wealth alone does not determine the success of a nation, a firm, or even an individual. Nations can be wealthy and not competitive. Living in Switzerland – a wealthy nation by many standards – I have often been at odds with the authorities and the business community when trying to alert them to the falling competitiveness of the nation. One of the typical reactions I encountered was: "What do you mean we are losing our competitive edge? Look how wealthy we are: the roads, the education, the technology, the money . . ."

True, Switzerland is extremely wealthy, but is it competitive? People who inherit $100 mn and decide to spend the rest of their days lying on a tropical beach, are definitely wealthy, most probably happy. But from a competitiveness point of view they are useless – they do not, through their own efforts, create any economic added value and, thus, do not contribute to the prosperity of any nation.

Wealth is largely the result of past competitiveness – the accumulated economic and business achievements of past generations. Wealth is also a function of *chance* – such as having natural resources for a nation, or being born into a rich family for an individual – yet such wealth is not sufficient to determine future competitiveness. Wealth helps – it gives nations, firms, and people a head start in economic development – but it does not guarantee that the prosperity of today will be perpetuated tomorrow.

Natural resources: a blessing or a curse?

Abundant natural resources are generally considered a blessing for a country. Saudi Arabia and Norway are wealthy countries in their own right, because they are world leaders in oil and gas production. Because their populations are wealthy, both nations give the impression of being competitive: Saudi Arabia has a per capita Gross Domestic Product (GDP) of $10 486 (purchasing power parity adjusted for 2001), while for the same year, Norway had a GDP per capita of $30 142. A regular flow of money from natural resources helps an economy, or rather provides a sense of security. Natural resources continue to play an important role in industrialised nations: the US and France are world-leading exporters of agricultural goods, while oil remains, with the automobile industry, one of the top exports of Britain. In a similar way, considerable exports of North Sea gas have sustained the competitiveness of The Netherlands.

However, natural resources don't necessarily lead to competitiveness. Iraq has huge reserves of oil but, unfortunately, cannot yet capitalise on this asset. Russia has the largest amount and diversity of natural resources of any nation in the world, yet it is only barely emerging as a competitive power. There is a long list of nations that seem to follow a similar pattern – South Africa, Brazil, India, Indonesia – immensely rich nations, endowed with considerable natural resources, but lagging in the development of their competitiveness. They have over-relied on the extraction of natural resources for their wealth, yet if they were to focus more on processing those resources into other products, they would increase their competitiveness.

Is it a "curse" to have natural resources? In contrast to nations richly endowed in natural resources, "poorer" nations in that sense – Singapore, Japan, Switzerland, and Ireland – have indeed thrived in competitiveness. These nations focused on the transformation of imported natural resources into manufactured products, and now dedicate themselves mostly to the provision of services.

Whether it is renewable or not determines the impact that a natural resource has on competitiveness. Forests are managed as renewable resources in many countries, and timber harvesting is highly regulated. Trees cannot be cut before a certain age, and new plantations are compulsory. In Europe, 31.1 % of the surface area is now covered by forest, a proportion that is increasing every year – partly because oil has replaced wood as a significant source of energy. As a consequence, and contrary to conventional wisdom, there are probably more trees in Europe today than one hundred years ago.

Unfortunately, such enlightened forestry policy is not applied everywhere. Brazil and Indonesia, for example, suffer the effects of severe deforestation because of unregulated, intensive timber exploitation, without appropriate replanting schemes. The former East Germany had one of the highest growth rates in the former Communist world. However, after German reunification, it became evident that East Germany had achieved its success at considerable environmental cost. The eastern part of a unified Germany was a land exhausted by pollution, careless exploitation of resources, and poorly planned urbanisation. The East German "economic miracle" depended on the abuse and depletion of nonrenewable assets. East Germany only performed, or rather boasted, at the expense of future generations – "selling the family silver to buy lunch."

Sustainable development

In 1987, the World Commission on Environment and Development, under the chairmanship of Dr Gro Harlem Brundtland from Norway, articulated a widely-accepted definition of sustainable development. The definition states that sustainable development "meets the needs of the present without compromising the ability of future generations to meet their own needs." The work of the Commission is considered a landmark, highlighting the long-term relationship between the exploitation of natural resources and prosperity [5].

Unless they are used to develop other activities, nonrenewable natural resources – oil, gas, or minerals – are not assets for competitiveness. If the proceeds from their exploitation and extraction are not invested for building future competitiveness, the depletion of nonrenewable assets represents a net loss of wealth for future generations. Although exports of nonrenewable natural resources can contribute significantly to the Gross Domestic Product of a nation, they cannot, as such, be considered drivers of future competitiveness, unless used wisely.

Nonrenewable natural resources can, nevertheless, provide a window of opportunity to develop future competitiveness if the wealth derived from their exploitation is invested in means of future production, such as human capital, plant, and equipment. Dubai, one of the United Arab Emirates, unlike its wealthy neighbour Abu Dhabi, only has a limited amount of oil left – perhaps 20 more years of production. The leadership of Dubai has thus decided to use current oil revenues to diversify its economy, promoting the development of technology-based activities, such as the Internet and multimedia, together with an offshore financial centre and a booming tourist industry [6]. Norway is following a slightly different strategy, although the purpose is similar. The Norwegian government has created a special fund – financed mainly by the country's considerable oil revenues – with the objective of preparing for when oil revenues dry up.

The experiment of Dubai

Dubai is conducting an impressive experiment in shifting its competitiveness away from oil, to a diversified economy. Dubai's GDP, estimated at $16.4 bn in 2000, has been growing at 8 % over the past ten years. Today, only 10 % of the GDP is derived from the oil sector – manufacturing, trade, finance, real estate, tourism, and transportation have all become more important than oil. The non-oil sector is now growing by almost 10 % per year. Dubai is a remarkable example of the strategic decision to use nonrenewable natural resources (oil and gas) to finance the transition toward a more sustainable and advanced competitiveness model, thriving on skills and knowledge.

Although clearly a source of wealth, natural resources should be perceived as an *enabler* of competitiveness. The true value of natural resources for competitiveness exists only if such resources are made renewable, or if the nation uses the revenues generated by natural resources to diversify the economy into added-value activities that can last into the future.

It is mainly nations that need to have natural resources policies but very similar basic underlying principles apply to firms. In 2004, oil giant Shell got into deep trouble because it had misstated its proven oil reserves and mismanaged oil exploration efforts, jeopardising the future source of revenue of the company. Shell certainly still has a strong balance sheet (wealth), but under these circumstances, it was not very competitive.

Sustainability has thus a special appeal for today's customers and businesses. Our modern value system increasingly emphasises that we don't actually own assets – we are just custodians for future generations. Patek Philippe, the Swiss watch company, runs an advertisement that capitalises on such new trends: "You never actually own a Patek Philippe. You merely look after it for the next generation."

Past competitiveness – an unbearable burden?

A link between past competitiveness and present wealth is relatively easy to establish. Competitiveness ultimately aims at increasing the prosperity of a nation and its people. In theory, a competitive nation generates a certain amount of economic value every year, which appears in the national accounts as an increase in GDP. In turn, this increase in GDP adds to the existing wealth of the nation, which is accounted for . . . well, actually, nowhere!

The GDP data of a nation indicates an added value. It does not reflect in any way the accumulation of valuable assets, such as roads, buildings, transportation, schools, or universities, which are key parts of the wealth of a nation. Some nations – New Zealand, Italy and, more recently, Great Britain – are trying, not without difficulty, to assess the value of their total wealth. These projects attempt to fill a vacuum in national accounts. Accumulated wealth is a very important portion of a nation's prosperity, which remains unaccounted for. Using GDP alone to determine the prosperity of a nation is akin to calculating the prosperity of an individual solely on the basis of their current yearly income, omitting any wealth accumulated over time.

Wealth, if it is not a direct consequence of natural resources, is the cumulative result of the competitiveness of years past. Wealthy nations, such as Great Britain, Japan, and Germany, owe a great deal of their present standard of living to the competitiveness of past generations. Today, these nations may or may not be competitive, regardless of the achievements of past generations. Past success is not necessarily a guarantee of present competitiveness.

For any nation, a mix of past wealth and present competitiveness determines current prosperity. Prestigious universities, such as Harvard, Oxford, or La Sorbonne, innovative firms, such as Siemens, and efficient infrastructure, such as the bullet train in Japan, are legacies of the past. Yet, they can also contribute actively to today's competitiveness. However, their historical value is neither a guarantee of their future competitiveness, nor of the prosperity of their home nation in the future.

Success will depend upon the efficiency of the present generation to use, expand, and transfer these assets to future generations.

Wealth can also be a *threat* to competitiveness. Wealthy nations, firms, and people run the risk of falling into complacency, arrogance, and apathy. Complacency and arrogance have indeed killed more companies than any strategic mistakes. Wealth can act as a sedative, inducing nations, firms, and people to become insensitive to change. "We are so good . . ." Competitive organisations are often *hungry* for success – wealthy ones are simply not as hungry. Such attitudes are understandable, but the hungry organisations have a stronger drive and motivation toward success, and this is a key determinant of competitiveness.

Wealth is a thus a double-edged sword, supporting or hindering competitiveness. The theory of competitiveness would summarise the issue as follows:

> *What you have does not matter as much as what you do with what you have . . .*

1.1.4 Competitiveness is more than power

For almost a decade, Japan has endured harsh economic conditions – 1996 was the last year when Japan showed a GDP growth rate above 3 % – 3.6 % to be precise. Since then, Japan has lingered on the borderline of recession. Although today, Japan's economic performance seems to be improving, the stigmas of these difficult years still remain. Japan – the unrivalled leader of competitiveness in the early 1980s – has lost its dynamism and aura. The elements of its competitiveness model, previously acclaimed the world over, are now widely criticised – the tight links between the banking and the business community; the famous, but now infamous, *keiretsu* family of companies; the long-term business investments perspective; active government support for research and industrial policy; the legendary cohesion of the Japanese firm and society. In short, all of the factors that made Japan "unique", and were researched thoroughly by scholars for decades, are now vilified.

Nonetheless, Japan remains a formidable economic power – it has the world's second largest GDP, just behind the US, at $4667 bn in 2004, far ahead of third-place Germany with $2704 bn (US GDP stood at $11 733 bn in 2004). Despite its economic woes, Japan remains a formidable force in the world economy that should not be written off.

The fate of Japan illustrates how a country can lose its competitiveness standing, while still remaining an economic power. The opposite can also be true: a country can display significant increases in competitiveness for a number of years, while being a smaller economic power, as illustrated by the case of Singapore. Since gaining independence from Malaysia on 9 August 1965, Singapore has displayed a remarkable economic performance – 10.3 % GDP growth in 2000 and 8.4 % growth in 2004. Yet, Singapore's potential as an economic power is inherently limited by the constraints of its relatively small population and land base. With a land area of only 692 km² – roughly 3.5 times the size of Washington, D.C. – Singapore has a population of 4.4 million inhabitants, producing a total GDP of $106 bn (2004). Singapore – with all the intelligence and astuteness of its government and people – can potentially match the power of a country like Sweden, with a GDP of $343 bn and a population of 8.9 m people. Yet, even with an aggressive international trade and foreign direct investment policy, it is highly unlikely that Singapore could ever match the economic power of China or the US.

Power, from an economic point of view, can be visualised as a function of a *country's wealth* and its *population size* (Figure 1.2). At first

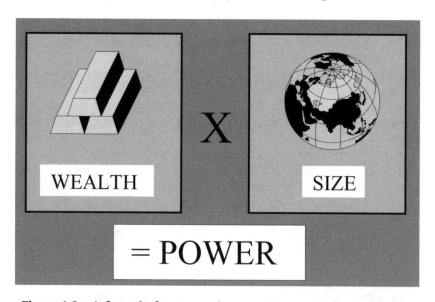

Figure 1.2 – A formula for economic power. Economic power is more than just the overall GDP data of a country. For example, despite the fact that the overall GDP of China or Russia is relatively modest, the potential economic power of these nations is determined partly by their enormous size: China in population, Russia in land. As shown by Singapore or Finland, wealth can only mitigate a lack of size to a certain extent. Ultimately, in a modern and global world, size is a key competitiveness factor.

glance, it might appear that the overall GDP of a nation could be a good approximation of a *country's wealth*. Unfortunately, GDP is an indicator of a *flow* of annual added value, and not of *accumulation* of wealth. Therefore, in the absence of any such direct measurement of a nation's wealth, we are obliged to use the overall GDP as a proxy: by taking separately the overall GDP of a nation and its relationship with the population, we can obtain an approximation of the potential economic power of a nation. It is the *combination* of these two components that actually defines the limitation, or the potential, for the power of a nation.

Let's compare The Netherlands and Russia as an example. In 2004, The Netherlands had a GDP of $579 bn, just slightly lower than that of Russia at $588 bn. These figures don't really tell us anything about the potential economic power of either nation. Why? Because, The Netherlands' economic power is based on a population of 16m and a GDP per capita of $35629, while Russia reached a comparable GDP with a population of 145m people and a GDP per capita of only $4083. It is safe to argue that, because of its limited land area, The Netherlands will never reach a population of 145m. Who is more competitive? Clearly, The Netherlands – it reached such a GDP with a population of 16 million, relative to Russia's 145 million. Dutch residents are, overall, individually more prosperous than those of Russia. Yet, in the perspective of economic power, Russia could potentially overtake The Netherlands. It is very likely that the GDP per capita of Russia will grow much faster in the coming years than the demography of The Netherlands. Hence, barring unforeseen circumstances, such as war, epidemics, or natural catastrophes, Russia has the potential to become a true world economic power, but The Netherlands does not.

Larger markets will dominate competitiveness

In 2050, the more developed regions of the world will account for 1155bn people, against 7754bn people in the less developed regions [7]. The labour force of China alone is estimated at 787 million people – approximately twice the labour force currently going to work in the entire industrialised world (Figure 1.3). China, because of its land area and the size of its population, can be turned more easily into a world economic power with a lower level of competitiveness per capita than would be required for a smaller nation. With a growth rate of 9.5 % in 2004 (and average annual growth rate of 8 % over the past decade), China is well on its way to becoming a considerable player in the world economy.

Size is an important determinant for the competitiveness of nations. During the early stages of economic development, the size of a country's domestic market can act as a magnet for foreign investment. Countries such as China, India, and Russia today are advancing their attractiveness

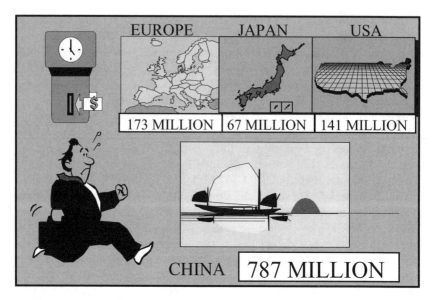

EUROPE   JAPAN   USA

173 MILLION | 67 MILLION | 141 MILLION

CHINA **787 MILLION**

Figure 1.3 – Going to work every morning. The size of the labour force in China (787 m) or in India (444 m) is a formidable reserve of development and power for these nations. Increasingly, the integration of Chinese and Indian workers into the global labour force will have important economic repercussions, including on the hourly salaries of workers worldwide.

by stressing the potential of their large domestic markets. At later stages of development, a nation's size encourages larger capacity for the production and export of goods, services, and investments. Advanced industrial economies like the US, Germany, and Japan rely upon the size of their domestic markets to build economies of scale in the production of their goods and services. Such large nations use their size as a means of achieving economic or political power.

Since the publication, in 1973, of the famous book *Small is Beautiful* by E.F. Schumacher, there has been a tendency to believe that size is no longer that important [8]. Modern communications and transport technologies, and the opening of world markets, have allowed small companies to play a significant role in international markets. Companies such as Nokia, Microsoft, eBay, and Vodafone can be world leaders in their fields without necessarily being large companies – this is one of the most interesting developments in modern management. We now see that small companies can be "big," and have a competitive edge over larger players – they can become significant actors in international markets. In the old days, the international game was the reserve of the very large organisation, which could devote important resources to the management of its international operations. Today, global niche firms, small but highly competitive, conquer the business world thanks to the development of the Internet and efficient logistics around the globe. Nowadays, the most competitive firms are far smaller than their predecessors of four decades ago. In an open world, firms have unlimited access to resources and talent wherever they are – a privilege that nations do not share.

The population boom changes the power game

Just five nations will account for 50 % of the world population growth during the next 50 years: India, China, Pakistan, Bangladesh, and the USA. In 2050, the world population will reach 8.9 bn people, almost a 50 % increase compared to the present (Figure 1.4). By then, the only industrialised nation that will make it onto the list of the 12 most populous nations of the world, i.e. having a population above 100 million people, will be the United States.

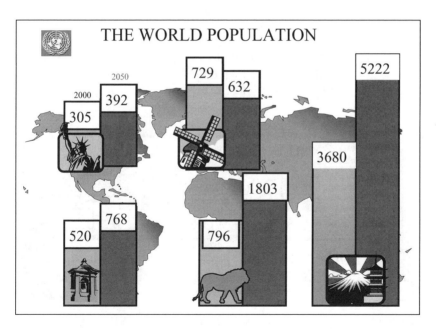

Figure 1.4 – World population growth between 2000 and 2050. According to the United Nations, with the exception of Europe, every part of the world will see an increase in population during the next 50 years. The most significant demographic explosion will occur in Asia, with 1542 m additional people, and in Africa, which will more than double in population size [7].

In Europe, only six countries (seven if one includes Turkey) have a critical mass of over 35 million inhabitants that could allow them to have some kind of weight in international economic affairs. They are: Germany, the United Kingdom, France, Italy, Spain, and Poland. All the other nations, more than 20 according to this definition, are small countries. They can legitimately hope to become highly competitive and to ensure the economic prosperity of their people, but, alone, they cannot expect to play a significant role on the world economic scene.

The world population has been growing faster and faster. From 1804 to 1927, it took 123 years to increase the world population by one billion people. However, in just 12 years, between 1987 and 1999, the world population increased by the same one billion people! Thus, the world population is growing more rapidly, but not everywhere. In Europe, during the same period of time, the population decreased by almost 100 million people. In addition, the "greying" of the population will have a huge economic impact. In 2050, for example, one out of every three people in Europe will be over 60 years old. By then, 10 % of the population in 21 nations around the world will be more than 80 years old.

The US and Europe produce two-thirds of global output, with only about one-tenth of the world's population. Yet, their share of the global population is falling – by 2050, their combined population is estimated to be only 7.7 % of the world's total (Figure 1.5). Will they maintain their current share of world GDP? Most likely not.

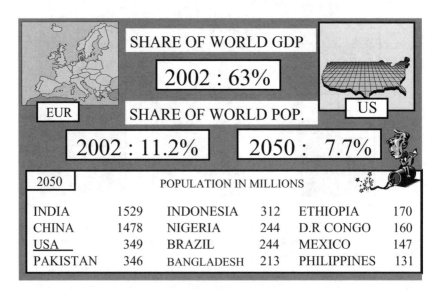

Figure 1.5 – Where will the markets be?

Can smaller nations survive?

Demographic perspectives are not encouraging for smaller nations. The clock is ticking against them – how will they continue to matter in the future? A small company has a better chance of becoming a significant player on world markets than a small nation. Such a situation is epitomised by the relationship between Nokia and Finland, both very competitive organisations in their own right. Nokia could theoretically be just as successful and powerful if operating from another home base, such as Denmark or Singapore. Thriving on technology and globalisation, Nokia represents a new type of competitor on world markets, somewhere between a large global player and a local niche player. This type of firm could be described as *global-niche players*, for whom location and size are less important.

The global marketplace

Figure 1.6 shows the world marketplace as it appeared in 2001. These figures, as well as their relative importance, have evolved in recent years. For example, the market capitalisation of listed companies worldwide is now generally superior to world GDP. Foreign direct investment (shown here as annual flows from countries to countries, and as stocks), which represents the foreign

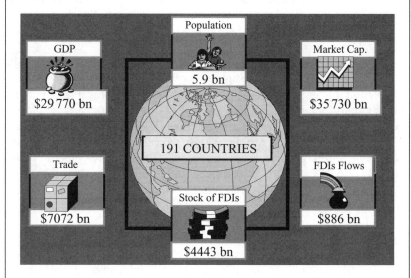

Figure 1.6 – How big is the global marketplace?

ownership of productive assets, has increased drastically as a result of globalisation. Trade is also expanding quickly as borders become more permeable to business, and trade barriers vanish.

In such a world, size matters. The US alone accounts for one-third of world GDP! Including Europe and Japan, the advanced industrialised nations represent three-quarters of world GDP. This is thus a world of big players. Interestingly, as mentioned already, small enterprises have more scope to impact the global world than small nations. Nokia, for example, a $30bn company, has rapidly become a global player. As a consequence, it has increased the competitiveness of Finland. In 1999, Nokia accounted for 25 % of Finnish exports, and contributed 1.5 % to the growth of GDP. It represented 60 % of the capitalisation of the Helsinki Stock Exchange, and had created more millionaires and big taxpayers than any other company in the country.

Small countries can host significant players, but the national ties of these firms can be weakened. Nokia can hire people from the world over to fuel its expansion, and to further develop a globalisation strategy. It can also acquire companies and, thus, new competencies and people. In Switzerland, Novartis and Nestlé, the two largest industrial companies in the country, generate less than 5 % of their turnover at home. The vast majority of their employees are non-Swiss. At Nestlé, even the majority of the managing board is non-Swiss, including both past and present presidents.

In contrast, the future development of Finland is restricted by the size of the population, which is slightly above 5 million. Switzerland has a population of slightly over 7 million, in a geographical space much smaller than Finland. A country can, of course, rely on immigration to expand its power base – the United States, Canada, and Australia have done so. However, such a policy doesn't produce results overnight and may have deep political consequences. Theoretically, Finland could increase its population, because its land area is reasonably large ($338000\,km^2$); however, Luxembourg ($2600\,km^2$), Hong Kong ($1100\,km^2$), and Singapore ($700\,km^2$) are stuck with their size, even if they are highly competitive.

The internationalisation of local firms, as well as increased attractiveness for foreign investments, can partially alleviate the constraints of size for a smaller nation. For places like Finland, Switzerland, and Singapore, future competitiveness can be achieved through the selection of activities with high added value and skills. Such policies will probably increase the general levels of prosperity in the countries. Nevertheless, the bottom line is that Finland, Switzerland, and Singapore don't have a future as world economic powers, as they are limited to their current respective sizes.

Switzerland, Finland, Singapore, and The Netherlands are homes to a large number of world-class, international companies that do not restrict their activities to the limited size of the domestic market. Companies from such countries are not subject to the same size restrictions that limit the power of their home countries. They can become significant global players: disproportionately influential in comparison to the small size of their home markets. Size is thus a constraint for a nation, but not necessarily for a firm.

1.2 Competitiveness: a change in the mindset

As we have just seen, the theory of competitiveness endeavours to go beyond the analysis of productivity, the accumulation of physical assets, the amassing of wealth, and the increase of power. Competitiveness is also about changing mindsets: looking at the world, nations, firms, and people from a different perspective. The wholeness of this view, the more holistic approach to the elements determining a firm's or a nation's prosperity, constitutes one facet of the theory.

Another important facet of the theory is how competitiveness profoundly modifies the frames of comparison used in examining these elements. Furthermore, competitiveness incorporates an analysis of time and space that is very different to that of conventional economics.

1.2.1 Forget the past, competitiveness is now!

In the mindset of competitiveness, we need to change our attitude to time and space as frames of comparison to measure our performance. As seen earlier, as a standard measure for the economic performance of a nation, GDP has multiple shortcomings – no accounting for the depletion of nonrenewable resources, no valuation of intangible assets, and no indication of accumulated wealth. The situation is similar when analysing firms – profit accounts show little or no regard for the value of brands and other intangibles, such as technology, processes, employees' skills – many of the elements that are crucial to the firms' ability to produce output. The other drawback with conventional measures, such as GDP or profit, is that they lead firms and nations to be *inward* and *backward* looking when assessing their performance. They are more likely to consider their performance in comparison with what they achieved in the past, and in isolation from the rest of the world. Such an introspective approach to performance represents one of the most treacherous menaces to competitiveness – often perpetuating an illusion of success when, in fact, the reality has changed.

Gross Domestic Product in short . . .

The GDP defines all the final goods and services produced in an economy in one year, measured at market prices or purchase power parity adjusted. It includes:

* personal consumption;
* government expenditure;
* private investment;
* inventory changes;
* trade balance.

Competitiveness is like a race. It's not just about *you* running faster today than *you* did yesterday; it's about *you* running faster today than *all the others* in the race (Figure 1.7). Benchmarking – central to competitiveness – tells a company or a nation how its performance measures up with what its competitors are achieving in the same timeframe. Unfortunately, many politicians and CEOs prefer to compare their present performance with their past performance. While it might be interesting, it is most often irrelevant from the point of view of competitiveness.

Suppose an athlete concentrates his efforts and trains regularly to boost his performance in the 100 m dash. As the days pass, he runs faster and faster; at the beginning of his training, he would run 100 m in 15 seconds, now it takes him 11 seconds. In the absence of any other frame of comparison, he takes the improvement of his current timing versus his previous one as proof that he is highly competitive, and decides to compete in the Olympic Games.

At that stage, our athlete encounters a basic principle of competitiveness – *the performance of others matters as much as yours*. In an Olympic final, running the 100 m dash in 11 seconds is not good enough to win. To have any chance of winning, you have to do it in less than 10 seconds.

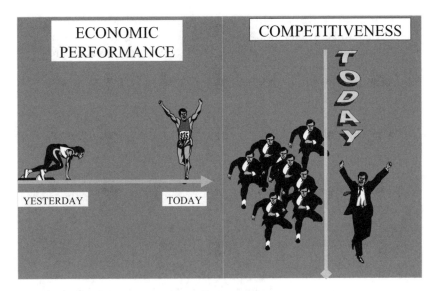

Figure 1.7 – Running against the others.

The frame of comparison is different. In the final, our athlete may very well achieve his best performance ever – perhaps running 100 m in less than 11 seconds – a major achievement for him, but not good enough to win. The winner most likely completed the race in less than 10 seconds. Both our athlete and the Olympic champion have excelled in their performance, but the *competitiveness* of one – the gold medallist – is greater than that of the rest of the field.

Nations can also succumb to the same delusion. In 2000, Switzerland posted 3.2 % growth in GDP – the first time since 1990 that the nation achieved a growth performance above 3 %. The Swiss business and political communities duly celebrated this "achievement." To really understand the implications, this apparent "achievement" has to be tempered by looking at the performance of Switzerland's competitors. During that very same year, forty out of the sixty economies that we monitor continuously at the IMD World Competitiveness Centre, displayed a GDP growth rate superior to 3 % (the same phenomenon occurred in 2004, globally a very good year for economic performance). The accomplishments of the Swiss economy were remarkable by Swiss standards and in comparison to the previous Swiss performances. However, when examined within the frame of comparison of *world* competitiveness, such "achievement" becomes markedly less impressive.

Disillusionment grew when the performance was assessed on a longer time scale – a decade. Within this timeframe, Switzerland only had one year of growth above 3 %. In comparison, Sweden had five such years; The Netherlands, 6; Finland, New Zealand, and the US, 7; Australia, 8. Switzerland performed well according to its own previous standards, but not according to those of its competitors. Assessing one's performance through the prism of competitiveness can indeed be a very informative, if frustrating, experience.

Competitiveness is thus about *benchmarking* one's performance with others today, and not with oneself yesterday. In the 80s, American and European firms began to notice a great fall in the demand for their products, coupled with a rise in demand for Japanese products. American and European firms realised that it was not enough to compare their present results with those of the past, or even to compare themselves with other domestic competitors. To really make a difference, they had to compare themselves with the "best in the class", i.e. the Japanese firms. This process, benchmarking, provided a serious wake-up call for both nations and firms. Japanese firms seemed to be better, faster and, especially, cheaper than their American or European competitors.

In the early 80s, John Young, then CEO of HP (Hewlett-Packard), understood the impact and magnitude of the effect low-cost Asian producers were going to have on the American IT industry [9]. Not only the IT industry was affected, the consequences reverberated throughout all US industries, such as transport, household goods, and telecommunications. American leaders were determined to crack the secret of Japan's recipe for success. Young was one of the founders of the US Council on Competitiveness, gathering leaders from business, government, and academia to find remedies for lagging American competitiveness.

Young also took the challenge back to his own company: he instigated an internal process at HP to achieve a ten-fold improvement in quality. The strategy required a company-wide examination of methods and processes, and *Quality Directors* were appointed to reinforce the company's commitment to a quality strategy. Senior HP executives had to adopt quality enhancement as their primary goal. Yet, while HP employees found numerous ways to improve quality, they still believed such a drastic ten-fold improvement was unattainable. Through benchmarking, managers and employees systematically examined the processes employed by other companies and their performances. Thus, HP unblocked an inward-looking culture and unleashed innovation. Employees realised that goals which seemed to be unattainable were, in fact, everyday occurrences elsewhere. Pride came into the picture; "Why can they do it and not us?"

Young's policy on quality improvement and benchmarking was a resounding success, forming the basis of HP's strong competitiveness during the 80s and 90s. HP *could* continue to compete, providing quality products at competitive prices. John Young had foresight and saw how the competitiveness of HP required a change in the *frame of reference.* To remain competitive, HP needed to break away from past moulds, challenge current practices, and question basic assumptions. It was competitiveness policy at its best!

1.2.2   Winning is not enough

The conceptual importance of winning is rarely challenged. However, in the competitiveness mindset, *winning may not be as good as you think.* Although being head of the class is certainly praiseworthy, nations and firms should also tackle a more fundamental question:

Are we winning the right race and, if so, by how much?

Choosing the right comparison basis, i.e. the right race to win, *and* defining the objective, i.e. by how much to win, are the two fundamental principles of competitiveness. The change in mindset produced by focusing on competitiveness can be seen through the following example.

Let's assume that a student wants to select her future career. While reviewing all her competencies, she assesses that, among other things, she is an excellent driver – she thinks, in fact, that it is what she does best. Thus, according to the conventional wisdom that a person should concentrate on what he or she does best, our student should become a driver. Yet, from a competitiveness angle, such a statement is terribly wrong. Millions of people around the world know how to drive a car; most think they are good drivers; a few even believe they are truly outstanding. However, being able to drive is not a competitive advantage – lots and lots of people know how to do it, and thus there is no uniqueness in being able to do so. In addition, even an excellent driver is not *that much better* than a good driver – or at least so much better that it actually makes an important difference. Most likely, the difference between a good driver and an excellent one is rather marginal. To really succeed in driving, one has to be at the level of a Michael Schumacher – little else will do.

Thus, when examining her career options with a competitiveness mindset, our student resolves that she should not earn her living from driving. So how should she decide on a career? The theory of competitiveness would suggest that she should look at all her other

MAXIMISING
THE DIFFERENCE
BETWEEN
1 AND # 2

#1

#2

Figure 1.8 – Competitiveness is also about maximising the difference with followers.

competencies and identify the one where she commands the biggest advantage *compared* to competitors (Figure 1.8). If our student considers that her next best competency after driving is tax law, then she should embrace a law career, even if her skills are only average, provided she is in an environment where tax lawyers are relatively scarce. For competitiveness, being good is not enough to bring about success – being *different* is what really matters.

In practical terms, competitiveness theory underlines that success is about differences, according to the following principle:

> *Competitiveness thrives on maximising the positive difference (or comparative advantage) between a nation, a firm, or a person and their most direct competitor.*

A competitiveness mindset can have a great impact on a firm's profitability. In business, a situation that resembles a compact sprint – like in a cycling race when there is little space between competitors – generally doesn't command high margins. The retail food and computer industries are examples of cutthroat competition with reduced profit margins. In these sectors, competitors are very close to each other in terms of product range, pricing, and strategy. The differentiating factors are minimal, and most often cost is the only thing that differs. In such situations, markets are unwilling to pay a premium for a firm's products if there is little uniqueness in comparison to those of competing firms. Whenever the customer enjoys a multiple choice of comparable propositions, prices and profit margins shrink inexorably.

In contrast, firms commanding a large advance on their nearest competitor generate high margins and earn strong profits. Luxury goods firms – because of their brand reputation – and software developers have enjoyed such privileged situations. Microsoft has a very large market capitalisation, as we have seen earlier, not only because the firm excels in technology and marketing, but also because the nearest direct competitors of Microsoft are much further behind in terms of market share. Some users may argue Microsoft's technologies are not the best around. While that may be the case, are there any other real alternatives open to consumers? Operating systems which could be considered as a threat to Microsoft's, such as Linux, have a very small market share in comparison to that of Microsoft – even if the adoption of Linux is growing quickly. Linux may well be a far better operating system than Microsoft's Windows. However, in a crude competitiveness approach, to safeguard the high valuation of the firm by stock markets, Microsoft should worry less about marginally improving technology, than about maintaining a huge competitive distance between the firm and its rivals.

Nations face a similar dilemma – their attractiveness is a key determinant of competitiveness. Foreign investments transfer capital, technology, employment, and skills into the host nation, thus contributing to its prosperity. Having recognised how foreign investments bring jobs, government leaders – generally preoccupied with unemployment, as it influences their re-election – actively support an attractiveness approach to competitiveness. During the past two decades, national investment agencies using incentive packages to lure foreign firms have proliferated; Ireland and Singapore being key references of such policies. However, the *packages* themselves are rather undifferentiated. Most nations promote the same advantages: grace period and preferential tax rates for investment, excellent infrastructure, low cost of operation, access to markets, government support, and so on. In this situation, firms have multiple locations to choose between for an investment, and can turn out to be tough negotiators in making their choice, pitting one nation against others to see who will provide the better bargain. When a situation of extreme and close competition occurs in a firm's context, the consequence for the supplying firm is generally that prices are reduced and margins are squeezed.

In the context of national governments, most likely tax revenues will be reduced. Governments today realise they have little choice but to be competitive in the area of corporate taxes if they wish to attract foreign investment – it is, after all, what every other nation is doing. As a result of this competition among nations and the increased mobility of corporations around the globe, the margin of manoeuvre on corporate taxes is increasingly limited for nations, practically leading to a convergence in corporate tax rates all over the world.

The *compact sprint* among nations illustrates how building up a distance from competitors is a key concept to competitiveness. Nations may escape the pressure of corporate demands by focusing on different competitive advantages – the ease of doing business, quality of life, an international culture, openness, protection of intellectual property, and security of goods and people – and build a different model based on a package of unmatched competitiveness advantages. However, most government leaders are elected to cure the "wrongs" of the previous administration. Understandably, these leaders concentrate on improving the past and showing their electorate how much better off they are now. In doing so, they favour pursuing a minimalist approach: *as long as it is better than before . . .*

The theory of competitiveness requires government leaders to change their own *frames of comparison*: they should examine the performance of their nation in light of the performance and achievements of other comparable, competing nations during a specific period in time, and then seek to maximise their advantage. Such a change in mentality constitutes a real challenge for leaders who have focused generally on local politics and issues. Nevertheless, in an exposed international environment, where information and capital flows around the world move even more freely and quickly than products, hiding from certain realities is no longer an option. Nations are also compelled to abide by the laws of competitiveness.

In summary, this first chapter illustrates how the theory of competitiveness provides a more comprehensive, holistic approach to those interested in identifying what drives prosperity, and how to enhance it. Firms and their managers cannot forever thrive on dividing up everything – production, markets, customers, goals, even business units and competencies. Neither can nations neglect the development of a common value system, a cohesive set of goals, and an established, widely-accepted blueprint for the creation of prosperity. Divergent goals and means need to be reconciled within any organisation – typically at the most senior leadership level – so that they can provide a guiding sense of purpose for the future.

The theory of competitiveness provides a framework for conducting this reconciliation process. The theory stresses the importance of:

1. *Going beyond* productivity, tangibles, wealth, and power as sole determinants of success.
2. *Shifting the frames of reference* from short-term benefits to long-term sustainability; from past individual comparisons to benchmarking performance with present competitors; from being complacent in success to maximising comparative advantages.

While competitiveness is a recent addition to the field of economics, the insights and the development of the theory did not occur overnight. The concepts that set the grounds for the theory have been in the making for most of the past three centuries. In the course of the next chapter, we will go through a brief overview of the long winding road to competitiveness, and see where it leads.

The Long and Winding Road to Competitiveness

2

"A day shall come when there will be no other battlefield than markets opening to trade and minds opening to ideas."

Victor Hugo (1802–1885)

Economics (from the Greek words *oikos* "house" and *nemo* "rules" – thus "household management") is the social science which studies how societies allocate scarce resources to satisfy the unlimited wants of consumers. Generally, scholars trace the birth of modern economics as a field of inquiry to 1776, when Adam Smith published his work *An Inquiry into the Nature and Causes of the Wealth of Nations* [1]. British philosopher David Hume had also touched upon economics in his *Political Discourses*, when he argued: "all conflicts spring from scarcity" [2]. Hume believed that the transition from an agricultural to an industrial economy was a precondition for the development of civilisation, but, unlike Adam Smith, he did not turn his ideas into an economic theory.

The term "economics" is little more than a century old. The English economist Alfred Marshall coined the term around 1880 in his seminal book *Principles of Political Economy*, in which he synthesised the theories of supply, demand, marginal utility, and the cost of production [3]. The title of his book reflects contemporary views on the subject, as it still uses the generic term *Political Economy*; the same term Adam Smith, David Ricardo, and Karl Marx had used previously. Sometimes economists such as these, and even politicians such as Thomas Jefferson, also used the term "economy of *polities*," an expression describing the administration of a government or a political organisation. However, for later editions of the book, Alfred Marshall had it renamed, *Principles in Economics* – the standard textbook title still often used today.

Competitiveness – most likely derived from the Latin verb *competere*, meaning to strive for something together with another – is a significantly more modern term. As a field of economics, competitiveness came to the foreground during the 1980s – two centuries after the founding analysis of Adam Smith, and one century after Alfred Marshall. It was easy enough to understand competitiveness as a concept by creating an analogy with the familiar Darwinian theory of evolution. Firms compete for survival: to succeed, they have to adapt better and faster than competitors; to prosper, they must innovate; and if they do not perform well within their environment, they will disappear. Nevertheless, the application of competitive analysis to firms was accepted much more readily than a similar analysis applied to nations.

Nations are different: they are less affected by the environment in which they operate than firms. A nation, even if it disappears from a political point of view, does not "disappear" as an entity. Take the Soviet Union for example; as a political entity, it disappeared, but in reality, 15 other nations were "born," inheriting its territory, economic base, and people as the basis of their nationhood. Even when nations converge into a supranational entity, such as the European Union, they still want to retain as much control as possible over their own identities. Nor do nations "disappear" for economic reasons. They simply decline into poverty. At the beginning of the 19th century, China was one of the wealthiest nations in the world, largely surpassing the then-emerging European industrial powers of Britain and France. Yet by 1950, China had fallen behind and had become one of the poorest nations in the world. Nevertheless, it continued to survive as a political entity.

The rise of competitiveness as a field of economics is the result of a shift in approach to the study of the drivers of prosperity. Competitiveness looks at nations from a global – even holistic – point of view. We saw in the previous chapter that this "wholeness" is an important characteristic of competitiveness.

It would, however, be an oversimplification to state that competitiveness appeared out of nowhere in the 1980s. Over the previous two centuries, the study and reflection of many economists, social scientists, and politicians planted the seeds for the development of a theory of competitiveness. Even if they did not use the term itself, many of their theories identified and articulated the fundamental components of the theory of competitiveness. The first step that needed to be taken was to *aggregate* into a coherent framework a number of ideas from the different fields of the social sciences, and then to *develop* the specificities necessary to have a coherent theory. Here is an attempt to summarise briefly some of these landmarks.

2.1   A short odyssey through competitiveness

2.1.1   Classical economics provides the ground work

The end of the 18th century and the beginning of the 19th century was a period of vast socioeconomic change in Europe. It was during this period, and throughout the Industrial Revolution, that capitalism emerged from what had been a feudal society and economic order. The new capitalist order seemed to be organised around a system in which every individual sought their own prosperity. The key question was: how could such a society avoid collapsing into chaos? The answer lay in understanding the factors driving growth and development, as explained by the classical economists. This approach is mainly found in the works of Adam Smith, Jean-Baptiste Say, and David Ricardo [1, 4, 5]. Their work identified the wealth of a nation as the *yearly national income*, rather than the size of the royal treasury. Their work defined the factors that are essential as "inputs" to the production process:

- land;
- natural resources (sometimes included under "land");
- capital;
- labour.

According to the classical economists, national income is the product of labour applied to land, capital, and natural resources. A competitive advantage in one or more of these factors would lead to increased competitiveness. They identified these four factors, since they were the ones most applicable to the extractive and manufacturing industries which prevailed during their time. Classical economics also stresses the benefits of trade. As principles, they still retain a lot of usefulness for economists today.

The main strategy of nations at the time was to sustain their competitiveness by gaining access to one or all of these input factors through industrial policy, or even war. Throughout history, securing *land*, even through conquest, has been a constant obsession of nations, from the Roman empire to the present day. As we saw in Chapter 1, size was identified early on as a key component of competitiveness.

Securing sources of *natural resources* became a top priority for countries from the 15th century onwards. The conquest of the Americas by Spain and Portugal was to seek new sources of gold and silver. The Netherlands and England created vast trading empires to gain access to spices from Asia. With the Industrial Revolution, it became even more important to secure access to natural resources in order to "feed" the production capacity of Europe. To be competitive during this period, some nations found it necessary to create and sustain networks of colonies, whose main purpose was to ensure the availability of natural resources to sustain the development of manufacturing industries at home.

Access to *capital* – conceived as accumulated wealth – has also been a preoccupation of countries and rulers. Throughout human history, seeking wealth has led to numerous clashes – the "People of the Sea" in the Mediterranean world of the 12th century BC, the Hittites in the 9th century BC, the Huns in the 5th century AD, and the Mongolians in the 13th century are just some examples of "hostile takeovers" of someone else's capital [6]. However, during the Industrial Revolution, capital took on a whole new meaning. It became less important to have capital as accumulated wealth, and more important to have capital *as a means of production* – whether it was used to produce more or not.

Access to *labour* has often been a corollary to gaining new land – especially if it means access to a cheap labour force. Slavery is linked intimately to the development of societies, including advanced ancient Greek and Roman civilisations. It also sustained the industrial development of Europe and the Americas up until the last abolitions of the 19th century, when it became untenable on philosophical, political, and economic grounds. The notion that labour could also be educated, and thus become more productive, only really appeared in the middle of the 19th century.

2.1.2 The law of comparative advantage: still the cornerstone

The law of comparative advantage has often been described as the most important theory in economics – being at the same time logical, simple, and equally applicable to nations, firms, and individuals. Although the English economist Robert Torrens had first described the law of comparative advantage in an essay he wrote concerning the trade of corn between England and Poland, the law is mainly associated with the work of David Ricardo [7]. In his book, *On The Principles of Political Economy and Taxation*, Ricardo states that the country with the lowest opportunity cost for producing a particular good should specialise in producing that good [5]. To illustrate his point, he used the trade of cloth and wine between England and Portugal. Even if Portugal can produce both wine and cloth cheaper than England can, Portugal should still concentrate on producing wine and not cloth, while England should focus on manufacturing cloth and not wine – Portugal can more easily "out-compete" England on wine than it can on cloth, and vice versa. The theory introduces the concept of *relative cost*, which, in turn, leads to the notion of *comparative advantage*. Nations should proceed to develop their exports of products where they would enjoy the largest relative comparative advantage, and import those goods where other nations have a better competitive edge. This theory of comparative advantage provides the intellectual foundations of international trade as a means of ensuring the prosperity of *all* nations, and not as a "zero sum game": the success of one nation is not necessarily built at the expense of another.

In the competitiveness mindset, the law of comparative advantage implies that a nation, firm, or individual should not focus automatically on activities it can perform *better* or *cheaper* than its competitors, but, rather, on those where its relative advantage is *larger*. The law entails two fundamental assumptions:

1. An organisation or an individual needs to identify, and then specialise in, the *uniqueness factors* setting them apart from competitors.
2. As we have seen in Chapter 1, the law underlines the importance of building a strategy which *maximises* the *relative* advantage between competitors – being number one is not such an enviable position if number two is very close behind.

The more modern concept of competitiveness builds on the law of comparative advantage, and expands on it by being more *proactive* in the management of the determinants of the law. In the classical context, the input factors – land, natural resources, capital, and labour – were mainly considered as a given. For example, the labour cost of a firm was entirely dependent on the wage level of the workforce within the borders of the nation where the firm operated. Today, however, firms can escape their local market conditions and *track* the access to input factors on a worldwide basis. A firm can thus locate operations in any nation: it can choose the one which provides the largest comparative advantage in specific factors, such as the extraction of raw materials, research, manufacturing products, or servicing customers.

The globalisation of business, the opening of world markets, and the wide availability of technology have considerably expanded the application of the law of comparative advantage, and modified some of its mechanisms. Nevertheless, the principles set forth by Robert Torrens and David Ricardo still continue to define some of the most fundamental attributes of competitiveness as we conceive it today.

2.1.3 The sociopolitical context really matters

The impact of social structures on the prosperity of a nation has long been an issue of interest to scholars. It was not until the 17th century, however, that the relationship started to be studied in greater depth, and much more systematically in the works of political theorists such as

Figure 2.1 – Karl Marx (1818–1883). He is, of course, well known for his analysis of history in terms of class conflict and the antagonism between capital owners and wage labourers. A key determinant in the competitiveness analysis of a nation today is the importance he gave to the impact of the sociopolitical environment on economic development.

Hobbes (1588–1679), Locke (1632–1704), Montesquieu (1689–1755), Voltaire (1694–1778), Burke (1729–1797), and de Tocqueville (1805–1859).

The most accurate, articulate, and critical description of the social impact of business and economic relations is provided by the theory of class struggle of Karl Marx (Figure 2.1) [8]. Marx's powerful analysis of the relationship between society, politics, and economics can be exemplified by developments in China.

I belong to a generation that grew up immersed in a mythical view of China. When I was young, I felt I knew better the streets of Cambaluc – the city of Kubilai Khan described by Marco Polo (1254–1324) in his *Book of Marvels* – today called Beijing, than the streets of my own town [9]. That idealised, Europeanised vision of China, a mixture of wonder and enigma, became part of European culture, as almost every European castle in the 18th century had a "Chinese room." Yet, it also immediately suggested a mystery – why didn't such a brilliant civilisation, more advanced than any other nation on Earth at the time, have its own industrial revolution?

When China was ahead of the world

Although it is widely recognised that the Chinese invented paper money (9th century) and printing (8th century) long before the West, other fundamental inventions they made are less well known. Here are some examples:

- the ploughshare (6th century BC);
- cast iron (4th century BC);
- double air bellows (4th century BC);
- the compass (4th century BC);
- transforming cast iron into steel (2nd century BC);
- the parachute (2nd century BC);
- the crank (2nd century BC);
- the suspended bridge (1st century BC);
- the wheelbarrow (1st century BC);
- the rudder (1st century AD);
- Chinaware (3rd century AD);
- the river lock (10th century AD);
- the spinning wheel (12th century AD).

Source: [10]

In his seminal work "*Science and Civilisation in China*," published in 1954, Joseph Needham compiled a list of some of the most striking technological innovations made by ancient China [11]. In almost every field of knowledge, China was ahead of the rest of the world at one point or another. Yet, despite its unprecedented and unmatched technological prowess, China did not sufficiently develop its agricultural base so that it could ensure enough food to feed its population, nor did it develop an industrial base to capitalise on its accumulated knowledge. The population theories of Malthus (1766–1834) also illustrate China's situation [12]. According to Malthusian principles, starvation and natural disasters regulate population growth, and thus define the fate of nations.

Voyages of discovery

Christopher Columbus sailed to the Americas, landing on the island he called Hispaniola in 1492 (Figure 2.2). His "discovery" of a new world is considered to be one of the most important dates in history. Christopher Columbus sailed with a fleet of three ships, the Niña, the Pinta, and the Santa María, which were, on average, 22 metres long.

Very few people know that some 71 years earlier, in 1421, Admiral Zheng He led an armada of four fleets (led by himself, Grand Eunuch Hong Bao, Eunuch Zhou Man, and Eunuch Zhou Wen), which sailed around the world and explored the Indian Ocean, Africa, South America, Antarctica, North America, and Australia (Figure 2.2). When they sailed back, Emperor Zhu Di of the Ming Dynasty, who had commissioned this voyage, had lost his throne. His successors, Zhu Gaozi and Zhu Zhanji, closed China to the rest of the world and ordered the destruction of most of the records of the expedition. Once again, China led the world in technology and discovery, but decided instead not to make the most of the breakthrough: a regular occurrence in Chinese history.

1492   1421

CHRISTOPHER
COLOMBUS

3 SHIPS:
~ 22 m LONG

ADMIRAL
ZHENG HE

100 JUNKS:
SOME 160 m LONG

Figure 2.2 – Two dates, two admirals. *Source:* **[13]**

For eleven centuries, the Chinese did not transform their technological advances and knowledge into economic competitiveness – they remained at a developmental stand-still. The sociopolitical environment that prevailed in China for many centuries, blocked aspirations and efforts to reap economic benefit from its knowledge-base, and serves as an example of how value systems influence competitiveness – a topic which we will develop further in Chapter 6.

Two major philosophical schools coexist within Asia: Confucianism and Taoism. Confucianism advances values such as hard work, loyalty, discipline, thrift, and education; values that are still very pervasive in Asia today. On the other hand, Taoism purports a less active approach: it encourages the attainment of an inherent harmony and stability between individuals and the environment in which they live. Perfection in Taoism can lead to non-action.

Taoism increasingly became part of the official philosophy of the Chinese empire from the Han dynasty. Yet, its drawbacks became especially clear during the Tang dynasty (618–907 AD), a time of great technological innovation. In the Taoist philosophy, the State is unalterable and has a command structure which places the emperor at the top of the power pyramid – the only intercessor with the heavens. Since new ideas presented an untenable challenge to the established order of society, economic and societal developments in China were halted for centuries; the Middle Empire thus became the "Immobile Empire."

Marxist philosophers quickly realised that knowledge of the sociopolitical environment is fundamental to the understanding of economic development. The Industrial Revolution in Europe was not only the result of technological revolutions, but also of the emergence of a new class of citizen: the *bourgeoisie*. Initially lacking the access to land and large estates of the privileged nobility, this new class focused its energy and inventiveness on trade and industry [14]. Gains in wealth, in turn, quickly triggered increasing demands for political rights, especially in England and France, where they led directly to the French Revolution.

Karl Marx always held that "philosophy is *praxis*" – the goal of philosophy is to lead to action. Marxist philosophers assumed that changing the root cause of society's problems, i.e. the sociopolitical order, would alter the outcome, i.e. the economic development of the nation. The concept of the class struggle was born.

The importance of Marxist thinking for competitiveness lies in the significance it gives to sociopolitical environment analysis in understanding the determinants of prosperity. The Marxist approach opens the path to understanding what is behind the structure of a sociopolitical environment, that is, the value system of a society. The relationship between value systems and society was investigated by another German philosopher, Max Weber (1864–1920).

The Industrial Revolution

Some scholars date the beginning of the Industrial Revolution by the invention of the steam engine with a piston, patented in 1769 by James Watt (1736–1819), and shown in Figure 2.3 in its 1774 version. But James Watt was not alone; he was part of a new class within English society, the *bourgeoisie*, which thrived on a passion for everything modern: it which was composed of inventors, scientists, and industrialists. In contrast with China, English technological innovations were turned immediately into mass-market products during the 18th and 19th centuries.

Industrialists such as Richard Arkwright, Matthew Boulton, and Josiah Wedgwood transformed what could have been mere scientific curiosities into a formidably competitive system for Britain. As industrial production exploded, Britain became the wealthiest and most powerful nation of the 19th century. In 1760, Britain imported only 1000 tons of raw cotton to supply its factories; by 1850, these imports had jumped to an incredible 222 000 tons!

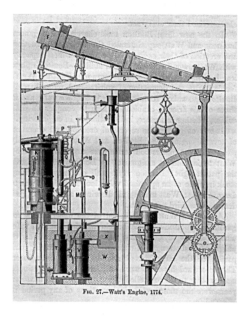

Fig. 27.—Watt's Engine, 1774.

Figure 2.3 – The Industrial Revolution in Britain.

2.1.4   Value systems are valuable

In 1905, Max Weber wrote *The Protestant Ethic and the Spirit of Capitalism* – a landmark book in both philosophy and economics [15]. In his work, he demonstrated that the so-called *Homo Economicus*, described by the classical economists, was not, after all, a completely rational and analytical machine. His thoughts and actions were influenced by emotions and values, which were deeply rooted in his religious and philosophical background. Assuming, as some Hegelian and Marxist philosophers had, that the environment would shape the mind, and that religion, as a provider of values, is a key determinant in any environment, Max Weber set himself the task of investigating the link between religion and economic development (Figure 2.4).

He tried to understand why the German Catholic states (the *Länder* in Germany), were less developed, from an economic point of view, than the Protestant ones. He concluded that a pure ascetic Protestantism, as expressed for example in Calvinism (derived from the name of Jean

Figure 2.4 – Max Weber (1864–1920). He argued that the "Calvinist" ethic of godliness, which fosters the dedication of the individual to one's present occupation – one's *beruf* ("call of duty") – leads to higher labour productivity in Protestant countries. By contrast, Catholic principles lead people to believe that their current occupation is only a step towards a better, more dignified position. By implication, today's job is not perceived meaningful, and productivity collapses.

Calvin, 1509–1564, a French pastor who emigrated to Geneva to teach a strict Protestantism), would better support entrepreneurial economic development. In the Protestant ethic, success is considered an earthly sign of being "elected" by God. Work creates a direct link between the individual and God. Success is a manifestation of God's "grace."

Max Weber took a philosophical approach. Economists, however, were quick to see the implications for the economic development of nations. More recently, Alain Peyrefitte, in his book *Le Mal Français (The French Disease)*, establishes a relationship between the early industrialisation of Protestant European states and the lethargy of those that had undergone the "Counter Reformation" of Catholicism in the late 16th century [16]. In the "pure" Catholic value system, money is considered a sign of greed, not a sign of God. Such a value system would not encourage risk taking and industrialisation. His conclusions are similar to those of Max Weber.

Obviously this doesn't mean that everyone should become Calvinist to support competitiveness. However, it does suggest that a good understanding of value systems is essential to competitiveness. Another French writer, Michel Albert (1930–), formerly High Commissioner to the French Plan and also a businessman, went one step further [17]. Within the Protestant value system, he made a distinction between what he called the Rhenan Continental European and the Anglo-Saxon value systems.

The paradigm that social and cultural values have an observable impact on competitiveness still holds to this day. Our own research on world competitiveness, using correlation analysis of the results of the *IMD World Competitiveness Yearbook*, has also highlighted three similar models [18]:

- a *"Southern Model,"* which is defined by little regulation, parallel unreported activities, and a high degree of volatility;
- a *"Continental European Model,"* which is highly regulated and emphasises stability and consensus;
- an *"Anglo-Saxon Model,"* which reduces the level of regulation and strives for flexibility, risk taking, and empowerment of people.

These models will be discussed further in Chapter 6, where values and competitiveness will be addressed in depth. Although such models can sometimes be perceived as a simplification of a complex reality, they underline the importance of value systems for understanding and managing competitiveness at the level of a nation or a firm.

Figure 2.5 – Joseph Schumpeter (1883–1950). For Joseph Schumpeter, entrepreneurs are the main drivers of economic development because they regularly disrupt the equilibrium advocated by the classic economists. Surprisingly, Schumpeter was not optimistic about the future of capitalism. He argued that, as capitalism advanced, it would not support entrepreneurship, and more egalitarian societies would prevail.

2.1.5 The destructive creativity of entrepreneurs

The sociological approach of the Marxists and Max Weber describes an environment that sets the framework for the action of the individual. The role of the individual as an entrepreneur was explained by the Austrian economist Joseph Alois Schumpeter (1883–1950) in his famous book, written in 1942, *Capitalism, Socialism and Democracy* [19]. Schumpeter (Figure 2.5) is remembered for his dynamic approach to capitalism. He emphasised that progress is the result of disequilibria, such as cyclical crises, which favour innovation and technological improvement. The key role in economic progress is thus played by the entrepreneur, through his ability to break the traditional mould with daring investments, technology, and business models. This is the well-known "creative destruction process."

Schumpeter's contribution was to link the notion of economic progress with breakdowns and breakthroughs. The classical economists could only conceive of the economy in terms of "perfect equilibrium" or smooth linear evolution. In Schumpeter's "brave new world," the breakdown of a model that has reached its limit, or the breakthroughs of entrepreneurs who reinvent a model by "thinking the unthinkable," are the true engines of economic progress. The "Internet bubble" is a perfect illustration of this theory. The old economic framework abruptly collapsed, and numerous new business models blossomed in enterprises.

The Schumpeterian entrepreneur theory is obviously central to the concept of competitiveness. It shows that "turning points" in industrial innovation, i.e. the unexpected emergence of a new technology, a new product, or a new business model, have a considerable impact – positive or negative – on the destiny of enterprises and countries alike. It also explains the formidable success of entrepreneurs who break from a traditional business model to play a kind of "catch me if you can" strategy.

I have always wondered how Ray Kroc, the developer of the McDonald's restaurant chain, would have explained his new business model to a group of potential investors [20]. Would he have described how, in his new type of restaurant, customers would queue up in front of the kitchen to get their little meal on a plastic tray, that they would then have to fight for a table, eat with their fingers, drink out of paper cups and that finally, at the end of their meal, they would be expected to bring back their empty tray? Who would have believed that he would find anyone to invest in this new undertaking? But, as we all know, it worked!

The same applies to Ingvar Kamprad, the founder of the Swedish furniture store chain Ikea. He too, would have had to explain to potential investors that, in his new type of store, customers would take their piece of furniture off the shelves in a package, that it would take them half an hour to fit it into their car, that once home they would spend two days trying to assemble everything, before realising that a screw was missing. And that, even more surprisingly, two weeks and a few extra scars on their hands later, the same customer would be back at the store for more. Crazy in theory, but it has been, and is, a huge success!

The problem with the Schumpeterian model is that a society, however competitive it may want to be, cannot be composed of only entrepreneurs. Indeed, only a few individuals have the ability to become "mould breakers." In addition, any society or enterprise needs administrators. Therefore, the key challenge arising from Schumpeter's theory is how to maintain a reasonably high level of efficiency, and not necessarily innovation, in the nonentrepreneurial part of society.

Schumpeter was unexpectedly quite pessimistic about the future of such a system. He, like Marx but for different reasons, felt that capital-

Breaking the mould

Figure 2.6 shows Microsoft's founding team in 1978, with Bill Gates in the front row, first from the left. Twenty years later, Microsoft was one of the most valuable companies in the world. In addition, its products have contributed to the development of a new industry, and to the creation of jobs for millions of people: a great example of the theory of Schumpeter!

Figure 2.6 – Radical ideas are not necessarily bad ideas. (Reprinted with the permission of Microsoft Corporation.)

ism would destroy itself. With success, the "bourgeoisie" would decompose. Success would bring complacency, arrogance, and emphasise security. Profits would diminish, and entrepreneurs would become bureaucrats, adverse to innovation. The whole system would collapse from inside. The only way to escape this inexorable fate was to maintain a high level of competitiveness among the elite. How?

2.1.6　The rational thinking of managers

In modern times, two men have addressed this dilemma with considerable success. They have invented the concept of modern "management," which I like to define as "day-to-day competitiveness without being a genius . . ."

Alfred P. Sloan Jr (1875–1965), in his book *My Years with General Motors*, was the first to advance classical concepts of modern management, such as organisations structured by divisions, financial control systems, incentive compensation, product management, and, of course, the well-known distinction between line and staff [21]. This book has fascinated generations of businessmen because it brought the concept of the Nietzschean–Superhero–Entrepreneur down to the level of our daily lives of competitiveness. Even today, Bill Gates is quoted as saying: "I think Alfred Sloan's *My Years with General Motors* is probably the best book to read if you want to read only one book about business" [22].

The other founding father of modern management is Peter Drucker (1909–) an economist of Austrian origin living in the US. In his book *The Age of Discontinuity*, he defined modern management, organisational structures, strategy, motivation, and societal responsibility as some of the main competitiveness factors of today [23]. I have only once had

---

The rationalisation of activities

In contrast to entrepreneurship, management aims at rationalising activities within an organisation. As such, management is not a new science. The Hanseatic League is an early example of a "managed" organisation. Created in 1241 as a treaty of mutual protection between Hamburg and Lübeck in North Germany, it was really a league of merchant associations which traded around the Baltic Sea. It had standard management rules and principles, as well as a board: the Hanseatic Diet.

Nearby in Sweden, Bishop Peter acquired, along with some other "business" partners (one was the King of Sweden), one eighth of Kopparberg Mountain and started mining operations, thereby founding Stora (now Stora Enso) in 1288. This company is generally considered to be one of the oldest companies in the West still in existence and operation.

Figure 2.7 – The Arsenal in Venice, one of the best-managed European companies of the Middle Ages.

In Venice, the Arsenal, or City shipyard (Figure 2.7), was established in 1104, and quickly became one of the largest enterprises in Europe, employing some 3000 workers by the 14th century. Standardisation was highly developed: every piece and part of the galleys was manufactured according to precise specifications that could be reproduced easily. The Arsenal was able to arm 100 galleys in seven weeks! In addition, the standardisation of processes allowed "spare parts" to be stocked in various warehouses around the Mediterranean Sea to repair vessels quickly. At the famous battle of Lepante in 1571, half of the Christian vessels which defeated the Turkish armada had been produced by the Arsenal.

the honour of sharing the stage with him when I was a young professor. Despite the fact that he was already getting on in years, he remained highly provocative: "So much of what we call management today consists of making it difficult for people to work!" So true . . .

The distinction between entrepreneurs and managers is not clear cut. It is correct that a company needs to balance both, or at least provide structures and processes that favour the work of both. To this extent, some companies are trying to breed "intrapreneurs," i.e. individuals who exercise their entrepreneurial spirit within the framework of a special entity inside the company. New ideas are tested and developed within the special structure, before being absorbed and implemented by existing operational units. Nokia's New Venture Organisation (a concept which will be developed further in Chapter 7) provides such a structure.

While working at Hewlett-Packard, I once had a discussion with the co-founder of the company, Bill Hewlett, about this issue. He had already retired from operational affairs, but his influence on the company was still considerable. He continued to be fascinated by the relationship between innovation and the obsolescence of products. He said: "At HP we kill our products ourselves, before the competition does it" – the closest I have come to an institutionalised Schumpeterian approach.

2.1.7   Knowledge and technology lead growth

Just after World War II, the various elements of the puzzle of competitiveness were almost in place. The next challenge was to define how they would *interact* with each other.

Robert Solow (1924–), professor at MIT, received the Nobel Prize in economics for the "Growth Model" that now bears his name. He studied the factors underlying the real growth in the US economy between 1948 and 1982 [24]. His contribution was to bring to light the main determinants of economic development. He classified them into three categories and attributed a relative impact to each:

1.   Additional labour and capital equipment: 20%.
2.   Improvement in the education level of the workforce: 30%.
3.   Technological innovation and increased know-how: 50%.

Without going into the detail of such a monumental analysis, it is important to realise that the work of Robert Solow underlines how much the economy has changed since the Industrial Revolution. The non-tangible aspects of the economy, such as education of the workforce, technological innovation, and increased know-how, have become key factors of competitiveness. With Robert Solow, *knowledge* becomes a central element of modern competitiveness. He, thus, laid the foundations for the reflection of many modern scholars who later capitalised on the *knowledge* factor.

Liberty Ships

Between 1941 and 1945, the United States launched 2571 "Liberty Ships" to transport goods for military operations in Europe and the Pacific (Figure 2.8). The first such ship launched was the SS Patrick Henry on 27 November 1941. It took 225 days to build. Soon, the shipyards adopted a standard mass-produced design to increase production. The 250 000 parts were prefabricated at several different sites within the US and then assembled at a central location. As a result, just a year later, a Liberty Ship could be built in only 70 days. The record is held by the SS Robert E. Peary, which was assembled in a mere 4 days, 15 hours, and 26 minutes! New management processes and the accumulation of manufacturing knowledge made the difference. This level of efficiency, which was only to be matched four decades later when quality methods were introduced, also produced a highly motivated workforce. "Praise the Lord and pass another section" was the motto. Their only drawback was the aesthetic qualities of the ships: President Franklin Delano Roosevelt nicknamed them "ugly ducklings."

Figure 2.8 – Knowledge and the Liberty Ships.

In 1973, for example, Ernest Gellner also argued that throughout the past two centuries, economies have become more and more driven by the importance of knowledge [25]. Agrarian societies were driven by mercantilism, which held that the accumulation of precious metal is the source of power. Spain went to the Americas to accumulate gold and silver. Mercantilism was a zero-sum game. The breakthrough came with Adam Smith, when he argued that the use of resources – the factors of production – is more important than their accumulation. David Ricardo took it one step further with the theory of comparative advantage. He tore down the zero-sum approach by arguing that all nations are better off by trading with one another. Gellner underlines that the transition to an industrial world could only be made possible by the wide dispersion of knowledge.

More recently, scholars such as Nicholas Negroponte, co-founder and chairman of the MIT Media Laboratory, have stated that knowledge is intrinsically valuable, aside from any immediate industrial application [26]. As such, knowledge has been acknowledged as a direct determinant of competitiveness, and thus prosperity.

2.1.8 Rivalry and clusters: The Diamond Theory of Michael Porter

One of the early attempts to systematise the various factors of competitiveness is the work of Professor Michael Porter of Harvard Business School. In his book, *The Competitive Advantage of Nations*, Michael Porter puts forward the now famous "Diamond Theory" (Figure 2.9) to highlight how the main determinants of competitiveness interact for nations [27].

The various components of the Diamond Theory are so well known that a only a brief summary is needed here:

- *Factor conditions*: the fundamental factors articulated by the classical economists – labour, land, capital, and natural resources – as well as basic and advanced infrastructure.
- *Demand conditions*: the composition of the home demand (structure and needs), the size and pattern of growth, and the internationalisation of home demand.
- *Related and supported industries*: this determinant includes, among others, the Cluster theory, which promotes a concentration of enterprises, which, in turn, coordinate or share activities in the value chain, or initiate technical interchange.

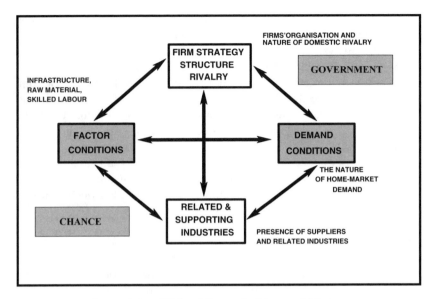

Figure 2.9 – Michael Porter's Diamond Theory.

- *Firm strategy, structure, and rivalry*: this part of the diamond looks at the intensity of domestic rivalry, as well as managerial attitudes and practices.

Michael Porter's analysis includes two additional factors that are not integrated fully into his model. They are:

- *Chance*, which comprises unforeseen events such as wars, earthquakes, shortage of a commodity (food, oil), and so forth.
- *Government*: Michael Porter did not believe that this could be a fifth determinant of competitiveness. However, in Europe, Latin America, and Asia, governments are often a driving force in the development of competitiveness (negative or positive), mainly through their industrial policies. In the US, government intervention is traditionally more limited. Incidentally, it is interesting to note that the US government, unlike most other nations, does not have a Secretary for the Economy!

It is always unfair and subjective to summarise a major book, in this case 855 pages long. But, to me, the most salient points that refine the notion of competitiveness are:

1. Competitiveness is a systemic approach. The relationship between the factors, or determinants of competitiveness, is just as important as the analysis of the factors themselves. The interaction of factors is the other facet of competitiveness.
2. It is not necessary to pursue an advantage in all the factors of competitiveness – only a few are needed. Nevertheless, it is a valid strategy to aim for a significant advantage in one, or many, of the determinants, as already suggested by the theory of comparative advantage.
3. As a consequence, for a competitive nation, a disadvantage in one determinant is usually offset by an important advantage in another.
4. The sustainability of a comparative advantage also determines its value above and beyond any immediate returns.

The next two points require more thorough explanation:

5. Intense rivalry between firms in the home market defines their competitiveness abroad. In other words, you can only be competitive in international markets if you have learned to compete at home.

Michael Porter studied the number of competing firms in various industry sectors at length. He found a correlation between the degree of rivalry a firm is exposed to in the home market and the level of competitiveness achieved abroad. The development of the computer industry in Europe is a case in point. In the 1970s and 1980s, computer companies were defined as "strategic" by European governments. As such, they received preferential treatment in their own national markets. This meant that public procurement favoured the "national champion." The French government bought only Bull computers, the Italians would only purchase from Olivetti, the Germans from Siemens, and so forth.

Such policies led to unexpected consequences. Bull, for example, became the strongly dominant leader in the French computer market, yet was completely unable to penetrate any other market in Europe. The reason was twofold: Bull became complacent on the French market, since contracts were more or less "guaranteed," and neighbouring countries retaliated by closing their public procurements to Bull. By the end of the 1980s, the situation in an emerging unified European market was absurd: the number one computer company in each country was always the national champion, but the number two was always a US company!

To illustrate this point of theory further, I often describe a conversation I had with Akio Morita (Figure 2.10), the legendary chairman of Sony, in his Tokyo office. He took me over to the window of his office (I later learned that he did this with almost all of his visitors) [28]. "What

Figure 2.10 – Akio Morita (1921–1999) is credited with developing Sony into one of the few truly multinational Japanese companies. He encouraged the invention of the Walkman, bringing him worldwide fame. In addition, he was a shrewd connoisseur of both Western and Eastern cultures, which gave him remarkable insights on both. For example, he felt that the decline in US and European competitiveness in the 1980s was due to a disinterest in manufacturing excellence.

do you see?" he asked me. Well, I could see a lot of billboards advertising all of Sony's competitors. Then he asked me, "Have you been to the Philips Headquarters in Eindhoven recently?" I had indeed. "What did you see?" Well, in fact, all I had been able to see there was Philips, Philips, Philips. He concluded by saying "If you operate in a highly competitive environment like Japan (even if only comprised of Japanese companies, I might add), then you will be competitive abroad . . ." This was a perfect illustration of the theory of rivalry in home markets.

This rivalry strategy has some important consequences for competitiveness. It means that any merger or acquisition inside the home market that leads to a consolidation of a business sector, and a reduction of domestic rivalry, is bad for the competitiveness of a nation. Switzerland experienced just such a situation with the merger of its two largest banks, the UBS and the SBS, in 1997. From a company competitiveness point of view, it may have made business sense to create a larger bank with more weight on international markets; but this merger also meant rationalisation of the work force, and reduction of competition on the home market. For the competitiveness of Switzerland, it would have been much better had the UBS and SBS each bought a foreign bank. The same can be said about the Deutsche Bank acquisition of Dresdner Bank in Germany.

6. Clusters are a key and powerful determinant in sustaining the competitiveness of a nation.

In advanced industrial economies, clusters are well established: Silicon Valley for the computer industry, Hollywood for movies, Detroit for cars, New York for finance, Ireland for IT assembling and call centres, the British Midlands for the car industry, Baden-Würtemberg and Bavaria in Germany for cars and electronics, Basel in Switzerland for life sciences, Bologna in Italy for design and steel, Osaka in Japan for mechanical electronics, and so on [29].

In industrialising nations, the concept is just as powerful. The formidable economic development of China as a manufacturing powerhouse for the rest of the world was based on the creation of Special Economic Zones on the east coast of China [30]. Shenzhen, near Hong Kong, is one of the most striking successes of this policy, and is a world leader in toy production, among others. Bangalore in India is now renowned for the vitality of its software companies, Dubai in the United Arab Emirates is breaking ground in Internet technology, multimedia and financial affairs.

A cluster approach to competitiveness has a number of characteristics:

1. It is a well-defined area where companies share and interface their value chain. They also develop common access to a skilled workforce, or knowledge base. Interaction between companies defines a cluster; it is not simply a concentration of enterprises.
2. There is often a knowledge nucleus at the centre of a cluster. It can be a prestigious university, such as Stanford for Palo Alto and Silicon Valley, or, surprisingly enough, a military complex. The success of Omaha (Nebraska) as a cluster for communications is closely linked

to the presence of the Strategic Air Command activities in the region. Military operations procure a lot in their direct environment, and create advanced knowledge.

3. In emerging countries, clusters must benefit from a special development policy, such as efficient infrastructure (traditional, such as ports, airports, or railways, and advanced, such as telecommunications), favourable employment regulations (for expatriates and locals), and tax incentives to lure foreign companies.

Clusters are an extremely efficient policy for the development of the competitiveness of a nation. They imply, however, a concept of competitiveness that is based on first developing "islands of competitiveness," then multiplying and rolling the concept out across the country. To be successful, it demands strong political involvement, which is not feasible everywhere. The success of the Special Economic Zones in China was linked to a restrictive government policy that controlled labour flows inside the country. A successful cluster can quickly attract a huge workforce, lured by higher wages and better living standards. This could potentially "kill" the cluster, while creating imbalances in the development of other regions of the country.

This is one of the strong limiting factors in a cluster policy. South Africa, for example, has all the ingredients to develop a competitive cluster in the Cape Town region: good infrastructure (roads, airport,

---

What's next?

The rise of clusters is often an early sign of the development of competitiveness. At first, nations provide low-cost inputs to foreign firms, for example, financial services and back-office operations in India. Then, they offer access to their own domestic market. In other words, they move from "market sourcing" to "market serving" foreign direct investment (Figure 2.11).

In due course, nations launch and export their own brands. Japan reached that stage in the 1970s, when companies such as Sony, Toyota and Panasonic became global premium brands to the world. South Korea, India, and China are moving quickly in that direction, and are becoming fierce brand providers to the rest of the world.

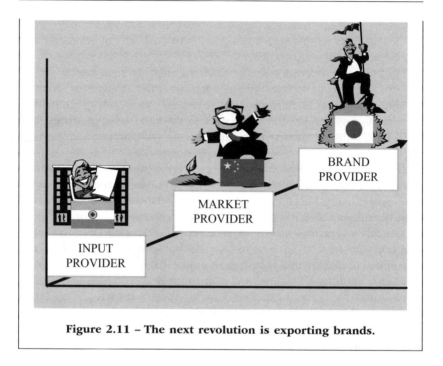

Figure 2.11 – The next revolution is exporting brands.

harbour), excellent language and working skills, a well-established financial centre, and a strategic location in Africa. However, such a strategy would imply giving Cape Town temporary preferential treatment in the competitiveness strategy of South Africa. In view of the history of the country, this would be politically unacceptable for the South African government.

By the 1990s, all the determinants that support the notion of competitiveness had been articulated, and could thus be integrated into a single definition – a definition that will serve as the basis of our discussion throughout this book.

2.2   Competitiveness of nations – a formal definition

The "one-liner" definition mentioned earlier can be supplemented by a more formal definition, which includes the multiple facets of competitiveness that we have been tracing as they developed over the years.

Competitiveness of Nations – the formal definition

"The theory of competitiveness is a field of economics which analyses the facts and policies shaping the ability of a nation to create and maintain an environment which sustains increasing value creation for firms and greater prosperity for its people."

Fundamentally, what differentiates competitiveness of nations and competitiveness of enterprises is *where* the creation of economic value takes place in society. Our assumption is that economic value is *only created by enterprises*. Nations can establish an environment that hinders or supports the activities of enterprises. However, a nation does not generate economic added value directly.

The ownership of enterprises should not blur this important distinction – an enterprise can be partly or fully State-owned and still be fulfilling its role of economic value creation. Indeed, in a socialist system, where all enterprises directly or indirectly belong to the State, enterprises continue to play their role as the only source of economic value creation. In a market economy, ownership of enterprises is in private hands. In both systems, however, enterprises perform the same function – they provide the framework in which labour and capital are combined to produce goods and services for other firms and households. The difference lies, therefore, in the *levels of efficiency* attained by enterprises in various systems, but *not* in the nature of the tasks they perform.

The longer definition is better understood by breaking it down into its individual components:

"the theory of competitiveness is a field of economics . . ."

Competitiveness of nations, as a field of economics, is relatively new in itself – it has only recently, in the early 1980s become a field of research and teaching. As we have just seen, the theory of competitiveness is built upon the aggregation of a number of ideas, developed over the past two centuries by leading thinkers. While they might not have explicitly used the term "competitiveness," they articulated its fundamental components.

"which analyses the facts and policies . . ."

A nation's business environment is the result of a combination of:

- facts, which have to be taken as given, and
- policies, which can be influenced by human effort.

Among the facts that affect the competitiveness of a nation are endowments in natural resources, land area, risk of natural disasters, such as earthquakes, floods, or El Niño, risk of human disasters, such as epidemics, war, and so on. A nation can try to manage the impact of these facts, for example, by constructing anti-seismic buildings, or by vaccinating the population. However, the potential for compensating for a lack of natural resources or size is limited. Policies, on the other hand, are entirely dependent upon the determination of people. They can be shaped and revised at will.

"shaping the ability of a nation to create and maintain an environment . . ."

Facts and policies together determine the strategic policy of a nation. Such a strategy has to be concerned with the long-term perspective, hence the use of the word "maintain." The concept of sustainability, mentioned in Chapter 1, emphasises this point.

"which sustains increasing value creation for firms . . ."

We have stressed so far that economic value is created only within firms. Here, the word to emphasise is "increasing." A nation could very well manage its competitive environment for mere survival. Some nations are quite satisfied with small, incremental rises in their economic performance. Such nations generally argue that they must preserve their quality of life, their cultural heritage, or they are simply wealthy enough to dispense with competitiveness. By their own standards, they appear to perform well, but, by competitiveness standards, they are gradually losing their comparative advantage to others. "Increasing" should also be understood as the possibility for a nation to exploit fully its competitiveness potential.

"and greater prosperity for its people."

Ultimately, competitiveness is about raising the prosperity of people, which can be defined as a combination of income, standard of living, and quality of life.

In this context, "prosperity" is important, because it emphasises the noneconomic side of competitiveness, while at the same time highlighting the unsustainable nature of any strategy of "competitiveness at all costs." Competitiveness cannot be reduced to productivity or profits. In the long term, a country that does not give its people fair access to

World wages

Although Figure 2.12 reflects a situation more than a decade old (1992), it indicates the vast differences in labour costs and in prosperity that existed in the world at that time. For example, OECD skilled workers represented less than 10% of the worldwide workforce, yet earned most of the global income. The globalisation of business, through trade and direct investments and strategies such as offshoring, have fully exploited these differences in revenues. As a result, the gap between world wages has narrowed, and will continue to narrow, during the coming decades.

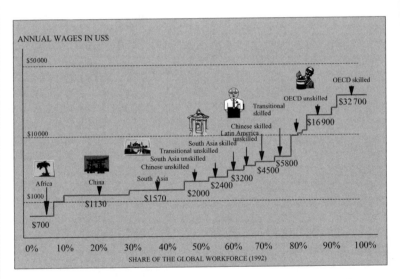

Figure 2.12 – Disparities in world wages. *Source*: **[31].**

the wealth it creates, that does not ensure an adequate health or education infrastructure, or does not maintain political or social stability, will not thrive. The government of Singapore, for example, has always been keen to "give back to the people" tangible signs of success of the economy – better housing, hospitals, and education. Other nations, mainly in Latin America, have undergone a bumpier road to competitiveness, because they have been less sensitive to sharing the fruits of success.

Having identified all of the components of competitiveness as a theory, the next step is to understand how competitiveness works, and how we can build upon it by using the Competitiveness Cube Theory.

Working Out National Competitiveness: The Cube Theory

3

> *"If it moves, tax it.*
> *If it keeps moving, regulate it.*
> *If it stops moving, subsidise it!"*

Ronald Reagan 1911–2004
(Describing government policy as he had seen it prior to his election to
the Presidency of the United States)

In Molière's play *The Bourgeois Gentleman* (1670), the main character, Monsieur Jourdain, wants to learn the arts [1]. In a discussion with his philosophy master on the different nature of verse and prose, he suddenly marvels: "I have been speaking in prose all my life without even knowing it!" before thanking his philosophy master profusely for this wonderful discovery.

Figuring out competitiveness bears some similarities to Monsieur Jourdain's discovery. Leaders with no knowledge of the theory of competitiveness have managed nations and companies for centuries, sometimes with great success. They relied on common sense, intuition, and a little experience. Historically, the management of a nation was really aimed at the management of power. *The Art of War* by the Chinese writer Sun Tzu (4th century BC) or *The Prince* by the Italian writer Niccolò Machiavelli (16th century) were remarkable analyses in their time, and gave leaders valuable advice on how to deal with, and crush, an enemy [2, 3].

Some scholars believe the theories contained in these masterpieces can be applied to competitiveness. After all, one of the objectives of competitiveness is to surpass, and even "eliminate," a competitor. However, competitiveness does not deal with power alone – it also deals with the management of prosperity by a nation or a company. Power, as we have seen in Chapter 1, can indeed be a means to achieve prosperity, but, in our modern world, power for its own sake is no longer a worthwhile goal for a society to pursue – prosperity is.

The works of Sun Tzu and Niccolò Machiavelli are also significant, because they systemise the actions of leaders, and they provide a basis for action. Although, over time, the vast majority of kings and traders have continued to manage their nations and their businesses in total ignorance of these writers, the few who read them were probably a bit more knowledgeable and efficient.

In certain respects, the *Competitiveness Cube Theory* follows a similar approach: it identifies the main components of competitiveness, establishes a simple model of their interaction, and works out the policy options and implications. Some parts of the model are the aggregation of existing facts (e.g. GDP, foreign direct investments, etc.). The objective is to place the pieces of the puzzle where they belong in the system, and to look at them from a competitiveness angle. Other parts of the model are more innovative, such as the *competitiveness forces*, which determine how competitiveness is managed.

Altogether, the Competitiveness Cube Theory aims at providing a simple understanding of the determinants of competitiveness, and how they can be used for policy purposes. The theory was formulated in the early 1990s to serve as a framework for IMD's research into world competitiveness. It has three objectives:

1. To identify the *four competitiveness factors*, which characterise how a nation's competitiveness is structured.
2. To highlight the *four competitiveness forces*, which determine how national competitiveness is managed.
3. To reveal the *interaction* between firm competitiveness and national competitiveness, and how competitiveness evolves over time.

The Competitiveness Cube Theory explains and illustrates the mechanism of competitiveness at a national level. It emphasises fundamental policy options and makes the link between the source of competitiveness, i.e., enterprises, and the ultimate goal of competitiveness, which is enhancing prosperity.

The competitiveness cube is shown in Figure 3.1. The cube models how a nation manages its competitiveness standing. The core of the model is the creation of value by firms. The *front* of the competitiveness cube represents the *four factors* and the *four forces* shaping the national competitive environment – this frontal face of the cube shows the wealth created in a nation within a given year. The *depth* of the competitiveness cube indicates the wealth accumulated by a nation over time. We can represent a country's competitiveness standing by a cube conveying wealth creation and accumulation – a larger face means more wealth creation, more depth means more wealth accumulated. For example, the face of the cube representing Switzerland is smaller than Singapore's, meaning Switzerland created less wealth during a given

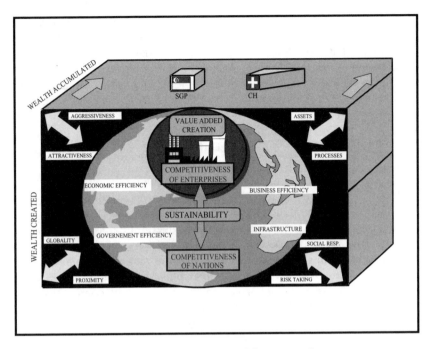

Figure 3.1 – The competitiveness cube.

period than Singapore did. Yet, its significantly deeper cube shows Switzerland's huge accumulated wealth.

In Chapter 2, we underlined that the competitiveness of a nation depends on its ability to combine given facts (for example, the availability of natural resources), and policies (for example, tax incentives) to create and maintain an environment that supports enterprises and enhances the prosperity of its people. It usually takes time to combine both facts and policies in a way that influences competitiveness – it is the *time* element that distinguishes competitiveness from mere economic performance.

At the core of the competitiveness cube we find firms – which, as we have argued, are the creators of economic value. The four factors of competitiveness form a circle surrounding this core, which have been identified by our research on competitiveness at IMD. They are: *economic efficiency, government efficiency, business efficiency* and *infrastructure*. We have identified the structure of these four factors by linking, through correlation analysis, economic theory and over 300 criteria that we use in IMD's *World Competitiveness Yearbook*.

The second circle illustrates how a given national environment can be "stretched" in one or another direction as a consequence of fundamental policies that have long-lasting impact. We have thus identified four dimensions in competitiveness describing the extent to which a nation emphasises some policies over others. These dimensions are *attractiveness vs. aggressiveness, social responsibility vs. risk, assets vs. processes*, and *proximity vs. globality*. These four dimensions are present in all nations to one extent or another – their relative importance varies – thereby painting a very different picture of how each individual nation manages its own competitiveness.

The depth of the competitiveness cube includes the time dimension within which a nation has been able to build its wealth endowment. The face of the competititiveness cube describes the "degree of competitiveness" reached by a nation within a given time period – the larger the face, the more competitive a nation. The depth of the cube shows the "accumulation of competitiveness" that the nation has inherited: i.e. wealth from the past. A young nation such as Singapore, however competitive it may be, does not have the same "depth" of competitiveness, or history, as Britain. Wealth, as indicated in Chapter 1, is not only about money or material resources, but includes the whole host of intangibles, such as education, infrastructure, or sciences, that reflect investments made by previous generations. Such wealth is a valuable base for future competitiveness, but only if it is well managed. For example, Britain has inherited a scientific tradition and an education system that are world-renowned. These are assets for the future competitiveness of Britain, although they alone cannot guarantee it. In a competitive mindset, accumulated wealth is only valuable if it is used to develop and enhance current competitiveness, and thus the prosperity of the people.

3.1 The firm: at the core of the Competitiveness Cube Theory

As we have mentioned before, the creation of economic value in a society takes place only at the level of the firm. The fact that only firms can create value is the key assumption of our model (Figure 3.2).

A nation's business environment, be it political, economic, or social, can be supportive or detrimental to economic value creation by firms – but the nation does not, *directly*, create economic value. There is an *indirect* creation of economic value by nations through their research, or education, policy. Even cultural policy can lead to the creation of economic value. For example, France's policy of strengthening its *cultural*

Figure 3.2 – Enterprises at the core of the model. Some scholars believed that nations did not compete; only enterprises did. While this viewpoint has become mostly obsolete, it did stem from a correct assumption: enterprises are the only place where economic value is created by combining the factors of production.

exception provides incentives for firms to produce films, books, or cultural events, which preserve French culture and language. Although the nation sets the course, the actual *transformation process* – taking labour, capital, and ideas and turning them into products – only takes place at the level of the firm.

The difference between a market economy and a State-planned economy lies in the ownership of enterprises, not in what those firms do. In a market economy, firms are in the hands of the private sector, while in State-planned economies, they are in the hands of the public sector. However, from a competitiveness point of view, as mentioned earlier, they perform the same function, perhaps with varying degrees of efficiency. In a mixed economy like China, the creation of added value by privately or State-owned enterprises is allocated to different sectors of the economy. Even in advanced market economies, the State has retained ownership of certain enterprises in so-called strategic industry sectors, such as defence. Therefore, from a competitiveness point of view, the ownership of enterprises is not an issue in itself. What really matters is the *level of efficiency* in enterprises as the main creator of economic added value in society.

Referring back to the definitions of competitiveness articulated in the previous chapters, one of the key objectives of a nation's competitiveness policy is thus to provide an environment which sustains the creation of economic value at the firm level. Thus, the competitiveness strategy of a nation has to correspond with the model of competitiveness in which its firms can thrive. While we will explore this further in the next chapter, dedicated to the *Extended Enterprise Model*, two key issues need to be stressed at this point:

1. Many nations' policymakers do not always grasp fully the evolution of the business model of enterprises, mainly because they do not have the professional background to do so. However, there are some exceptions, such as Singapore, where government officials have a high degree of business literacy.
2. While business models evolve quickly and react to market conditions, national competitiveness strategies take much more time and effort to be redesigned. There is a lack of synchronisation between the pace at which the business community works, and that of policy makers. Nations such as Japan and Germany have recently experienced difficulty in getting reforms in place quickly enough to match the fast-changing needs of business.

3.2 The four competitiveness factors

Viewing competitiveness can sometimes be likened to enhancing the clarity of a picture by increasing the number of pixels. The more pixels we use, in our case the criteria of competitiveness, the better the quality of the image we get. As mentioned before, IMD's *World Competitiveness Yearbook* uses more than 300 criteria of competitiveness, which can be grouped into the four main factors of competitiveness (Figure 3.3). These four competitiveness factors provide a simple and appropriate portrayal of the elements of competitiveness of a nation.

3.2.1 Economic efficiency

This first factor regroups all of the traditional macroeconomic evaluations of the *performance* of a nation, such as GDP growth, international trade, international investment, employment, and prices. While considerable research and literature has been produced on each one of these subfactors, research into their relationship with competitiveness is more recent.

International trade is a well-developed area of research for competitiveness, which can be traced back all the way to the Law of Comparative Advantage of David Ricardo. Not so long ago, it led some scholars to reduce the competitiveness of a nation simply to its capacity to export. Now, we take a more comprehensive view. The importance of the price

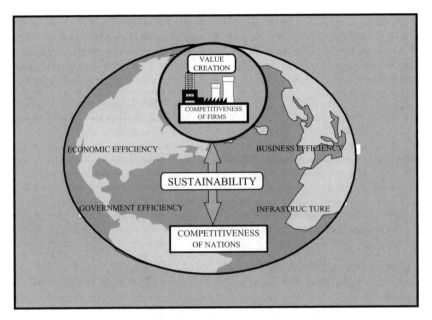

Figure 3.3 – Four competitiveness factors. The environment that sustains, or not, the competitiveness of a nation's enterprises can be analysed according to four input factors: economic efficiency, government efficiency, business efficiency and infrastructure.

factors (inflation, stability, low prices, etc.) has also been emphasised by many economists, and more recently by Milton Friedman of the University of Chicago [4]. It appears, correctly, that price performance is both a prerequisite and a consequence of a sound economic policy. The economic slump of the 1970s persuaded policy makers to include job creation and retention as an objective of competitiveness.

Today, the debate focuses on two issues which impact how competitiveness is measured and explained:

1. *Is GDP and its components input for, or a result of, competitiveness?*

Some scholars argue that the ultimate objective of competitiveness can only be measured in terms of GDP growth. They assume that there should be a direct correlation between a good competitiveness policy and a higher GDP growth rate. If GDP is a *consequence* of competitiveness, it cannot, logically, be included as an input factor that explains competitiveness. At first, such an approach is attractive because of its simplicity. However, excluding GDP and its components from the analysis of competitiveness means excluding growth, exports, and foreign direct investment. It would be hard to explain the competitiveness of a nation by omitting these fundamental factors: it would be like declaring irrelevant to their national competitiveness the fact that Britain has the world's second largest stock of direct investment abroad, or that Germany is the world's second largest exporter of manufactured goods.

GDP

The Gross Domestic Product is a good indicator of the size of the domestic market. However, rankings change depending on whether it is calculated at nominal prices, or adjusted to purchasing power parity. If adjusted to PPP, countries like China, India, Brazil, and Russia already perform like the largest world economies (Figure 3.4).

GROSS DOMESTIC PRODUCT (GDP)		GDP (PPP)	
	2004		2004
US$ billions		Estimates: US$ billions at purchasing power parity	

Ranking		US$ billions	Ranking		US$ billions
1	USA	11,733.5	1	USA	11,404
2	JAPAN	4,667.8	2	CHINA MAINLAND	7,058
3	GERMANY	2,704.3	3	JAPAN	3,661
4	UNITED KINGDOM	2,120.5	4	INDIA	3,287
5	FRANCE	2,019.0	5	GERMANY	2,328
6	ITALY	1,678.7	6	FRANCE	1,689
7	CHINA MAINLAND	1,649.4	7	UNITED KINGDOM	1,662
8	CANADA	994.1	8	ITALY	1,582
9	SPAIN	992.1	9	BRAZIL	1,447
10	KOREA	679.9	10	RUSSIA	1,418

Figure 3.4 – The GDP of the ten largest economies. (Reproduced from [5] by permission of IMD.)

The truth is probably that GDP, and its components, is *both* a cause and a consequence of competitiveness. A high growth environment provides a dynamic framework for a competitiveness policy. As we have seen earlier, during the 1990s, Australia posted eight years of GDP growth above 3 %, the US, Finland, and New Zealand had seven such years, The Netherlands six, and Sweden five. This growth context has an enormous impact on competitiveness. It gives a country a margin of manoeuvre to conduct infrastructure investments, or to enhance research and social policy, *without* increasing taxes. In contrast, a slow growth country can only undertake such investments through additional taxes or increased debt.

2. *What is the real impact of foreign direct investment (FDI) on competitiveness?*

What is a foreign direct investment?

"Foreign Direct Investment reflects the objective of obtaining a lasting interest by a resident entity in one economy ("direct investor") in an entity resident in an economy other than that of the investor ("direct investment enterprise"). The lasting interest implies the existence of a long-term relationship between the direct investor and the enterprise and a significant degree of influence on the management of the enterprise."

Source: [6]

Foreign direct investment (FDI) has changed the face of modern competitiveness, and altered the way we assess the economic efficiency of a nation. We will use the IMF's definition of FDI for our study of competitiveness. Two fundamental characteristics, underlined by the International Monetary Fund's definition of FDI, illustrate its importance to competitiveness:

1. FDI has a longer time perspective than a portfolio (or financial) investment. Investment in financial instruments is very liquid – during the 1990s, shareholders kept a share on the New York Stock Exchange for only nine months on average. When a firm undertakes an FDI, it takes a long-term perspective.
2. An FDI is not a passive investment – it implies a voice in management. Tax authorities often define a direct investment as any participation in the capital of a company above a certain threshold (on average, 10 % in the OECD region). In addition, many countries require the disclosure of the identity of any buyer who acquires more than 5 % of the capital of a company, assuming that the objective of such a move goes beyond a simple financial investment.

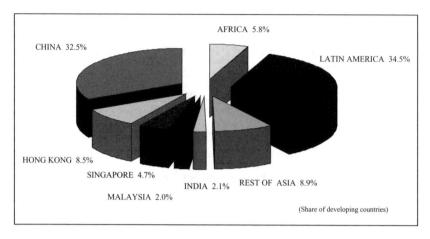

CHINA 32.5%

AFRICA 5.8%

LATIN AMERICA 34.5%

HONG KONG 8.5%

SINGAPORE 4.7%

INDIA 2.1%   REST OF ASIA 8.9%

MALAYSIA 2.0%

(Share of developing countries)

Figure 3.5 – Today, Asia attracts most of the FDI going to developing nations. China is particularly attractive for manufacturing investments. *Source:* **[5].**

While FDI increasingly defines the activities of global companies, sources tend to be limited to only a few nations. The US, UK, Japan, Germany, and France account for two-thirds of FDI outflows; only ten nations (among them China (Figure 3.5), The Netherlands, Brazil, Ireland, and Canada) receive two-thirds of total inflows. FDI distorts the picture we can draw of the competitiveness of a nation, because a nation's accounting system values trade on the basis of the origin of goods, and not on the basis of the ownership of goods.

The direct investment flow inside a country, and as a proportion of GDP, is a also a good indicator of the attractiveness of a country (Figure 3.6).

When a product passes through a customs authority, it is accounted in the national statistical system on the basis of its geographical origin. The reason is, obviously, that different tariff rates or non-tariff measures, such as quotas, apply for different countries. This system for determining the origin of traded goods has been in place for many centuries, and assumes a product was made entirely in the country from which it comes. Today, this is less and less the case – components are procured internationally, and assembled in another country. The car, or the computer, industry illustrates this point very well. It means that the "nationality" of a product is not necessarily that of its country of origin.

DIRECT INVESTMENT FLOWS INWARD

2004

Percentage of GDP

Ranking			%
1	HONG KONG		20.68
2	SINGAPORE		15.03
3	IRELAND		14.33
4	CHILE		8.08
5	SLOVAK REPUBLIC		7.52 ⁱ
6	ESTONIA		5.85
7	ZHEJIANG		4.92
8	CZECH REPUBLIC		4.67
9	HUNGARY		4.41
10	MALAYSIA		4.01
11	SWITZERLAND		3.99
12	JORDAN		3.78 ⁱ
13	CHINA MAINLAND		3.76
14	PORTUGAL		3.63
15	ICELAND		3.57
16	ROMANIA		3.22 ⁱ
17	NETHERLANDS		3.06 ⁱ
18	BRAZIL		3.00
19	SAO PAULO		3.00 ₚ
20	AUSTRIA		2.85 ⁱ
21	NEW ZEALAND		2.81
22	RHONE-ALPS		2.71 ₚₗ
23	MEXICO		2.66
24	COLOMBIA		2.62
25	UNITED KINGDOM		2.59
26	FINLAND		2.46
27	POLAND		2.11
28	BELGIUM		1.99
29	ILE-DE-FRANCE		1.73 ₚ
30	FRANCE		1.73
31	RUSSIA		1.70
32	KOREA		1.23
33	VENEZUELA		1.05
34	CATALONIA		1.03 ⁱ
35	USA		1.03
36	SPAIN		0.99
37	INDIA		0.95
38	NORWAY		0.93 ⁱ
39	ITALY		0.89
39	LOMBARDY		0.89 ₚ
41	TURKEY		0.86
42	AUSTRALIA		0.81
43	MAHARASHTRA		0.73 ₚₗ
44	ARGENTINA		0.71
45	CANADA		0.66
46	SLOVENIA		0.64
47	TAIWAN		0.62
48	THAILAND		0.61
49	DENMARK		0.56 ⁱ
50	ISRAEL		0.47
51	GREECE		0.41 ⁱ
52	INDONESIA		0.41
53	PHILIPPINES		0.40 ⁱ
54	SOUTH AFRICA		0.27
55	SCOTLAND		0.25
56	JAPAN		0.15
57	BAVARIA		0.07 ⁱ
58	SWEDEN		−0.00
59	GERMANY		−1.81

Figure 3.6 – Investment flows inward (as % of GDP). (Reproduced from [5] by permission of IMD.)

The Multi-Fibres Agreement, for example, which had been in effect since 1995 under the auspices of the World Trade Organisation (WTO), determined quotas for countries exporting textiles and clothing. Having exhausted China's quota for exports of certain types of cashmere sweater, Chinese firms shipped their sweaters to Indonesia. There, the label "Made in Indonesia" was sewn onto them, as Indonesia's quota had not been exhausted. The sweaters were then re-exported from Indonesia to the rest of the world . . . with a new nationality!

The Osaka Convention, approved in 1977, defines the origin of a product as "where the last, most substantial transformation process takes place" [7]. While a step in the right direction, the convention did not really elucidate what it meant by "the last, most substantial transformation process" in cases such as the assembly of a car or a computer. To clarify the definition, policymakers introduced notions of deciding the origin of a product on the basis of "national percentage" (50 to 60 % of assembled parts), or through where specific processes were done (for example, wafer diffusion in the manufacturing of microchips).

The proliferation of FDIs over the past two decades has obscured things for customs authorities. For example, Nissan manufactured the Bluebird in its British factories in the 1980s for the European market. Investing in Britain was an attractive option, because the cars could enter the European Common Market as a British-made product, rather than as a Japanese export that would be subject to a higher tariff. While the British authorities considered a car to be British if it had "local content" of 50 %, on the other side of the Channel, the French inspectors thought it should be 60 %. Calais customs authorities blocked the first cars arriving from Dover! Meanwhile, the Nissan management in Japan quietly observed the then British Prime Minister fighting with her French counterpart to allow "British" exports to enter the French market.

Investing abroad

The stocks of investment abroad is a good indicator of the aggressiveness of a country and its economic power (Figure 3.7). Such investments also extend the reach of the power of countries of origin. (Reproduced from [5] by permission of IMD.)

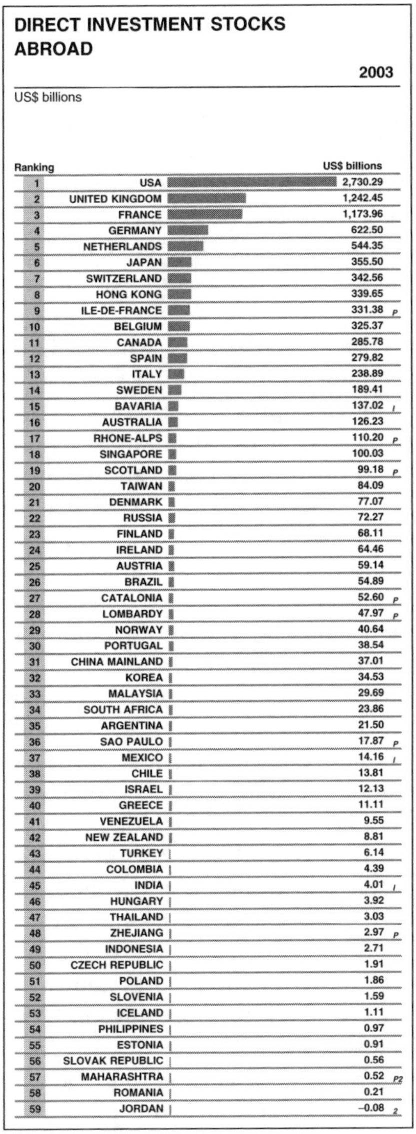

**DIRECT INVESTMENT STOCKS
ABROAD**

2003

US$ billions

Ranking		US$ billions	
1	USA	2,730.29	
2	UNITED KINGDOM	1,242.45	
3	FRANCE	1,173.96	
4	GERMANY	622.50	
5	NETHERLANDS	544.35	
6	JAPAN	355.50	
7	SWITZERLAND	342.56	
8	HONG KONG	339.65	
9	ILE-DE-FRANCE	331.38	p
10	BELGIUM	325.37	
11	CANADA	285.78	
12	SPAIN	279.82	
13	ITALY	238.89	
14	SWEDEN	189.41	
15	BAVARIA	137.02	i
16	AUSTRALIA	126.23	
17	RHONE-ALPS	110.20	p
18	SINGAPORE	100.03	
19	SCOTLAND	99.18	p
20	TAIWAN	84.09	
21	DENMARK	77.07	
22	RUSSIA	72.27	
23	FINLAND	68.11	
24	IRELAND	64.46	
25	AUSTRIA	59.14	
26	BRAZIL	54.89	
27	CATALONIA	52.60	p
28	LOMBARDY	47.97	p
29	NORWAY	40.64	
30	PORTUGAL	38.54	
31	CHINA MAINLAND	37.01	
32	KOREA	34.53	
33	MALAYSIA	29.69	
34	SOUTH AFRICA	23.86	
35	ARGENTINA	21.50	
36	SAO PAULO	17.87	p
37	MEXICO	14.16	i
38	CHILE	13.81	
39	ISRAEL	12.13	
40	GREECE	11.11	
41	VENEZUELA	9.55	
42	NEW ZEALAND	8.81	
43	TURKEY	6.14	
44	COLOMBIA	4.39	
45	INDIA	4.01	i
46	HUNGARY	3.92	
47	THAILAND	3.03	
48	ZHEJIANG	2.97	p
49	INDONESIA	2.71	
50	CZECH REPUBLIC	1.91	
51	POLAND	1.86	
52	SLOVENIA	1.59	
53	ICELAND	1.11	
54	PHILIPPINES	0.97	
55	ESTONIA	0.91	
56	SLOVAK REPUBLIC	0.56	
57	MAHARASHTRA	0.52	pg
58	ROMANIA	0.21	
59	JORDAN	−0.08	2

**Figure 3.7 – Direct investment stocks abroad. (Reproduced from
[5] by permission of IMD.)**

Let us now assume that a US company exports computers to China. This would be accounted as a positive factor for the US balance of trade, and for its competitiveness. However, if business turns out to be very good in China, the company might very well decide that it is time to serve the Chinese market more closely through a direct investment. Despite the fact that the market share of the company might increase in China, the move would be accounted as a *drop in exports* from the US, and thus as a decrease in its competitiveness. Even if the balance of payments improved over time through the remittance of dividends, it would still be accounted as a negative development for the competitiveness of the US.

The situation becomes even trickier when a US company operating abroad ships a component or product back to its home market for assembly or sale. Should such a product be considered as an import from Singapore or China if it originates from an American company, operating with American capital, technology, and skills? It is estimated that more than 20 % of the "imports" in the US originate from American subsidiaries operating abroad, while the vast majority of the exports accounted for Singapore or Ireland, are indeed produced by American companies.

It would be more accurate to analyse the competitiveness of a nation, and specifically, its trade performance, *on the basis of the ownership* of products, and not on the basis of their geographical origin. From the point of view of assessing competitiveness, it would make more sense to take everything a nation's companies sell worldwide, independently of the locations of their subsidiaries, and subtract everything a nation's companies buy from the rest of the world.

An attempt to do so was made in 1990 in a book by British economist Deanne Julius entitled *Global Companies and Public Policy* [8]. It was based on 1986 data for the US, but one can assume that, although the numbers have certainly changed today, the principle remains the same. In 1986, the US was running a trade deficit of $144 bn. Many will remember that, in those days, the monthly trade results were awaited with anxiety, since an excessive deficit would lower the exchange rate of the dollar. However, during that same year, the sales of US companies abroad amounted to $1145 bn, while the purchases of US companies worldwide represented only $1088 bn. In short, despite the trade figures, the US was running a "business" surplus of $57 bn on an ownership-of-goods basis.

Britain's famous 19th century Prime Minister Benjamin Disraeli had the perfect phrase to apply here: "There are three kinds of lies – lies, damned lies, and statistics." Accounting for the economic efficiency of a nation is an exercise plagued with uncertainty. International and national accounting systems are far from perfect. In this respect, the magnitude of the line "errors and omissions" in the US national accounts is quite telling! A similar observation can be made about national accounts within the European Union. The addition of total exports from member countries to other EU nations does not equal the addition of total imports from these same countries! As for inflation or GDP figures, they are constantly revised, even years later.

Nevertheless, however imperfect it may be, the picture provided by GDP and FDI is not entirely wrong. Despite the various shortcomings described above, the statistical tools we have available to approximate the economic performance of a nation serve as the best indicators for economic efficiency – until something better is found.

3.2.2   Government efficiency

This second factor groups together public finance, fiscal policy, the institutional framework, and business legislation. In most regions of the world, the role of government is such that its level of efficiency has a direct impact on the competitiveness of a nation, or of enterprises. Political instability, administrative inefficiency, corruption, lack of transparency, and unequal treatment of companies (private and public, local and foreign) are all factors that can create more competitiveness problems than a higher business cost structure.

Governments have problems of their own, not only because they have specific responsibilities, but also because they simply do not operate like companies. The objective of modern public management, which attempts to introduce some of the management practices used by enterprises, such as quality, processes, customer orientation, and accountability, into the public sphere, is certainly commendable. However, a possible similarity of methods does not imply an alignment in objectives. A government is neither a firm nor a household.

The key issues in this factor are as follows:

1. *Should public finance be balanced?*

The politically correct answer is, obviously, yes. This is because a deficit in public finance triggers debt, which, in turn, reduces the financial alternatives of a nation, while often increasing exposure on financial markets and dependency on international organisations, such as the IMF and the World Bank.

A world of sinners?

Governments have a tendency to overspend, and deficits seem to be the norm (−4.3 % of GDP in the OECD area in 2003), as shown in Figure 3.8. A distinction should be made between deficits that are the results of investment spending, and which can create long-term wealth, and operating deficits, which may indicate a lack of efficiency.

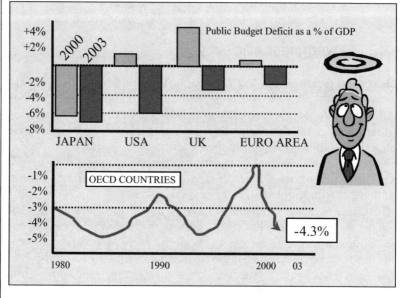

Figure 3.8 – Budget deficits.

Who you owe money to is important – you need to make a distinction between domestic and foreign debt. Belgium is highly indebted; in 2004, its central government debt amounted to $340.9 bn, which is almost as large as the total GDP of the country. However, of this amount, the government owed $336.7 bn to domestic institutions, and only $4.2 bn to foreign creditors. The Japanese government is in the same situation: it has a colossal debt of $5861 bn to domestic institutions, and less than $10 bn to foreigners. The situation is very different for Russia. The country owes just $28.2bn at home, and the majority of its debt, $107.7 bn, to foreign institutions. Foreign debt is obviously more dangerous for a nation's economic independence. Multilateral institutions (such as the IMF or the "Paris Group") can force a country to adopt restructuring measures, which influence its competitiveness. Domestic creditors are less dangerous, as long as they receive interest payments on their debts. Sovereign debt is generally seen as an acceptable investment risk.

A key element to monitor is the percentage of government revenues devoted to interest payments. In 2004, Turkey directed 58 % of its revenues to interest payments, while the US, which has one of the highest debt levels in the world, only devoted 8 % of its revenues to interest payments.

To complicate things further, a budget surplus is not necessarily a sign of competitiveness. In 2004, Denmark, which is generally considered as being a very competitive country, was running a budget surplus of 2.3 %. However, the same year, Russia, a country perceived as being less competitive, ran a bigger budget surplus of 4.1 % of GDP. In addition to the size, the origin of a budget surplus or deficit is thus important. In the case of Russia, the budget surplus was the result of higher tax revenues on oil and gas exports, and less investment in infrastructure.

In the long term, most countries are in debt and run budgetary deficits. These deficits can be the result of applying anticyclical policies in periods of economic difficulty (Keynesian approach), or being confronted with steadily increased public demand for infrastructure (health, education, security, etc.) The real issue, therefore, is not to balance public finances, but to find the means to afford the cost of such deficits. Competitiveness theory is concerned with the two possible ways to pay for such regular imbalances: taxation and economic growth.

2. *Are high taxes and competitiveness compatible?*

Intuitively, the answer would be no; but more correctly, it depends on what you tax and how you tax it. First, within a nation, it is possible to have differing levels of personal taxation compared to corporate taxation. Some countries, such as Sweden and Denmark, have high levels of personal taxes (34 % of a revenue equal to the average GDP per capita), but are very competitive on corporate taxation. In contrast, there is little personal income taxation in Hong Kong and Taiwan. In the future, strong competition for "attractiveness" will force nations to reduce corporate taxation disparities further, or to increase the allocation of tax incentives. A nation will find it hard to remain competitive with high corporate taxes.

Tax

The tax pressure of a country, i.e. the total revenues collected by the State as a % of GDP, is regularly quoted as being a key factor of competition (Figure 3.9). The trend during the past decade has

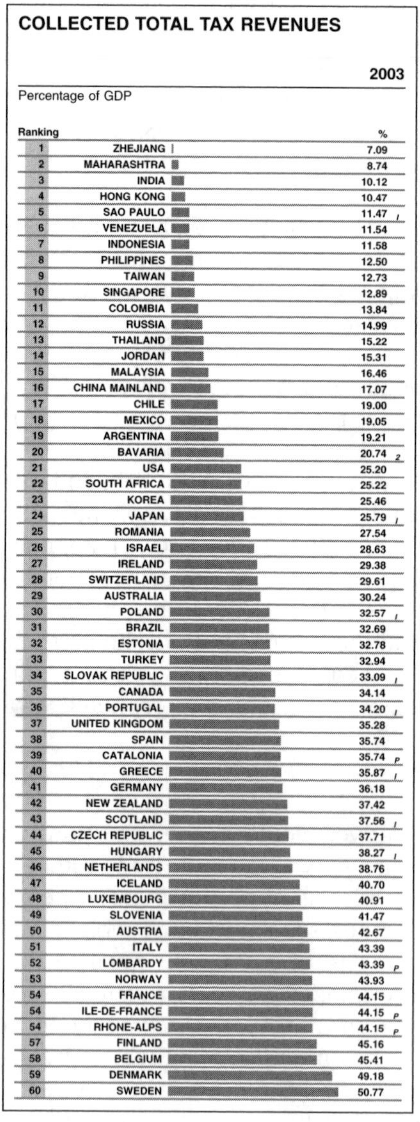

COLLECTED TOTAL TAX REVENUES		
		2003
Percentage of GDP		
Ranking		**%**
1	ZHEJIANG	7.09
2	MAHARASHTRA	8.74
3	INDIA	10.12
4	HONG KONG	10.47
5	SAO PAULO	11.47
6	VENEZUELA	11.54
7	INDONESIA	11.58
8	PHILIPPINES	12.50
9	TAIWAN	12.73
10	SINGAPORE	12.89
11	COLOMBIA	13.84
12	RUSSIA	14.99
13	THAILAND	15.22
14	JORDAN	15.31
15	MALAYSIA	16.46
16	CHINA MAINLAND	17.07
17	CHILE	19.00
18	MEXICO	19.05
19	ARGENTINA	19.21
20	BAVARIA	20.74
21	USA	25.20
22	SOUTH AFRICA	25.22
23	KOREA	25.46
24	JAPAN	25.79
25	ROMANIA	27.54
26	ISRAEL	28.63
27	IRELAND	29.38
28	SWITZERLAND	29.61
29	AUSTRALIA	30.24
30	POLAND	32.57
31	BRAZIL	32.69
32	ESTONIA	32.78
33	TURKEY	32.94
34	SLOVAK REPUBLIC	33.09
35	CANADA	34.14
36	PORTUGAL	34.20
37	UNITED KINGDOM	35.28
38	SPAIN	35.74
39	CATALONIA	35.74
40	GREECE	35.87
41	GERMANY	36.18
42	NEW ZEALAND	37.42
43	SCOTLAND	37.56
44	CZECH REPUBLIC	37.71
45	HUNGARY	38.27
46	NETHERLANDS	38.76
47	ICELAND	40.70
48	LUXEMBOURG	40.91
49	SLOVENIA	41.47
50	AUSTRIA	42.67
51	ITALY	43.39
52	LOMBARDY	43.39
53	NORWAY	43.93
54	FRANCE	44.15
54	ILE-DE-FRANCE	44.15
54	RHONE-ALPS	44.15
57	FINLAND	45.16
58	BELGIUM	45.41
59	DENMARK	49.18
60	SWEDEN	50.77

Figure 3.9 – Collected taxes as a % of GDP. (Reproduced from [5] by permission of IMD.)

been to roll down taxation, especially corporate taxes, since this is a key incentive to attract and retain enterprises. Nevertheless, since governments continue to face rising expenditure, it is likely that either indirect taxes will rise, or, alternatively, deficits will surge.

Second, a shift will occur between direct taxes, which affect a person or a company, and indirect taxes, such as VAT or sales taxes, which apply to transactions. Although it could be argued that an indirect taxation model is socially unfair, since it does not take into account differences in consumer income, indirect taxation is far more efficient from a competitiveness point of view, since it shifts the tax pressure from the production to the consumption of goods.

3. *How much growth is needed?*

The growth league over a decade

Cumulative growth 1993–2003 (%)

Ireland	79.8
Luxembourg	44.3
Finland	35.4
USA	32.5
Spain	31.4
Sweden	29.0
UK	28.6
Denmark	25.8
The Netherlands	25.4
European Union	22.5
France	21.1
Austria	20.8
Germany	14.4
Japan	13.2
Switzerland	10.7

The growth deficit of countries such as Germany, Japan, and Switzerland is a very visible indicator of a slide in competitiveness. For these three nations, economic problems have been compounded by considerable difficulty in introducing rapid reforms of the State. The capacity of a nation to "reform itself" is an important element of competitiveness.

Source: [5]

All countries should have a growth objective that takes into account the natural increase in infrastructure spending (for the economy and for society), the sustainability of economic expansion (environmental impact, for example), the sociopolitical context, and a competitive level of taxation. Yet, surprisingly, most countries do not have a growth target! Instead, they take as a given a rate of growth that stems from the international and domestic economic environments.

But with a competitive mindset, one has to define the measures that have a direct impact on growth, and act accordingly. For example, full privatisation of the rail network will have a very limited impact on the growth of a country – it is simply a transfer of assets from the State to the private sector. As Britain has experienced, it can produce more headaches than revenues and jobs. The change of ownership did not lead to a multiplier effect in the economy – such as the creation of more jobs or a significant number of new firms. On the other hand, the privatisation of telecommunications networks, including the "last mile," led to the unleashing of a great deal of innovation, which created new markets, jobs, and companies. Privatisation strategies that unleash innovation are the ones that influence competitiveness, and help a country reach a growth objective.

The "growth yardstick" is a very important metric for defining whether or not a policy decision is appropriate for a competitiveness strategy. If the economic benefits of an action are smaller than the social problems it engenders, then it should probably be abandoned. Take the case of the rationalisation of postal networks. In most countries, the post office is a State-run service to ensure proximity and cost efficiency. Today, it is fashionable to slash costs by getting rid of postal workers (often the last link with a society of ageing people), and closing down small post offices. Does such a policy increase the likelihood that a country will increase its growth rate? Probably not. Does such a policy irritate people? Yes. So why do it?

The *institutional framework* and *business legislation*, as subfactors of government efficiency, also define the context of growth. From a competitiveness point of view, such an environment doesn't necessarily have to be completely "business friendly." But for the benefit of competitiveness, the institutional and legislative business environment needs to be stable and predictable. China and Malaysia are not the most "pro-business" administrations in the world. However, they are stable. In contrast, India has changed direction many times during the past few decades – its inconsistency in the treatment of business caused some major companies, like IBM and Coca-Cola, to leave the country several years ago (they are now back). Firms are able to adapt to any environment as long as it is transparent and stable – erratic changes in policy harm competitiveness more than any other single factor.

Finally, competitive nations make it simple and cost-effective to do business. In a competitive mindset, the ease of doing business is an important objective. Competitiveness is not hindered by high taxes or labour costs, as long as there are other compensating mechanisms in place. Some relatively expensive nations, such as The Netherlands and Denmark, are attractive as locations for investment because they are extremely transparent and swift at coordinating and simplifying procedures and transactions. For example, they have "one-stop shop" agencies, which look after and facilitate all the transactions required for entering their markets.

In summary, nations can hasten their growth by:

- systematically analysing the impact on economic growth of every legislation, regulation, or policy (a cost/benefit approach); and
- institutionalizing, at the parliamentary and administrative level, the consistent simplification and streamlining of procedures.

The ability of a government to adapt to new economic realities often defines the quality of the relationship between a state and the business community (Figure 3.10).

3.2.3 Business efficiency

This third factor groups all the determinants whereby business has a direct impact on the national environment: business adaptability and effectiveness, labour relations, management practices, and skills. Business, and not just government, shapes the national competitiveness environment. The impact of business is perceived primarily in the competitiveness of enterprises. This explains why, as indicated before, some scholars simplified the concept of competitiveness of nations to the aggregate sum of local firms' competitiveness. However, business also has an influence on the development and the operation of a competitive environment. Strongly competitive nations have a certain degree of partnership between local business and the government in establishing the competitive strategy of a nation. Thus the question:

What is the most suitable relationship between business and government for the development of competitiveness?

In a market economy, the partnership between business and government is quite subtle. Japan, after World War II, was notorious for

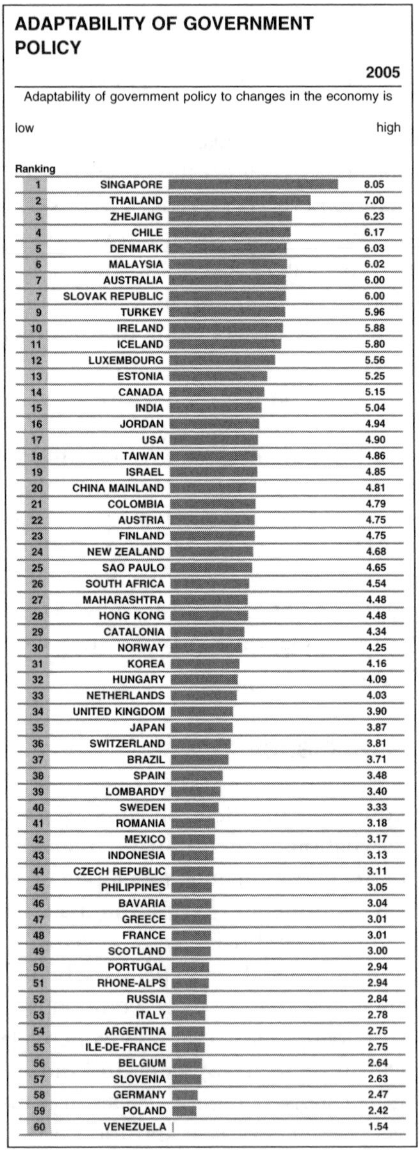

ADAPTABILITY OF GOVERNMENT POLICY

2005

Adaptability of government policy to changes in the economy is

low   high

Ranking			
1	SINGAPORE		8.05
2	THAILAND		7.00
3	ZHEJIANG		6.23
4	CHILE		6.17
5	DENMARK		6.03
6	MALAYSIA		6.02
7	AUSTRALIA		6.00
7	SLOVAK REPUBLIC		6.00
9	TURKEY		5.96
10	IRELAND		5.88
11	ICELAND		5.80
12	LUXEMBOURG		5.56
13	ESTONIA		5.25
14	CANADA		5.15
15	INDIA		5.04
16	JORDAN		4.94
17	USA		4.90
18	TAIWAN		4.86
19	ISRAEL		4.85
20	CHINA MAINLAND		4.81
21	COLOMBIA		4.79
22	AUSTRIA		4.75
23	FINLAND		4.75
24	NEW ZEALAND		4.68
25	SAO PAULO		4.65
26	SOUTH AFRICA		4.54
27	MAHARASHTRA		4.48
28	HONG KONG		4.48
29	CATALONIA		4.34
30	NORWAY		4.25
31	KOREA		4.16
32	HUNGARY		4.09
33	NETHERLANDS		4.03
34	UNITED KINGDOM		3.90
35	JAPAN		3.87
36	SWITZERLAND		3.81
37	BRAZIL		3.71
38	SPAIN		3.48
39	LOMBARDY		3.40
40	SWEDEN		3.33
41	ROMANIA		3.18
42	MEXICO		3.17
43	INDONESIA		3.13
44	CZECH REPUBLIC		3.11
45	PHILIPPINES		3.05
46	BAVARIA		3.04
47	GREECE		3.01
48	FRANCE		3.01
49	SCOTLAND		3.00
50	PORTUGAL		2.94
51	RHONE-ALPS		2.94
52	RUSSIA		2.84
53	ITALY		2.78
54	ARGENTINA		2.75
55	ILE-DE-FRANCE		2.75
56	BELGIUM		2.64
57	SLOVENIA		2.63
58	GERMANY		2.47
59	POLAND		2.42
60	VENEZUELA		1.54

Figure 3.10 – Are governments adaptable enough? (Reproduced from [5] by permission of IMD.)

steering its economy toward the path of world competitiveness through the coordinating actions of MITI (the Ministry of International Trade and Industry, recently renamed METI, Ministry of Economy, Trade, and Industry). MITI decided where industry should concentrate its competitive efforts. At the opposite end of the spectrum, the US business community is adverse to government involvement in guiding business priorities. In between, mixed systems, such as the French *Plan*, aim at providing a general framework for the economy, allowing the government to plan and undertake the necessary infrastructure investments for such an industrial policy.

Whatever system is adopted, a permanent, open, and efficient relationship between the business community and government policy makers is essential for competitiveness. Countries that succeed in the competitiveness scale, such as Ireland and Singapore, maintain such relationships, and it doesn't mean that one party is less important than the other. In other countries, the relationship between the business community and government is much more tenuous. The positions taken are much more antagonistic – it is not "what can we do together to make our country more competitive?", but "if you do not provide me with the right business conditions, I leave!" Such a confrontational approach widens the existing gap between government and business priorities, harming competitiveness.

The second key impact of business is on the labour markets:

What is the most suitable relationship between business and labour for the development of competitiveness?

There seems to be a direct correlation between the competitive success of a nation and its labour relations (Figure 3.11). The competitiveness of Switzerland has very much been a consequence of the "Labour Peace" system, which was implemented more than 50 years ago. It is based on a system of industry sector agreements, which guarantee a conflict-free environment for a certain number of years until they are renegotiated. Germany and Sweden have a very similar social-contract approach to labour relations.

Realising that Dutch competitiveness was in decline during the early 1980s, government, business, and labour leaders together developed the *Polder Model* to restore the competitiveness of the country. Under this agreement, the State, when necessary, eases the pressure of taxation and social premiums, increasing net disposable personal income. Such a policy is especially helpful when corporate profitability is under pressure, and firms cannot increase both labour productivity and wages. In such situations, the consensus is that the standard of living of workers

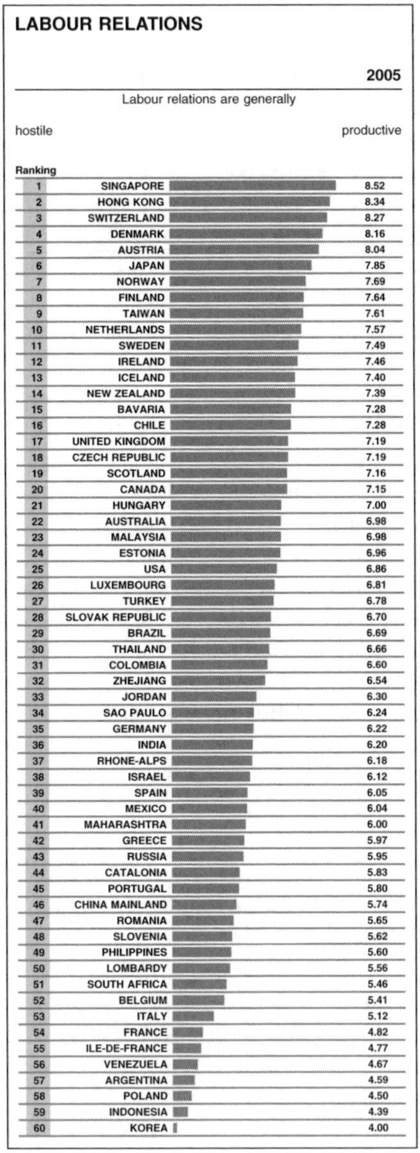

LABOUR RELATIONS

		2005

Labour relations are generally

hostile   productive

Ranking

1	SINGAPORE		8.52
2	HONG KONG		8.34
3	SWITZERLAND		8.27
4	DENMARK		8.16
5	AUSTRIA		8.04
6	JAPAN		7.85
7	NORWAY		7.69
8	FINLAND		7.64
9	TAIWAN		7.61
10	NETHERLANDS		7.57
11	SWEDEN		7.49
12	IRELAND		7.46
13	ICELAND		7.40
14	NEW ZEALAND		7.39
15	BAVARIA		7.28
16	CHILE		7.28
17	UNITED KINGDOM		7.19
18	CZECH REPUBLIC		7.19
19	SCOTLAND		7.16
20	CANADA		7.15
21	HUNGARY		7.00
22	AUSTRALIA		6.98
23	MALAYSIA		6.98
24	ESTONIA		6.96
25	USA		6.86
26	LUXEMBOURG		6.81
27	TURKEY		6.78
28	SLOVAK REPUBLIC		6.70
29	BRAZIL		6.69
30	THAILAND		6.66
31	COLOMBIA		6.60
32	ZHEJIANG		6.54
33	JORDAN		6.30
34	SAO PAULO		6.24
35	GERMANY		6.22
36	INDIA		6.20
37	RHONE-ALPS		6.18
38	ISRAEL		6.12
39	SPAIN		6.05
40	MEXICO		6.04
41	MAHARASHTRA		6.00
42	GREECE		5.97
43	RUSSIA		5.95
44	CATALONIA		5.83
45	PORTUGAL		5.80
46	CHINA MAINLAND		5.74
47	ROMANIA		5.65
48	SLOVENIA		5.62
49	PHILIPPINES		5.60
50	LOMBARDY		5.56
51	SOUTH AFRICA		5.46
52	BELGIUM		5.41
53	ITALY		5.12
54	FRANCE		4.82
55	ILE-DE-FRANCE		4.77
56	VENEZUELA		4.67
57	ARGENTINA		4.59
58	POLAND		4.50
59	INDONESIA		4.39
60	KOREA		4.00

Figure 3.11 – Quality of labour relations. (Reproduced from [5] by permission of IMD.)

should be maintained at a constant level. The State thus agrees to a temporary reduction in payroll taxes, while unions contain wages and business tries to preserve employment. All parties review the agreement on an annual basis – a model of negotiation that has proven to be very successful. Economic growth in The Netherlands has been substantially higher than in most other EU countries, while unemployment has remained considerably lower. Ireland followed a similar strategy a few years later. Once it had established an industrial relations agreement, quite similar in spirit to the Dutch agreement, its competitiveness really took off.

Britain and the US took a different approach. Margaret Thatcher's Britain, and Reagan's US, crushed centralised industrial labour relations. In these two countries, the labour movement as a national political force, if not completely dismantled, was weakened significantly. However, there are still important differences on either side of the Atlantic. In Britain, the trade union movement (mainly represented by the Trade Union Congress) had been a political force to reckon with. The Labour Party was born out of trade unionism, and historically unions had the ability to block the whole country with a strike. In the US, the trade unions, like the AFL-CIO, are now less directly involved in politics. After President Reagan quashed the air controllers' strike in 1981, which had, in effect, brought US commerce to its knees, unions were never again able to bring the US economy to a standstill with a single blow.

In both countries, the power of trade unions was reduced significantly at the national level – unions still remain strong at an industry sector, or firm, level. In 2000, the US lost 72.1 working days per 1000 inhabitants to strikes, compared with only 15.3 in Italy, a country often perceived as being the champion of strikes! (However, it is true that on an average of several years, Italy has more strikes than the US, but less than Canada . . .)

What is the most suitable relationship between business and society for the development of competitiveness?

The ability of business to influence the competitive environment of a country relies not only on its competencies, but also on its sense of social responsibility: both of which lead to credibility.

The perception of the competence of managers is very important in building the credibility of the business community within a nation; it is also a factor in attracting foreign investment. The US, Sweden, The Netherlands, Singapore, Hong Kong, and India are renowned for the competence of their senior managers. Switzerland and Germany used to be in the same group, but, for a time, Swiss and German managers have had a tough time in adapting to changes in the business environment. Recently, however, they have made major efforts to address their lack of flexibility.

The influence of business in shaping the national environment depends also on the availability of opportunities for business leaders to occupy government positions. In the US, and to a lesser extent in other Anglo-Saxon countries, it is common practice to have business leaders taking on significant responsibilities in the administration. Such fluidity between business and government jobs is much less frequent in Continental European countries. Contrary to the US, where business leaders enter government positions, France, for example, has a long tradition of putting senior civil servants in charge of its leading companies. In Singapore, to attract the best talent, the salaries of government ministers are in line with those of CEOs in the private sector.

A commitment to social responsibility is the result of a cultural background. The Nordic and Continental European countries are particularly concerned with the social responsibility of business leaders. In a consensus approach in labour relations, business leaders enhance their standing when they are also judged to be "social" leaders, concerned with those around them. In their day-to-day behaviour, business leaders have to show their "solidarity" and commitment to social principles.

Giving such importance to the "common good" dimension contrasts with the more individualistic approach of the Anglo-Saxon leadership style, especially the American one. In the Anglo-Saxon leadership model, there is a clear distinction between the individual as a *moneymaker* – a role with less social constraints – and the individual as a *money-owner* – who is expected to play a leadership role in social issues. In the US, making money is a socially acceptable goal in itself. But once you have made your money, there is strong social pressure to share your wealth, find a social cause, and devote yourself and your money to it. This mindset descends from the nation's Puritan roots, which held that if success is an act of recognition by God, then one should, as an individual, "pay back" this success to society, particularly through philanthropic actions. The extraordinary development of philanthropy and donations of all kinds by wealthy people in the US cannot only be seen as the result of a favourable tax system – more importantly it is linked to the American value system. Andrew Carnegie, in his essay *The Gospel of Wealth*, written in 1889, said: "The man who dies thus rich dies disgraced" [9]. He gave away 90 % of his wealth during his lifetime.

Corporate governance is another way by which business expands its focus from the creation of value for shareholders to the creation of value for stakeholders. The exuberance of the Internet years, as well as the complacency of certain boards, led to negligence and misconduct that badly hurt the credibility of business in the public eye. To avoid such misconduct, some basic principles need to be respected:

- The disclosure of information related to the financial performance of the firm has to be transparent and accurate.
- Disclosing financial information is not enough – firms need to report nonfinancial performance and measure the impact of their activities. Such an approach is gaining in momentum – pioneering annual reports already include a larger section on environmental behaviour, social responsibility, ethical standards (Figure 3.12), and community involvement.
- Senior executives have a fiduciary duty to those whose assets they manage, and need to be held accountable for their statements, actions, and performance. The Sarbanes–Oxley Act in the US incorporates strict rules to force CEOs and CFOs personally to stand by and guarantee the integrity of the figures they publish, and the processes used to collect the data [10].
- Objectivity in auditing is paramount. Business relationships, which could cause conflicts of interest, such as providing both auditing and consulting services to the same firm, are to be avoided in order to assure the integrity of the auditing systems.
- Management and board members are both in charge of making sure they have a going concern. When a company collapses, it is the result of both bad management and insufficient oversight by the board.
- Board members are ultimately responsible for the firm's future. Board membership is not solely an honour, it also means taking on significant responsibilities toward shareholders, and increasingly toward other stakeholders.
- To best serve their function, boards need to be truly independent. Co-opting board members, or having the CEO of the company on the nomination committee, reinforces the presence of "yes-men." Cross-board memberships, and the confusion of advisory interests, blur the picture even further.
- The credibility of a board relies upon the independence of its directors, especially those on the audit, nomination, and compensation committees. Again, the goal is to avoid conflicts of interest by implementing guidelines regarding presence on the board of current or former company executives, or even suppliers of the firm. Policies that boost the "activism" of the board, such as convening meetings without the presence of management, should be promoted.
- To ensure good governance, there should be a separation between the people holding the titles of CEO and Chair of the Board of

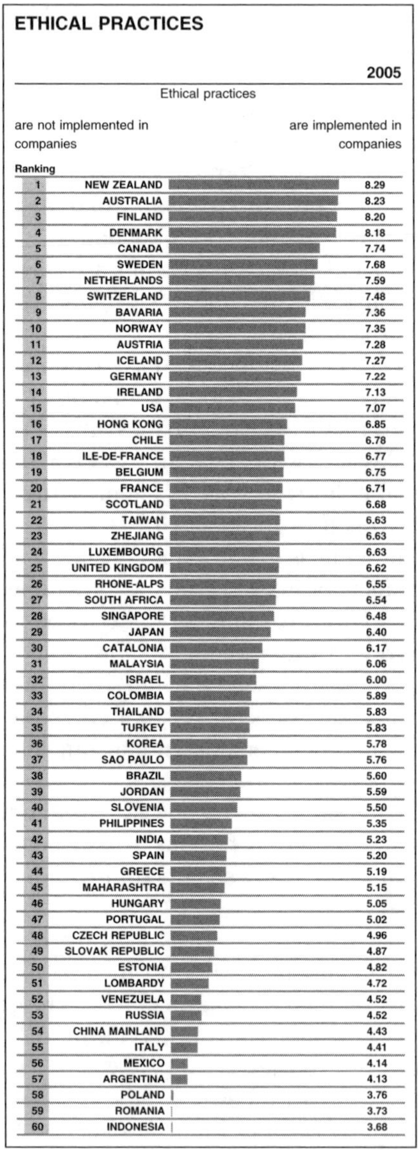

ETHICAL PRACTICES

2005

Ethical practices

are not implemented in companies   are implemented in companies

Ranking		
1	NEW ZEALAND	8.29
2	AUSTRALIA	8.23
3	FINLAND	8.20
4	DENMARK	8.18
5	CANADA	7.74
6	SWEDEN	7.68
7	NETHERLANDS	7.59
8	SWITZERLAND	7.48
9	BAVARIA	7.36
10	NORWAY	7.35
11	AUSTRIA	7.28
12	ICELAND	7.27
13	GERMANY	7.22
14	IRELAND	7.13
15	USA	7.07
16	HONG KONG	6.85
17	CHILE	6.78
18	ILE-DE-FRANCE	6.77
19	BELGIUM	6.75
20	FRANCE	6.71
21	SCOTLAND	6.68
22	TAIWAN	6.63
23	ZHEJIANG	6.63
24	LUXEMBOURG	6.63
25	UNITED KINGDOM	6.62
26	RHONE-ALPS	6.55
27	SOUTH AFRICA	6.54
28	SINGAPORE	6.48
29	JAPAN	6.40
30	CATALONIA	6.17
31	MALAYSIA	6.06
32	ISRAEL	6.00
33	COLOMBIA	5.89
34	THAILAND	5.83
35	TURKEY	5.83
36	KOREA	5.78
37	SAO PAULO	5.76
38	BRAZIL	5.60
39	JORDAN	5.59
40	SLOVENIA	5.50
41	PHILIPPINES	5.35
42	INDIA	5.23
43	SPAIN	5.20
44	GREECE	5.19
45	MAHARASHTRA	5.15
46	HUNGARY	5.05
47	PORTUGAL	5.02
48	CZECH REPUBLIC	4.96
49	SLOVAK REPUBLIC	4.87
50	ESTONIA	4.82
51	LOMBARDY	4.72
52	VENEZUELA	4.52
53	RUSSIA	4.52
54	CHINA MAINLAND	4.43
55	ITALY	4.41
56	MEXICO	4.14
57	ARGENTINA	4.13
58	POLAND	3.76
59	ROMANIA	3.73
60	INDONESIA	3.68

Figure 3.12 – Ethical practices. (Reproduced from [5] by permission of IMD.)

Directors, as well as better disclosure of salaries, stock options exercises, and so on, for the firms' directors and management.

These principles, which are currently discussed in many nations, reinforce the fact that the business community needs to be better attuned to the evolution of society. Peter Drucker highlights this fact: "Changes in society have a deeper impact on companies today than changes in management." Competitiveness is also about the ability of a business community to understand, and react to, the new expectations of the society in which it operates.

3.2.4   Infrastructure efficiency

This fourth competitiveness factor groups all the determinants requiring the long-term investments that shape the physical environment of a nation. Infrastructure can be divided into three categories.

Basic infrastructure

This comprises roads, railways, ports, airports, canals, and other means that enable the movement of people and goods across a nation and to the rest of the world. The availability of basic commodities, raw materials, and energy are also included within the basic infrastructure. Finally, this factor also accounts for the relative weight of urbanisation in national development – particularly important in countries such as Mexico, Egypt, and China, where large cities are a heavy burden on national resources. In 1800, only 2 % of the world population lived in cities; today more than 50 % do. Despite the fact that it is just being documented, it is likely that competitiveness today is linked to the development of an urban society that thrives on physical proximity and efficient infrastructure.

Scientific and technological infrastructure

This subfactor addresses the level of resources devoted by a nation to developing fundamental research through investments in its research centres, universities, and companies. It also looks at applied research and technology, and at the transformation of ideas into patents and marketable products.

The large industrialised nations lead the world in total expenditure on research and development (R&D). In 2003, the US topped the scale in absolute terms, having spent $284bn on R&D, followed by Japan with $124bn, with Germany, France, and the UK completing the top five (Figure 3.13). In relative terms, with R&D spending as a percentage of

TOTAL EXPENDITURE ON R&D

2003

US$ millions

Ranking		US$ millions	
1	USA	284,584	
2	JAPAN	124,113	1
3	GERMANY	60,294	
4	FRANCE	32,564	1
5	UNITED KINGDOM	29,434	1
6	CHINA MAINLAND	18,601	
7	CANADA	16,072	
8	KOREA	16,011	
9	ILE-DE-FRANCE	12,652	2
10	ITALY	12,162	2
11	BAVARIA	9,695	2
12	SWEDEN	9,364	2
13	NETHERLANDS	7,238	2
14	BELGIUM	7,084	
15	TAIWAN	6,997	
16	SPAIN	6,748	1
17	SWITZERLAND	6,320	3
18	BRAZIL	6,260	3
19	AUSTRALIA	5,977	3
20	RUSSIA	5,768	
21	AUSTRIA	5,550	
22	ISRAEL	4,803	
23	FINLAND	4,550	1
24	DENMARK	4,354	1
25	INDIA	3,703	2
26	NORWAY	3,186	1
27	LOMBARDY	3,054	1
28	RHONE-ALPS	2,990	2
29	MEXICO	2,542	
30	SCOTLAND	2,157	1
31	CATALONIA	2,119	
32	SAO PAULO	2,108	P2
33	SINGAPORE	1,966	
34	TURKEY	1,219	1
35	IRELAND	1,168	2
36	CZECH REPUBLIC	1,146	
37	PORTUGAL	1,142	
38	POLAND	1,123	1
39	HONG KONG	962	1
40	ZHEJIANG	909	
41	SOUTH AFRICA	872	2
42	HUNGARY	784	
43	GREECE	759	2
44	MALAYSIA	658	1
45	NEW ZEALAND	602	2
46	VENEZUELA	571	2
47	CHILE	504	
48	MAHARASHTRA	473	P2
49	SLOVENIA	415	
50	ARGENTINA	400	1
51	THAILAND	374	
52	LUXEMBOURG	335	3
53	COLOMBIA	334	3
54	ICELAND	263	1
55	ROMANIA	174	1
56	SLOVAK REPUBLIC	140	1
57	PHILIPPINES	107	1
58	ESTONIA	75	
59	INDONESIA	59	2
60	JORDAN	32	1

Figure 3.13 – Total expenditure on R&D. (Reproduced from [5] by permission of IMD.)

GDP, the smaller European nations perform very well. Sweden devotes 4.2 % of its GDP to R&D, followed by Finland and Switzerland. While in absolute terms, the US and Japan lead the world in the number of patents, on a per capita basis, Switzerland, Sweden, Belgium, and The Netherlands are global leaders.

However, financial and human resources do not entirely define the nature of a scientific and technological environment, and its importance for competitiveness. We should bear in mind four key considerations:

1. *The distinction between basic and applied research.* Both the US and Japan spend huge amounts of money on the sciences; while the US focuses its efforts on basic science research, Japan leans more towards applied research. As a result, between 1950 and 2004, the US had earned 220 Nobel Prizes in physics, physiology, medicine, and economics, while Japan had only earned 8.

2. *The distinction between product innovation and process innovation.* In 2002, 110053 patents were awarded in Japan, compared to 86551 in the US. However, Japan's patents apply mainly to processes, while the US has a significant number of product-related patents. Tellingly, very few product innovations have originated from Japan since World War II – its competitive edge is based on the innovation and improvement of transformation processes, rather than creating new products.

3. *The distinction between private and public research funding.* In 2003, Germany spent $60.3bn on R&D, of which $41.7bn was business spending. For the same year, India devoted a total amount of $3.7bn to R&D, but only $851mn was financed by business. Empirically, the more a country develops, the more R&D is carried out by the private sector. The rule of thumb is roughly one-third of research in government-sponsored institutions, and two-thirds in business.

4. *The blurred distinction between local and foreign R&D.* Countries can import the fruits of R&D efforts, since the ultimate "national" ownership of R&D is always difficult to assess. Ireland accounted for $1.168bn in business R&D in 2003. Yet, large foreign techno-logical firms operating in the country, such as Intel and HP, perform much of this research. Foreign-born scholars working in the US in fact won many of the US Nobel Prizes mentioned earlier. The R&D community is very global in nature. The transparency and the free flow of information supported by modern technology makes it very difficult today for a country to claim a scientific breakthrough as proprietary knowledge.

Access to, and availability of, technology, rather than its ownership, influences competitiveness. While Singapore devotes half of the amount of Sweden to R&D, as a percentage of GDP (2.1 %), the technological infrastructure it has developed is just as impressive. The Singaporean blueprint to becoming a networked society is a model that could be applied by many other countries. *Access to technology*, therefore, is perhaps more important for the immediate competitiveness of a nation than spending on fundamental research.

The free flow of science and technology in a society is critical for competitiveness, and relies on the existence of strong communications infrastructure. Government, academia and business need to develop a coherent national strategy for scientific and technological development.

Social infrastructure

This third type of infrastructure concerns health, education, the environment, and security.

Health care expenditure is exploding, especially in industrialised nations. In 2002, health expenditure represented 14.6 % of GDP in the US, 11.2 % in Switzerland, and 10.9 % in Germany, and growing. In Japan, overall life expectancy is increasing to 81.1 years, while "healthy life" expectancy is already at 73.8 years. There is popular demand for high-quality, efficient health care – a service that is considered a reward for achieving prosperity. In Singapore, the government has always had a policy of "returning" the tangible benefits from its competitive success to the population, in the form of better health care, housing, education, and so on. Such efforts sustain the vision of a socially cohesive society. Further, having a healthy population is an asset for competitiveness, as it directly affects the productivity of labour, such as reducing absenteeism and controlling health care costs.

Education is fundamental to competitiveness – in a knowledge society, being competitive means having skilled people. Denmark, Canada, Israel, and Sweden all spend more than 8 % of GDP on education. Yet, high spending does not mean necessarily getting good results. International programmes measuring educational achievement, such as the Foundation for the Assessment of Educational Achievement in the US, or the OECD PISA (Program for International Student Assessment) show that several advanced nations have serious issues to tackle regarding the secondary school performance of their pupils, especially in science and maths [11]. Japan and Korea traditionally perform very well, and former European communist countries still benefit from a long tradition of good education in science. At university level, however, the advanced nations, especially the US, perform very well.

There is, of course, a cultural aspect in supporting education which cannot be denied, and which will be highlighted when we look at the relationship between competitiveness and value systems. Nonetheless, competitiveness needs educated people. Ireland benefits from a dynamic education system, which is perceived, after Finland, as one of the best in the world for supporting competitiveness (Figure 3.14). The US university system continues to attract and develop some of the world's best talent.

On the other hand, education can be an underutilised investment if it is not synchronised with a competitiveness policy. India has some highly educated people and has undertaken remarkable policies to promote public education, with great success. For example, the state of Kerala boasts one of the highest literacy rates on the subcontinent. While India has one of the largest concentrations of engineers in the world, as well as some of the best mathematicians and astronomers, and some of the leading software experts, it fails to provide sufficient job opportunities at home for those it has educated. Lack of opportunities has led to a significant brain-drain, to the benefit of other countries. Thus, the investment in education made by India can be considered to have been partly unproductive, in terms of its national competitiveness, as it does not benefit from it immediately.

Environmental issues have risen to the top of the agenda in competitiveness policies. The concept of sustainable development is linked to the long-term approach of competitiveness (Figure 3.15). Special attention needs to be devoted to the environmental impact of human activities, since such costs are not included in most accounting practices, such as GDP. Environmental costs concern not only pollution, but also the excessive utilisation of resources. The impact of the degradation of the environment on a nation's competitiveness is a major and well-documented problem in countries such as Brazil and Indonesia. The World Wildlife Fund (WWF) conducts an *ecological footprint* analysis each year, assessing the number of hectares of biologically productive space (at home and abroad) consumed per person in a country. Singapore and the US have the largest ecological footprints, consuming more than 12 hectares per person, followed by Denmark, New Zealand, Ireland, Australia, and Finland [12].

The exploitation of the environment is often related to the level of economic advancement of a nation. However, if a competitiveness policy doesn't integrate environmental management, it simply leaves bigger problems to be solved in the future. In the near future, the number and scope of international environmental agreements, such as the Kyoto Protocol, will increase – to remain competitive, nations and enterprises will be more and more inclined to abide by stricter environmental standards [13].

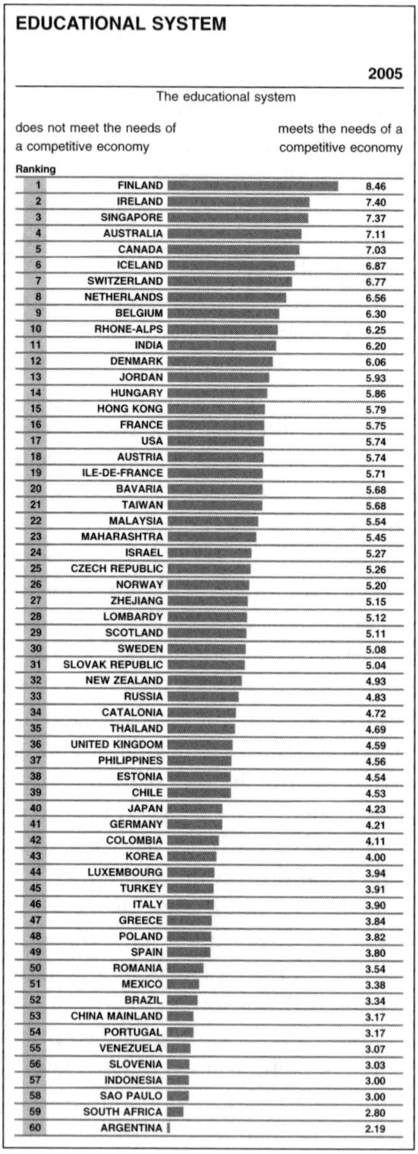

EDUCATIONAL SYSTEM

2005

The educational system

does not meet the needs of
a competitive economy

meets the needs of a
competitive economy

Ranking		
1	FINLAND	8.46
2	IRELAND	7.40
3	SINGAPORE	7.37
4	AUSTRALIA	7.11
5	CANADA	7.03
6	ICELAND	6.87
7	SWITZERLAND	6.77
8	NETHERLANDS	6.56
9	BELGIUM	6.30
10	RHONE-ALPS	6.25
11	INDIA	6.20
12	DENMARK	6.06
13	JORDAN	5.93
14	HUNGARY	5.86
15	HONG KONG	5.79
16	FRANCE	5.75
17	USA	5.74
18	AUSTRIA	5.74
19	ILE-DE-FRANCE	5.71
20	BAVARIA	5.68
21	TAIWAN	5.68
22	MALAYSIA	5.54
23	MAHARASHTRA	5.45
24	ISRAEL	5.27
25	CZECH REPUBLIC	5.26
26	NORWAY	5.20
27	ZHEJIANG	5.15
28	LOMBARDY	5.12
29	SCOTLAND	5.11
30	SWEDEN	5.08
31	SLOVAK REPUBLIC	5.04
32	NEW ZEALAND	4.93
33	RUSSIA	4.83
34	CATALONIA	4.72
35	THAILAND	4.69
36	UNITED KINGDOM	4.59
37	PHILIPPINES	4.56
38	ESTONIA	4.54
39	CHILE	4.53
40	JAPAN	4.23
41	GERMANY	4.21
42	COLOMBIA	4.11
43	KOREA	4.00
44	LUXEMBOURG	3.94
45	TURKEY	3.91
46	ITALY	3.90
47	GREECE	3.84
48	POLAND	3.82
49	SPAIN	3.80
50	ROMANIA	3.54
51	MEXICO	3.38
52	BRAZIL	3.34
53	CHINA MAINLAND	3.17
54	PORTUGAL	3.17
55	VENEZUELA	3.07
56	SLOVENIA	3.03
57	INDONESIA	3.00
58	SAO PAULO	3.00
59	SOUTH AFRICA	2.80
60	ARGENTINA	2.19

Figure 3.14 – Education and competitiveness. (Reproduced from [5] by permission of IMD.)

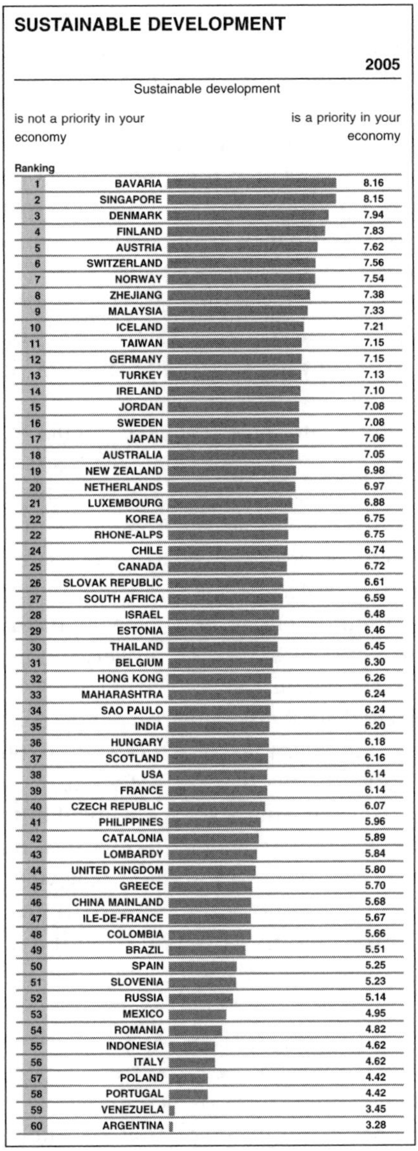

SUSTAINABLE DEVELOPMENT

2005

Sustainable development

is not a priority in your economy | | is a priority in your economy

Ranking			
1	BAVARIA		8.16
2	SINGAPORE		8.15
3	DENMARK		7.94
4	FINLAND		7.83
5	AUSTRIA		7.62
6	SWITZERLAND		7.56
7	NORWAY		7.54
8	ZHEJIANG		7.38
9	MALAYSIA		7.33
10	ICELAND		7.21
11	TAIWAN		7.15
12	GERMANY		7.15
13	TURKEY		7.13
14	IRELAND		7.10
15	JORDAN		7.08
16	SWEDEN		7.08
17	JAPAN		7.06
18	AUSTRALIA		7.05
19	NEW ZEALAND		6.98
20	NETHERLANDS		6.97
21	LUXEMBOURG		6.88
22	KOREA		6.75
22	RHONE-ALPS		6.75
24	CHILE		6.74
25	CANADA		6.72
26	SLOVAK REPUBLIC		6.61
27	SOUTH AFRICA		6.59
28	ISRAEL		6.48
29	ESTONIA		6.46
30	THAILAND		6.45
31	BELGIUM		6.30
32	HONG KONG		6.26
33	MAHARASHTRA		6.24
34	SAO PAULO		6.24
35	INDIA		6.20
36	HUNGARY		6.18
37	SCOTLAND		6.16
38	USA		6.14
39	FRANCE		6.14
40	CZECH REPUBLIC		6.07
41	PHILIPPINES		5.96
42	CATALONIA		5.89
43	LOMBARDY		5.84
44	UNITED KINGDOM		5.80
45	GREECE		5.70
46	CHINA MAINLAND		5.68
47	ILE-DE-FRANCE		5.67
48	COLOMBIA		5.66
49	BRAZIL		5.51
50	SPAIN		5.25
51	SLOVENIA		5.23
52	RUSSIA		5.14
53	MEXICO		4.95
54	ROMANIA		4.82
55	INDONESIA		4.62
56	ITALY		4.62
57	POLAND		4.42
58	PORTUGAL		4.42
59	VENEZUELA		3.45
60	ARGENTINA		3.28

Figure 3.15 – The impact of sustainable development. (Reproduced from [5] by permission of IMD.)

Security infrastructure, measured both by resources and policies, affects competitiveness. The protection of the physical and intellectual property of people, enterprises, and products is paramount to the smooth functioning of a market economy.

During recent decades, the world has become more open and transparent, as it has been immersed in the globalisation process. In addition, recent events, such as terrorist attacks, computer viruses, and international crime, have shown that, with increased openness, we have also become more exposed and vulnerable. We have become much more aware of the importance of security infrastructure, including the law enforcement system, in protecting business and personal wellbeing. Thus, the level and quality of safety infrastructure has become a key aspect of competitiveness.

The protection of private property is particularly well enforced in Austria, Finland, Singapore, Iceland, Denmark, Canada, and Switzerland (Figure 3.16). The level of personal security is an important determinant in attracting well-educated people and foreign senior executives. Obviously, Colombia, South Africa, and Russia are confronted with a more challenging situation in this respect – firms find themselves paying a significant premium to attract talent, and even then find it difficult to fill key positions. In a world of spreading anxiety, being a haven of security secures and retains talent.

Protecting intellectual property must be a key priority in view of its impact on a firm's value. Many Asian nations are confronted with large-scale piracy and fraud: luxury goods, software, music or videos, and even pharmaceuticals. Latin America, especially after the signature of the Andean Pact (Cartagena Agreement, 1969), has had an ambiguous approach [14]. The authorities of the region believed that strict enforcement of the protection of technological property owned by foreign enterprises was not essential, and that not enforcing this would facilitate the development of local technology (especially in the case of IT and pharmaceuticals). The opposite occurred – foreign firms became reluctant to invest and transfer technology to Latin America, precisely because their intellectual property would not be protected. When investing abroad, companies generally favour a 100% owned investment (seldom joint ventures), with an emphasis on full protection of patents, copyrights, and trademarks. Policies that do not protect or enforce intellectual property laws jeopardise the future competitiveness of a country.

Protecting intellectual property also protects people. Rolex watches, Cartier bags, or Gucci clothing, are not the only things that are imitated and passed on as the real thing. Fake pharmaceuticals are a much more dangerous threat. Reports indicate that, in Nigeria today, two medicines out of three are imitations of the original product. About 19 million

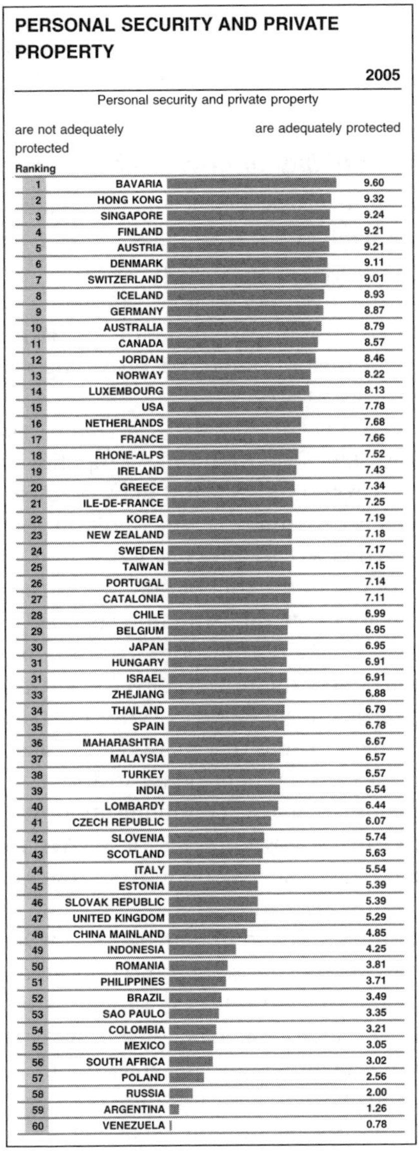

PERSONAL SECURITY AND PRIVATE PROPERTY

2005

Personal security and private property

are not adequately protected   are adequately protected

Ranking		
1	BAVARIA	9.60
2	HONG KONG	9.32
3	SINGAPORE	9.24
4	FINLAND	9.21
5	AUSTRIA	9.21
6	DENMARK	9.11
7	SWITZERLAND	9.01
8	ICELAND	8.93
9	GERMANY	8.87
10	AUSTRALIA	8.79
11	CANADA	8.57
12	JORDAN	8.46
13	NORWAY	8.22
14	LUXEMBOURG	8.13
15	USA	7.78
16	NETHERLANDS	7.68
17	FRANCE	7.66
18	RHONE-ALPS	7.52
19	IRELAND	7.43
20	GREECE	7.34
21	ILE-DE-FRANCE	7.25
22	KOREA	7.19
23	NEW ZEALAND	7.18
24	SWEDEN	7.17
25	TAIWAN	7.15
26	PORTUGAL	7.14
27	CATALONIA	7.11
28	CHILE	6.99
29	BELGIUM	6.95
30	JAPAN	6.95
31	HUNGARY	6.91
31	ISRAEL	6.91
33	ZHEJIANG	6.88
34	THAILAND	6.79
35	SPAIN	6.78
36	MAHARASHTRA	6.67
37	MALAYSIA	6.57
38	TURKEY	6.57
39	INDIA	6.54
40	LOMBARDY	6.44
41	CZECH REPUBLIC	6.07
42	SLOVENIA	5.74
43	SCOTLAND	5.63
44	ITALY	5.54
45	ESTONIA	5.39
46	SLOVAK REPUBLIC	5.39
47	UNITED KINGDOM	5.29
48	CHINA MAINLAND	4.85
49	INDONESIA	4.25
50	ROMANIA	3.81
51	PHILIPPINES	3.71
52	BRAZIL	3.49
53	SAO PAULO	3.35
54	COLOMBIA	3.21
55	MEXICO	3.05
56	SOUTH AFRICA	3.02
57	POLAND	2.56
58	RUSSIA	2.00
59	ARGENTINA	1.26
60	VENEZUELA	0.78

Figure 3.16 – The importance of security. (Reproduced from [5] by permission of IMD.)

people around the world can develop computer viruses, which attack personal and company computers. Therefore, the protection of data, personal or corporate, is becoming a serious concern for business and governments alike.

The role and responsibility of government in infrastructure

A nation's infrastructure policy, be it basic, scientific, technological, or social, is a key element of its competitiveness – and, ultimately, the responsibility of government. Even if the State is not involved directly in its implementation – the operation or the maintenance of infrastructure can be delegated to the private sector – it is perceived by public opinion to bear overall responsibility for providing such public services. There are two reasons:

1. During the early stages of a nation's competitiveness development, the government's role is direct and active. Since infrastructure is a "precompetitive" investment – a precondition for competitiveness – government is expected to provide for it. For example, an active cluster policy in a country cannot succeed if the chosen area does not benefit from adequate infrastructure such as good transport hubs – a harbour, rail, roads, and airports – to import components and to ship products. Many attempts to develop clusters, even with good tax incentive policies, have failed because of the lack of initial infrastructure investment. There are many such cases in Russia, where potential areas of development failed in the absence of other necessary investments to allow communication with the rest of the world. In contrast, the governments of Malaysia, Singapore, China, Hong Kong, and Dubai have all understood the necessity of the early development of infrastructure.

2. As a nation matures in its competitiveness development, the role of the government becomes more and more indirect and passive – that of a monitor. If infrastructure breaks down, people naturally expect the government to intervene. The government is perceived as the ultimate safety net guaranteeing the integrity of the infrastructure of a country – even if such infrastructure is operated by the private sector, such as in the case of airlines, hospitals, postal services, railways, airports, and so on. While citizens, overall, have faith in the market system, when the railway system breaks down in the UK, or when the airline companies are bankrupt in the US, public opinion always expects the government to intervene. During this mature stage, government intervention can also be linked to the emergence of new infrastructure, such as the Internet. The government provides a vision and a blueprint for implementation of new technologies,

and the development of an appropriate legislative and regulatory framework.

3.3 The four competitiveness forces

The four competitiveness *factors* describe the nature of a nation's competitiveness environment. We now turn to the four competitiveness *forces*, which reveal how nations *manage* their competitiveness. The four competitiveness factors are *descriptive*. The four competitiveness forces are *policy-oriented*. These forces are often the result of tradition, history, or value systems, and are so deeply rooted in the "modus operandi" of a country that, in most cases, they are not clearly stated or defined. Integrating these forces into an overall theory reveals how they interplay. Such a theory does not seek to quantify the competitiveness of a country, but rather to uncover the "competitiveness profile" that sets an economy apart, and to envisage how it might behave under certain conditions.

The four forces of competitiveness are:

1. Attractiveness vs. aggressiveness.
2. Proximity vs. globality.
3. Assets vs. processes.
4. Individual risk taking vs. social cohesiveness.

3.3.1 Attractiveness vs. aggressiveness

Nations vary in the way they manage themselves within the global business community (Figure 3.17). Traditionally, a nation's competitiveness was linked to its international aggressiveness – exports and outward foreign direct investment (FDI). Germany, Japan, and Korea followed an export-led strategy. Germany is still today the second largest exporter of goods ($569bn in 2000), after the US and before Japan. It has the largest positive trade balance in the world ($76bn in 2001).

More recently, some nations have managed their competitiveness through their investment attractiveness. For example, Ireland and Singapore have based their competitiveness on incentives to attract foreign direct investment. In 2000, the flow of direct investment to Ireland was in the order of 24.2% of GDP.

While aggressiveness generates income in the home country, especially when foreign earnings are repatriated, the benefits for job creation are not as visible (Figure 3.18). Exports certainly have a positive impact on the labour market of a country – they generate jobs and expertise –

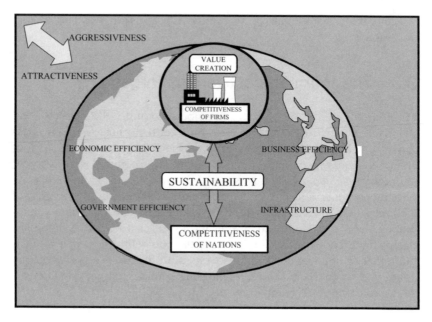

Figure 3.17 – Aggressiveness vs. attractiveness.

yet, the net result of an outward foreign direct investment is different. If a company shifts its strategy from exporting to a country, to investing directly there to satisfy local demand, it may deprive its home country of the exports it previously made, and thus of currency earnings and jobs. Some revenues may eventually come back as dividends.

Understanding where the costs and benefits are accrued becomes trickier when it comes to a direct investment that is not aimed at serving the local market, but rather at taking advantage of lower production costs. The goods produced may then be re-exported to the home market, as has been the case in Europe and the US for TV sets, toys, computers, etc. This strategy can lead to an export loss, an increase in imports, and some job destruction in the home country.

From the company's point of view, foreign direct investment is positive, since it usually results in increased market share. But, for the country, the benefits are not as clear-cut at first glance. Nevertheless, in the long term, nations certainly benefit from the aggressiveness of their companies on international markets, even if done through foreign direct investment.

Some scholars believe that foreign investment allows an extension of the power of the home country through the activity of its firms abroad – this thinking is considered a foreign policy tool by certain countries.

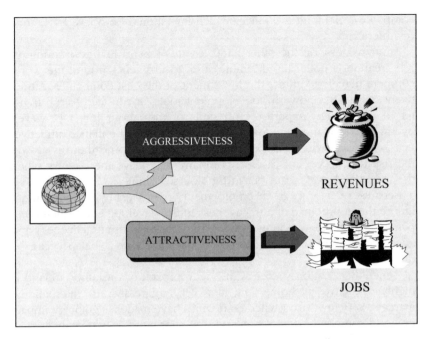

Figure 3.18 – Impact of attractiveness and aggressiveness.
Aggressiveness generates revenues for a nation, while attractiveness
generates jobs. In view of the rise of unemployment in recent years,
governments have re-emphasised their attractiveness policies,
providing more incentives for investors. As a result, today, nations
compete fiercely to lure foreign investors.

The US often uses the concept of the "extraterritoriality of the law." For instance, the Trading with the Enemy Act forbids trade relations with countries the US deems to be hostile nations. Other regulations administered by the Office of Foreign Assets Control in the US Treasury Department prohibit financial transactions with countries such as Sudan, Cuba, and North Korea [15]. Such regulations apply to foreign subsidiaries of American companies, despite the fact that, legally, they have the nationality of the host country.

Obviously, such policies can lead to political tension among nations. The US tried to force American companies operating abroad to implement US trade sanctions against the Soviet Union after it invaded Afghanistan in 1980. Host countries ordered companies of US parentage operating on its territory not to follow such instructions. France was particularly adamant in enforcing the primacy of its national law over such companies. It presented an interesting dilemma for the local CEO of US companies operating in France: which law should be obeyed – French or American?

Attractiveness, on the other hand, creates jobs in FDI host countries. Job creation is politically desirable, and governments around the world compete fiercely to attract the investment of the best companies. Attractiveness is also a powerful development tool – it can lead to the transfer of technology, expertise, and skills of the labour force. However, overly generous incentive packages that temporarily enhance attractiveness, can also reduce net benefits for the country. And there is always the risk that, in certain cases, a company may leave the country when the incentive benefits run out in the course of time.

Because of its impact on employment, even wealthy nations cannot ignore the importance of attractiveness in the development of their competitiveness strategy. Countries need to balance both attractiveness and aggressiveness in order to compete today, but such a balance can be difficult to achieve.

Generally, a nation succeeds in one approach or the other. Ireland is highly attractive at home, but not very aggressive in international markets. Very few Irish-owned companies have made a significant impact in world competitiveness. Korea, on the other hand, is extremely aggressive globally, both with trade and FDI, but it is far less attractive to hosting foreign investments. The UK used to be aggressive, and has now become a very attractive place for investments. Switzerland has followed the opposite path, and has moved from attractiveness (numerous European headquarters of foreign enterprises are located there) to aggressiveness. The United States seems to be the only country that displays a good balance in being both attractive and aggressive.

3.3.2 Proximity vs. globality

The economic system of a country is not homogeneous. As a result of the opening of borders and the globalisation of business, nations must now deal with two types of coexisting economy: the economy of proximity, and that of globality (Figure 3.19).

The *economy of proximity* is comprised of conventional activities, such as crafts and shops; personal services, such as doctors and social help; and administrative activities, such as government and justice. It also consists of technologically advanced companies in, for example, telecommunications, health, customisation of products, or after sales services. The economy of proximity is geographically close to the end-user, where it provides its added value. This type of economy is traditionally protected, and is not very price-competitive (Figure 3.20).

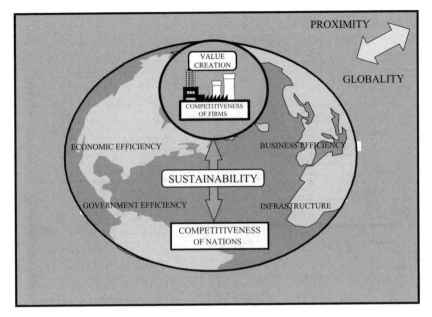

Figure 3.19 – Proximity vs. globality. The distinction between proximity and globality has become more acute in the past decade, with the considerable power accumulated by global companies, not only on foreign markets, but also at home.

The *economy of globality* is comprised of companies operating on a global scale, be it through trade or investments. Their production need not necessarily occur close to the end-user. The consumer can thus benefit from having access to competitive products developed for worldwide markets. A global approach also leads to comparative advantages, especially with regard to operational costs. This type of economy is generally open and price-competitive (Figure 3.20).

The contribution of these two economies to the competitiveness of a nation varies according to the size and the economic development stage of a country. On average, two-thirds of Western European GDP is generated by the economy of proximity, and the remaining one-third by the economy of globality. Smaller countries are often much more dependent on their economy of globality, which means a higher vulnerability to the volatility of international markets. Larger countries, such as the United States, can rely on a huge domestic market to act as a buffer during periods of economic slowdown abroad.

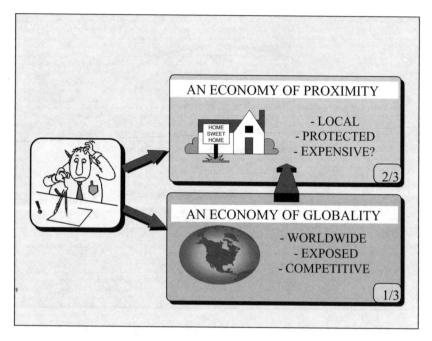

Figure 3.20 – Two sides of an economy. The intrusion of globality in the economy of proximity has recently created many social tensions. It often implies deregulation, privatisation, and a tougher competitive environment. Jobs are often lost. The privatisation of national telecom industries offers an illustration of this process. However, since most voters are to be found in the economy of proximity, politicians have a tendency to give particular attention to such disruptions.

Over the past 25 years, the economy of globality has shown considerable vitality, and has invaded the turf of the economy of proximity. A number of policies have supported this trend, such as the lowering of trade barriers, linkages through regional economic agreements (e.g. EU, NAFTA), the privatisation of enterprises, and the deregulation of markets. The globalisation of business activities exercises strong pressure on prices, profits, and wages. Consequently, the overall price level is falling in the economy of globality, thus keeping inflation under control. For example, many products, such as computers, mobile phones, cars, and consumer electronics, which originate in the economy of globality, are significantly cheaper and better performing today than five years ago.

Nations with high domestic standards of living, coupled with high operating costs, such as Germany and Switzerland, are going through a harsh adaptation process: the closure of local ineffective entities, and the entry of new competitors on the home markets. Other countries, such as Ireland, Chile, and Singapore, seem to be more at ease with the globalisation of their economies (Figure 3.21).

From a policy point of view, this two-tier economy means that government and business must identify clearly which competitiveness strategy applies to which part of the economy. The Netherlands has excelled in managing the coexistence of these two economies. On one hand, it has liberalised and privatised the part of the Dutch economy that is involved totally with global markets (telecommunications, logistics, etc.), while maintaining an active social policy in the economy of proximity, which has a more visible impact on local people. For example, besides providing generous social benefits and incentives, The Netherlands has developed one of the most flexible work structures in the world, responding to the changing needs of local people.

To force a "globality approach," for the sake of efficiency, on activities that are purely of proximity, such as post offices, education, or health services, can create social tension, especially since they also provide some social benefits. Countries need to juggle globality and proximity, creating a balance that takes into account private and public interests. The "cultural exception" policy introduced in France, to protect its culture from excessive Anglo-Saxon influence, illustrates such an approach.

Tensions between the two economies are on the rise. The antiglobalisation movement resonates the concerns and fears of a significant part of the population. Such movements question the legitimacy and benefits of competitiveness as a means of development. At the same time, it is imperative to remember that an efficient competitiveness policy also generates vitality and innovation in the economy of proximity. No country can survive in isolation today by focusing only on its economy of proximity; nor can a country succeed in the long term if its prosperity is based solely on globality. Large companies that claim to be "global" and relinquish their national origin are probably following a dangerous path – "Big trees need strong roots!"

3.3.3 Assets vs. processes

As we have seen earlier, nations also manage their competitive environments by relying more on either their natural assets, or in using efficient processes (Figure 3.22). Some nations are rich in assets – land, people, and natural resources – yet not necessarily competitive; such is the case for Brazil, India, and Russia. Other nations, such as Singapore,

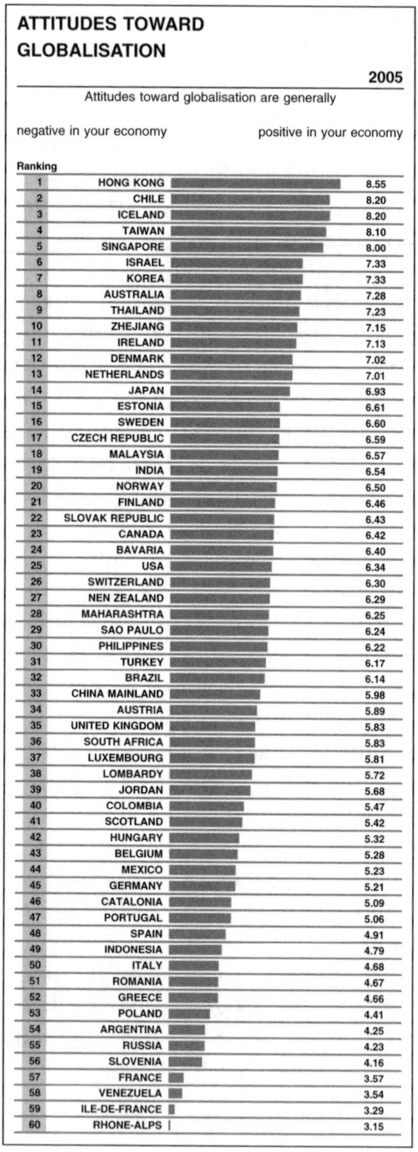

ATTITUDES TOWARD
GLOBALISATION

2005

Attitudes toward globalisation are generally

negative in your economy   positive in your economy

Ranking		Value
1	HONG KONG	8.55
2	CHILE	8.20
3	ICELAND	8.20
4	TAIWAN	8.10
5	SINGAPORE	8.00
6	ISRAEL	7.33
7	KOREA	7.33
8	AUSTRALIA	7.28
9	THAILAND	7.23
10	ZHEJIANG	7.15
11	IRELAND	7.13
12	DENMARK	7.02
13	NETHERLANDS	7.01
14	JAPAN	6.93
15	ESTONIA	6.61
16	SWEDEN	6.60
17	CZECH REPUBLIC	6.59
18	MALAYSIA	6.57
19	INDIA	6.54
20	NORWAY	6.50
21	FINLAND	6.46
22	SLOVAK REPUBLIC	6.43
23	CANADA	6.42
24	BAVARIA	6.40
25	USA	6.34
26	SWITZERLAND	6.30
27	NEN ZEALAND	6.29
28	MAHARASHTRA	6.25
29	SAO PAULO	6.24
30	PHILIPPINES	6.22
31	TURKEY	6.17
32	BRAZIL	6.14
33	CHINA MAINLAND	5.98
34	AUSTRIA	5.89
35	UNITED KINGDOM	5.83
36	SOUTH AFRICA	5.83
37	LUXEMBOURG	5.81
38	LOMBARDY	5.72
39	JORDAN	5.68
40	COLOMBIA	5.47
41	SCOTLAND	5.42
42	HUNGARY	5.32
43	BELGIUM	5.28
44	MEXICO	5.23
45	GERMANY	5.21
46	CATALONIA	5.09
47	PORTUGAL	5.06
48	SPAIN	4.91
49	INDONESIA	4.79
50	ITALY	4.68
51	ROMANIA	4.67
52	GREECE	4.66
53	POLAND	4.41
54	ARGENTINA	4.25
55	RUSSIA	4.23
56	SLOVENIA	4.16
57	FRANCE	3.57
58	VENEZUELA	3.54
59	ILE-DE-FRANCE	3.29
60	RHONE-ALPS	3.15

Figure 3.21 – Attitudes toward globalisation. (Reproduced from [5] by
permission of IMD.)

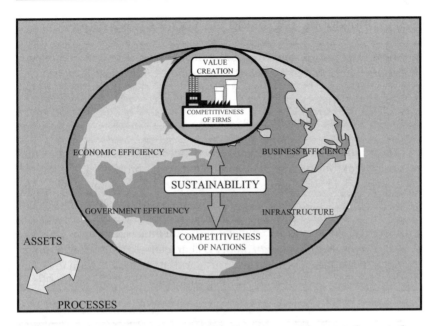

Figure 3.22 – Assets vs. processes. Endowment with natural assets has long been considered a key factor for competitiveness. Empires and colonies were conquered to ensure the supply of natural assets. Today, processes are more important for competitiveness, since raw materials and commodities can be procured freely around the world.

Japan, and Switzerland, are poor in natural assets but more competitive: they have developed the capacity to *transform* their natural assets into finished, or semi-finished, products. They are competitive in processing. Overall, nations that rely on processes for their competitiveness are more successful than those that rely on nontransformed natural assets.

Britain had steel and coal, and transformed them into steam engines, railways, and enterprises. The Industrial Revolution in Britain was born when the country began to rely more on transformation processes than on the exploitation of resources. Other nations have followed a similar path, among them, the US and Canada. The availability of natural resources indirectly supports the competitive performance of economies such as Norway, the UK, The Netherlands, and, today, Dubai. While these nations rely mostly on process competitiveness, the revenues gained from their natural resources have served as a base from which to develop their competitiveness, not as substitutes for creating economic added value.

3.3.4   Individual risk taking vs. social cohesiveness

The next force that defines the competitive environment of a country is the distinction between a system that promotes individual risk, and one that preserves social cohesiveness (Figure 3.23). The work of Max Weber (see Chapter 2) opened the way to a classification of business behaviours that can be summarised as follows:

1. *The Southern Model* is characterised by underdeveloped infrastructure, weak business regulation, limited social protection, low labour costs, and, in some cases, a significant parallel economy. Italy, Spain, Portugal, Turkey, and many industrialising nations are examples of such a model. The pre-eminent competitive features are the resourcefulness and inventiveness of individuals and firms.
2. *The Continental European Model* is characterised by a strong emphasis on stability, social consensus, and regulation. Germany, The Netherlands, Scandinavia, Austria, and Switzerland are examples of

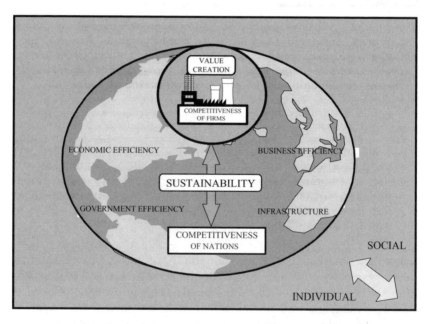

Figure 3.23 – Social vs. individual values. Economists and philosophers have always been keen to explain the development of nations in terms of behaviours and values. There is no doubt that there is a correlation between the attitudes of people, and their ability to compete worldwide.

such a model. The pre-eminent competitive feature is the long-term perspective.

3. *The Anglo-Saxon Model* is characterised by deregulation, extensive private ownership, flexible labour markets, and a higher tolerance for risk. The US, Canada, Britain, Australia, New Zealand, and Ireland are examples of such a model. The pre-eminent competitive feature is the entrepreneurial spirit.

As a nation moves along its developmental path, it is confronted with a stark choice between shaping itself according to the Anglo-Saxon, or the Continental European, Model. In the past, Japan and Taiwan have opted for the Continental European Model, while Hong Kong and Singapore have chosen the Anglo-Saxon Model (Figure 3.24). Nevertheless, countries can shift from one model to the other. Britain under the Labour governments of the 1970s was pursuing the Continental European Model; Margaret Thatcher brought it back into the Anglo-Saxon fold. New Zealand experienced a similar fate – it shifted course and has become one of the most privatised economies in the world today.

The Continental European and the Anglo-Saxon models have been in contest with each other for many years. From the 1980s to the early

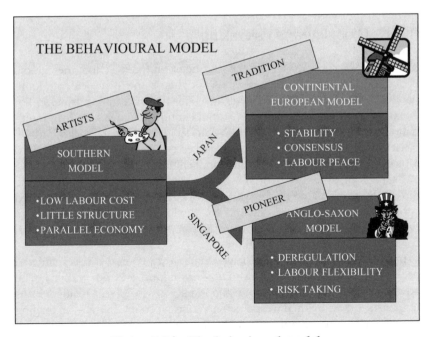

Figure 3.24 – The behavioural model.

1990s, there was a sharp increase in the acceptance and adoption of the Anglo-Saxon Model, as a result of the globalisation of markets led by Anglo-Saxon companies. However, today, a new pattern is emerging, where countries are trying to correct the imbalances created by a "pure" global Anglo-Saxon Model. The "Third Way" advocated by UK Prime Minister Tony Blair leans in this direction [16].

One of the major challenges for business and government leaders is striking the right balance between a hyper-competitive global business approach, along the lines of the Anglo-Saxon Model, and a more socially responsive, localised approach, along the lines of the Continental European Model.

3.4   Combining the four forces of competitiveness

The interplay between these forces, and the relative importance of each, sets a country's competitive landscape. We now move away from the *trade-off* within a single force (proximity *versus* globality), to the *combination* of various aspects across the model (globality *and* risk-taking).

3.4.1   Globality *and* risk taking

The Anglo-Saxon Model is the strongest reference for the global economy. One of the main reasons for this is the historical predominance of British and American firms in international business. For example, in the late 19th and early 20th centuries, many American multinational enterprises emerged and began to invest abroad – Standard Oil of New Jersey, Singer, International Harvester, Western Electric, and Ford Motor Company had major production facilities outside the United States. For such companies, the global economy was riskier and less predictable than their home market. The world of overseas business was uncharted – operations had greater demand for flexibility and entrepreneurship. Opening and running operations in remote parts of the world was perceived as a modern-day adventure.

In this historical context, global companies favoured a less-regulated economic system, which allowed for risk-taking and adaptability. The advantage of what later became the Anglo-Saxon Model resided in its emphasis on individual responsibility and accountability – managing global operations required a high degree of trust and delegation of authority to local managers. Even in today's world, where email, voice mail, and videoconferencing are tightening the grip that central management exercises on foreign operations, a competitive global company still promotes a pioneering culture – people posted abroad have to be able to take care of things themselves.

3.4.2   Proximity *and* social cohesiveness

In contrast, social cohesiveness has long been associated with the management of an economy of proximity, where the social consequences of competitiveness matter. The Continental European Model epitomises an approach that also pays special attention to values and cultural heritage. Europe has experienced many episodes of political revolution in the 18th and 19th centuries, and social upheaval in the 20th century. Almost every single European nation has experienced periods of brutal change, triggered by violence erupting in the streets. Monarchs have been beheaded, people have been exiled, and governments have fallen – all victims of violent demonstrations or strikes. As a consequence, in the collective memory of most European nations, the "street" has, at one time or another, overthrown the political system.

For these reasons, governments and leaders in Europe pay very close attention to social issues. In certain countries, such as the UK and Germany, trade unions have even created their own political parties to defend their position (respectively the Labour Party and the SPD). Leaders care about how people perceive their policies, and will tend to retreat quickly when they sense strong opposition. The Continental European Model is slow at producing government reforms in areas such as the tax or pension systems, because they have the potential to upset a subtle social balance. Thus, labour peace, social responsiveness, stability, and sustainability become central priorities. Such an approach creates an environment that tends to be more risk averse, where the interests of the community prevail over the needs of the individuals.

The American version of the Anglo-Saxon Model provides a remarkable contrast. The US is a land of *pioneers*. It has been built by people who, by emigrating, were willing to confront adversity, develop a sense of risk, accept the unknown, and above all, take care of themselves. The vastness of the country exacerbated the importance of these values. The conquest of the West in the 19th century epitomised a sense of adventure and entrepreneurship. It also fostered the notion of mobility and boundless possibilities, which is often so absent in the Continental European Model.

The US model also ignores the power of the "street," which is so feared by European governments. Being part of a nation founded by immigrants and pioneers, individuals are generally very self-reliant and mobile. When adversity strikes, they confront it directly and personally. Or they move on and start over. On the contrary, Europe has preserved a system of localised client–patron relationships, hindering mobility and risk-taking. Throughout history, individuals and communities relied on the protection of a lord, a prince, or a king. In many ways, the modern notion of the State in Europe has taken over this responsibility. When things go wrong, Europeans turn to the State.

Therefore, although large demonstrations are not uncommon in the US (e.g. civil rights and against the Vietnam War), the "street" has never uprooted an American government – the demonstrations are against policies, not the system. Trade unions have seen their power reduced significantly, especially after President Reagan broke the air traffic controller strike in August 1981. In addition, the US model glorifies individual success, regardless of origin. The 134 "dime novels," written by the 19th century American writer Horatio Alger, laid the foundations of the "American Dream," featuring, as they did, stories of young boys born in misery who reach success and fame [17]. Bill Gates is an example of a modern day Horatio Alger hero.

Nowadays, the gap between the models, and that between the economy of globality and proximity, is not as a clear-cut as it used to be. It would be absurd to generalise and to assert that there is no sense of social responsiveness in the US, or that there is no entrepreneurship in Europe. Nevertheless, one should not underestimate how much the fundamental roots are ingrained in people's attitudes. An attempt to apply the Anglo-Saxon Model in a country or an enterprise that thrives on consensus, can lead to social disruptions and upheavals. On the other hand, the pursuit of consensus at all costs, and adherence to the Continental European Model in an environment (for example, a high-tech company) that thrives on deregulation, speed, and flexibility, can kill competitiveness. In each case, governments and enterprises need to identify which model prevails, and adapt their strategy accordingly.

3.5   Competitiveness in perspective: the depth of the cube

Taken together, the *four competitiveness factors* and the *four competitiveness forces* define the degree to which a country can become competitive, and the strategies it could follow. The objective for a country to increase its competitiveness, is to enable its firms to create more added value today, while increasing the prosperity of its people. Such strategies, when repeated year after year, lead to accumulated "added value" over time, and thereby create wealth. The depth of the cube provides a general overview of the relationship between competitiveness and wealth.

A country like Singapore, which has been highly competitive during recent years, will be visualised as having a larger face for its cube. However, Singapore was only founded in 1965, and has only had a relatively short amount of time to accumulate wealth [18]. Therefore, the depth of the cube is relatively small. Switzerland, on the other hand, slowed its progress in competitiveness, so the face of its cube has become smaller. Historically, however, Swiss competitiveness has been built over more than 100 years – the depth of its cube is greater (representing a larger amount of accumulated wealth) than that of Singapore (Figure 3.25).

The relationship between the face of the cube and its depth – between competitiveness and wealth – is a theoretical illustration placing the competitiveness of a country within a historical perspective. Countries such as New Zealand, Australia, Iceland, Sweden, and the US have already

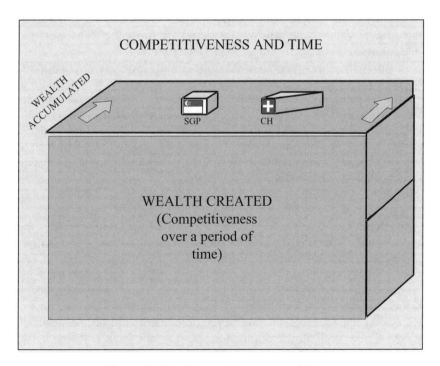

Figure 3.25 – Competitiveness and time.

attempted to give some statistical measurements of the assets they own, i.e. they have tried to measure their accumulated wealth.

Italy has just completed a study that estimates the value of the assets owned by the central and local governments to be $2100bn. This figure does not include artistic and environmental assets. The UK has also performed such an exercise. It is more comprehensive in scope, and it reaches a figure of $8800bn assets owned by Britons in 2003. Private homes represent more than half of this amount, while commercial and public property are valued at $1000bn. The country's roads, bridges, pipelines, and other infrastructure are estimated at $961bn. Such valuations are, of course, debatable. Indeed, much of the investment made by a country can neither be resold, nor generate revenues, unlike a private company's investment (although paying tolls for the use of bridges or roads, or the privatisation of public assets like railways, could be viewed as an attempt to correct this fact).

National accounts mostly treat investment spending as expenditure. The notion of placing a value on the aggregate assets accumulated by a nation is still in its infancy. Nevertheless, most would agree that a country which invests for decades in infrastructure, education, or scientific research, also invests in its future competitiveness, and the future prosperity of its people. The competitiveness created today will constitute the wealth of tomorrow. The depth of the cube illustrates that dimension.

In summary, the competitiveness Cube Theory explains what happens *between* the primary source of competitiveness, i.e. enterprises creating economic value, and the ultimate goal of competitiveness, i.e. enhancing the prosperity of people. In between, the role of the State is critical. First, the State provides the framework within which firms perform their activities. It then guarantees that the value created by firms will, in one way or another, contribute to the prosperity of people. The State has a delicate balancing act to perform, which cannot be tilted excessively one way or the other without running the risk of social destabilisation.

In such a systemic model, a change in one of the components of the model affects the behaviour of all the other components. For example, if the population demands more social welfare and protection, it can have a direct impact on the taxation of enterprises, or on labour legislation. On the contrary, if enterprises change their business approach drastically, for example through more investment abroad, it can have a significant impact on State revenues, employment, and on the development of new skills in the population. Both trends have happened, and had a huge impact on competitiveness. In the 1970s, a change in the value system of the population in most industrialised nations forced enterprises and governments to be sensitive to new issues such as social welfare, environmental protection, gender, racial, and minority discrimination, diversity, and work–life balance.

Equally important is the fact that enterprises have changed their fundamental business model radically over the past two decades – enterprises have become more global and more stretched. The fall of communism has reinforced the supremacy of open and global market economy as the business model of choice for the world. Outsourcing, and more recently, offshoring, has changed the profile of many enterprises – they have transferred assets and activities to partners worldwide in order to reduce costs.

Globalisation and outsourcing have created a new business model of competitiveness for the firm – the *Extended Enterprise Model*. Extended is a better term than stretched, as it implies that things are still under control. However, the situation it describes is the same: a firm that transfers some of its activities from its core to an expanding periphery of global and local partners.

The relationship between governments, firms, and people has been altered completely by current trends – globalisation and restructuring have acquired negative connotations in public opinion. Nations can no longer count on the allegiance of their leading firms – do they still have a home country in such a global world? To answer this question, we will now explore the structure, functioning, and consequences for competitiveness of this new business model – the *Extended Enterprise Model*.

4 The Extended Enterprise

*"Drive thy business
or it will drive thee!"*

Benjamin Franklin 1706–1790

As we have seen before, the firm – the "core engine" that drives value creation – is at the centre of any competitiveness model. From a theoretical standpoint, every company performs the same function: the transformation of ideas and technology into marketable products and services. While the economic purpose is identical, the means of achieving it are very different. Firms strive to be unlike any other – differentiation is central to a firm's strategy.

However, the globalisation of markets has led to convergence into a business model in which a series of key features are consistently deployed – the implementation of quality standards, the global management of a network of suppliers and distributors, the drive to keep customers loyal, and so on. Firms find that their viability is at stake if they do not rely on a common business model – an approach initiated by large global companies, and increasingly pervasive today. Large firms require their suppliers and distributors, many of which are small companies, to adapt to their new business model.

4.1 What is the Extended Enterprise Model?

The model relies on two key assumptions:

1. *Enterprises create more value by sharing knowledge.* Microsoft's stroke of genius was to make its DOS operating system easily available, thereby allowing third parties to develop numerous applications on this platform, and thus creating an industry standard. Today, Linux is applying a similar strategy. Apple, by contrast, controlled access to its proprietary system and limited its availability to a few selected partners. That choice discouraged growth in the number of

third-party developers, significantly limiting the appeal of Apple products and threatening the company's long-term survival.

2. *By linking their value chains, enterprises create more value.* Technology has allowed companies to interconnect their value chains, thus allowing all to benefit from the comparative advantage of each firm in the network, and to increase the efficiency and speed of business transactions. Electronic Point of Sales (EPOS), or Dell's "Direct Model" illustrate this strategy [1].

As indicated at the end of the preceding chapter, globalisation and the extension of the value chain through outsourcing drives the Extended Enterprise Model. The model is cost-efficient because it exploits fully the comparative advantages across nations and partners, allowing a company to produce in the most attractive locations around the world, and to collaborate with the most efficient suppliers or distributors.

This Extended Enterprise Model is based on a series of concentric circles stemming from a core enterprise, expanding into a periphery of partners operating at different distances from the core (Figure 4.1). *Ownership of assets* and *knowledge* by the core firm is the foundation of the model. The most fundamental decision a company can make is whether or not it retains exclusive ownership of certain types of assets and knowledge relating to its operations. In general, the decision to retain full ownership defines the type of activities that remain at the centre of the model, the *core enterprise*. The willingness to share, or shed, the utilisation of assets or knowledge determines the activities managed in the periphery, in cooperation with partners.

Nevertheless, firms operating according to this model have to tackle complexity, and thus require sophisticated processes and management skills, which may not be available in either the core or the periphery. In addition, the model is transaction-based. Transactions in the corporate world are notoriously inefficient. Companies master the new techniques of manufacturing, such as quality or reengineering, quite well; however, they often relatively underperform in managing transactions with suppliers or customers. If enterprises succeed in overcoming the efficiency hurdle posed by transactions, then, in the future, the model will produce even greater gains in productivity.

To explore the model, we will start from the core and move towards the periphery.

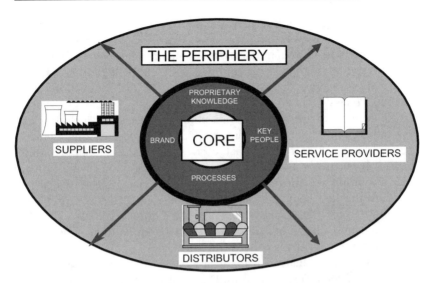

Figure 4.1 – The extended enterprise. The model portrays a core enterprise getting smaller over time and focusing on resource optimisation, such as the ownership and management of assets and proprietary knowledge. Through outsourcing, the core enterprise transfers sections of its supply and distribution chain to a network of partners, which are providers of assets, knowledge, and processes. A closer relationship also exists with customers, who seek value and satisfaction. The model operates across a common, Internet-based technological platform, either internal or external.

4.1.1 The core enterprise and the periphery

The core enterprise

The *core enterprise* is composed of the assets and knowledge over which the firm has chosen to retain ownership. In the past, everything was core enterprise, with full vertical integration. In the early 1980s, while on a trip to China, I visited the Beijing Ice-Box factory, then just opening to the world. The visit was a formidable experience, a true return to the past of industrialisation. We started the visit at the foundry, continuing through the assembly plant, and finally ending with the painting of the refrigerators! Everything was produced in one place, in complete autarchy, and with no knowledge of what other companies were doing. The State decided the cost, the price, and the quantity of goods to be produced. Those were the good old days . . .

For the Beijing Ice-Box factory, the boundaries of core and periphery were not an issue: everything was core. Firms today rely on a different model – the most important decision a company takes is to define which activities should be outsourced and which should be kept in-house. The wrong decision can deprive the enterprise of the foundation of its competitiveness.

The usual path for making core–periphery decisions includes analysing the value chain of the enterprise and how its various elements create added value, and at what cost. The value chain model, summarised by Figure 4.2, defines the relative contribution of the primary and supporting activities of a firm to its profit margin. The objective is to locate the key competencies of the firm, and determine how they contribute to its overall competitiveness. As a corollary, it also identifies which activities can be outsourced or shared with partners, whose level of efficiency is higher than that of the firm.

The value chain analysis leads to a strategic reflection on which are the core competencies of the firm. Deciding which activities a firm can,

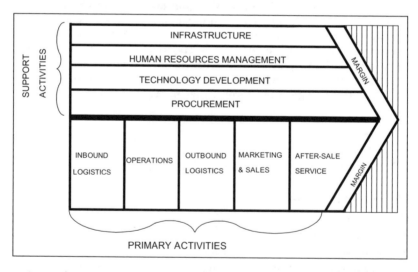

Figure 4.2 – The value chain. This model divides the company into primary activities – those in direct contact with products and services – and support activities – those allowing primary activities to be performed. Each activity, in theory, should add value in the overall process. If it does not, or is not cost-effective, it is a good candidate to be outsourced. Each company has one or more special strength(s) within its value chain. For example, Wal-Mart excels at *inbound logistics*, Toyota at *operations*, Nestlé at *procurement* and Procter and Gamble at *marketing and sales*.

or should, outsource does not necessarily tell the firm on which future activities it should concentrate its attention. Gary Hamel and C.K. Prahalad addressed this issue in various articles in *Harvard Business Review* and their book *Competing for the Future* in 1994 [2, 3]. They drew an analogy between the core competency concept of the firm and a tree. In their model, the leaves are the end products. Products, like leaves in the autumn, come to obsolescence, fall, and are replaced by other products in the following season. The branches are core products and the trunk is the core business – hopefully lasting longer than the leaves. The roots are the permanent sources of competitiveness of the firm and must be nurtured and developed constantly. If the roots rot, then the company dies, just like a tree (Figure 4.3). Managing the key competencies in the

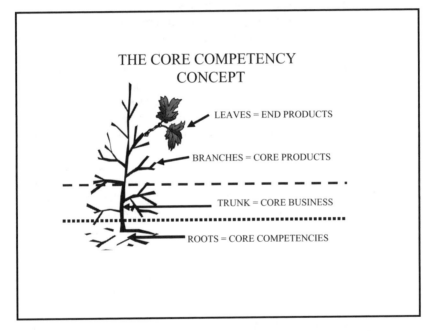

THE CORE COMPETENCY CONCEPT

LEAVES = END PRODUCTS

BRANCHES = CORE PRODUCTS

TRUNK = CORE BUSINESS

ROOTS = CORE COMPETENCIES

Figure 4.3 – The core competency concept. The analogy of the core competencies of a company with the roots of a tree is powerful. Core competencies, like roots, are less visible than leaves – products – but need to be nurtured constantly and developed. The top management of a company should own the process of taking care of the roots, while the development of core and end products can be left to strategic business unit managers. Companies usually disappear when they mismanage or ignore their core competencies. Kodak, for example, is struggling today because the company concentrated on conventional photography products, and failed to develop its core competencies in digital pictures, home printing, etc.

roots of the business, as well as creating new ones, are both key factors in the future competitiveness of the firm, and a fundamental responsibility of senior management.

A company should focus its activities primarily in business areas where it can build on a few of its core competencies. For example, the core competencies of Sony can be defined as entertainment, sound and image, and miniaturisation. A few years ago, Sony was a key supplier to the computer industry for disk drives and flat screens. A core competence analysis would have demonstrated clearly that Sony had the knowledge to enter the PC market itself, especially at a time when quality of sound and visual content were becoming a key competitive factor for consumers. Sony did not do so, initially, probably because of its strategic business unit (SBU) structure, which did not encourage executives to seek innovative business opportunities beyond their own turf. The same was true for electronic games, digital, and video cameras: Sony had the technology and mastered the processes to enter these markets in a competitive way, but it did not do so. Sony finally realised that it had more competencies than many other companies, and that the company could be more than just a supplier of digitalised components. Today, Sony has developed a strong business in PCs, games stations, and digital cameras. The firm revived its competitiveness by making better use of its core competencies in sound, image, and miniaturisation, combining them in every possible way.

Proprietary knowledge, which can be technology (through patents and processes), brand management, or customer intelligence, accounts for a significant portion of the core value of a firm. Part of the rest of the core value is driven by the ownership of assets (Figure 4.4).

The periphery

The key question is: *"how many physical and intangible assets does a company need to own in order to be competitive?"* The answer to this question defines which assets and activities can be transferred to the periphery of the firm.

The first part of the answer, and the easiest one, is based on costs. The relationship between cost efficiency and the ownership of assets is central to competitiveness. The financial community follows this marker for competitiveness closely by using a very powerful measure of company performance: ROA (return on assets). ROA implies that you should maximise profits, while minimising the assets the firm owns – such a strategy increases the value of the firm. As a consequence, many firms strategically replace *ownership of* assets with *access to* assets.

For example, let's examine whether there is a competitive advantage to owning a warehouse. A simple, yet efficient, business objective could

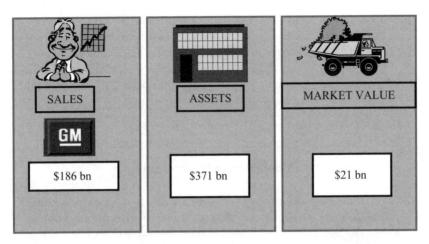

Figure 4.4 – Financial markets hate physical assets. A snapshot of the relationship between sales, assets, and the market capitalisation (number of outstanding shares multiplied by the average share price) at GM, fall 2003. (Sales and assets are for 2002.) The relationship between the market value of GM and the assets it possesses is striking. At that time, the financial markets did not believe that GM used its assets in an optimum way. In other words, GM probably did not need to own so many assets to make $186 bn in sales – as a consequence, its market value was $21 bn. At the same time, Microsoft had sales of $30 bn for a market capitalisation of $277 bn!

be to have access to storage facilities through a contract with a provider, but not actually to own the warehouse. A similar strategy can be deployed for computers – the machines can be leased by the firm, and the contractor could even go as far as directly employing the IT staff working on the company site. Ross Perot had this idea and developed it into his huge business empire (EDS, then Perot Systems) [4]. In short, he managed the computer departments for companies. As a consequence, assets disappeared from the firm's books, increasing the return on assets for a given level of profits. Of course, the cost of the service replaces the cost of ownership. But such moves make financial markets happy: return on assets increases.

The problem with physical assets is not only their *cost*, but also their *rigidity*. If a car company decides to expand its production facilities because it foresees an upturn in demand, it may take 18 months before the new plant is operational. If a company sells products on the Internet, such as Dell, Amazon, or eBay, and it decides to expand its product line, it takes only a few days to add these product listings to the website.

In contrast, when a car company has excess capacity and wants to close a production site, it could take as long as two or three years, depending on country regulations and the flexibility of trade unions. When an Internet company wants to align its product mix with declining demand, it only takes a few minutes to close a site. *Adaptability* – the avoidance of rigidity – is a key factor in competitiveness.

How deep is the bottom?

Companies that do not own assets are likely to suffer extreme volatility in their share price during market swings. From its peak in March 2000 until August 2001, Yahoo lost 90 % of its value. Most of the drop occurred in less than one year – from August 2000 to April 2001, as shown in Figure 4.5. When the market collapses, financial analysts are at a loss to define the "bottom" value of a company, especially if they cannot rely on the resale value of physical assets as a last-resort valuation.

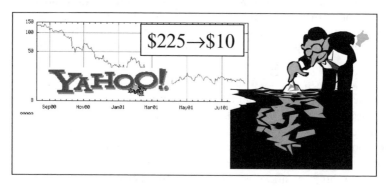

Figure 4.5 – How deep is the bottom?

Because their business model relied very little on physical assets, while providing maximum flexibility to adapt to demand changes, Internet firms reached extraordinary valuations during the recent stock market boom. Many analysts even argued that such a strategy would reduce the risk of being severely hit by economic cycles. Financial markets quickly came to hate physical assets and put formidable pressure on traditional companies to get rid of them, and firms complied. Just a few years later,

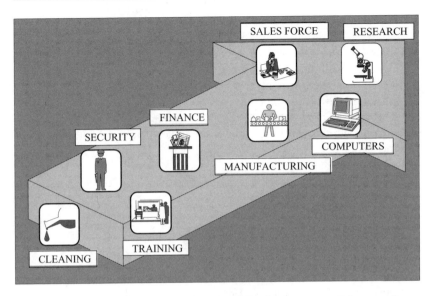

Figure 4.6 – How much to outsource? In theory, everything can be outsourced, from lower value-added activities, like cleaning, to higher value-added activities, such as research. The real issue is where to stop. In many companies today, a decision to outsource is purely financial. If it is cost-efficient, it is done. However, such a decision should also consider whether or not it weakens the core competencies of the company, its vulnerability to competitors and, above all, its relationship with customers.

however, at a time when many Internet companies lost 90 % of their market value, financial markets rediscovered a taste for assets . . .

Clearly, companies should retain the ownership of some assets. The dilemma is where and when to stop outsourcing (Figure 4.6). In theory, everything can be outsourced, such as:

- *Cleaning*: to specialised firms such as ISS, a Danish-based company, which specialises in cleaning everything from offices to airports to hospitals.
- *Security*: to firms such as Securitas in Sweden.
- *Training*: to business schools like IMD and Harvard.
- *Finance*: to financial institutions or banks.
- *Manufacturing*: to professional assemblers, such as Flextronics for the computer industry.

- *Transportation and delivery*: to FedEx and UPS.
- *Information systems*: to EDS, IBM, or Perot Systems.
- *Sales force*: to dealers, wholesalers, or value-added resellers. Supermarkets (Wal-Mart, Tesco, etc.) can be considered the result of the decision of the garment and food industry to outsource their sales force and distribution.
- *Research*: to universities or research centres.
- *Management*: to professional consultancies, such as McKinsey & Co. and DTT.

And so on. An outsourcing strategy, however, implies clear decisions on certain issues.

How far before it is too far?

There is a true danger in outsourcing a core competency – firms must analyse continuously and identify their core competencies, as well as their evolution. The results of core competency analysis can vary across firms, even when they are in the same business line or industry. Nevertheless, each firm needs to delineate *its own* answer to core competencies, upon which it will build its future competitiveness. Not knowing the answer to this question may be a most dangerous threat to the existence of a firm.

What is our business?

A firm's traditional line of business can become an obsolete competency, since it no longer creates added value or differentiates the firm in the marketplace. Manufacturing and assembling, which used to be the core competencies of automotive or computer firms, are most commonly outsourced today. An airline core competency is not just flying the planes: it is about providing a total travel solution to passengers – limousine service, check-in, lounges, luggage retrieval, car rental, and hotel accommodation – under a single brand. Their core competency is moving people – not only planes. Recently, Procter and Gamble has outsourced part of its account payable activities to HP, and part of its HR administration to IBM, two IT companies very unlikely to have performed such a service a few years ago.

Who are our friends, who are our enemies?

While outsourcing some physical and human assets and sharing information can increase a firm's productivity, they can also increase vulnerability. Today's partners could tomorrow become partners of the competition, or competitors themselves. Shared information can also be disseminated further, and even used against you! The volatility of business relationships has arisen as one of the key dilemmas of an outsourced world.

The survival of the core company not only depends on cost efficiency, but also on its stability. An over-extended enterprise with little core competencies at the centre is a vulnerable enterprise, as experienced by Valujet, a low-cost US airline in the 1990s. Valujet had been developed on a business model that outsourced everything – from flying planes to ground handling to passenger services. Managers found it difficult to maintain control of the overall system: a situation that, at a certain stage, threatened the viability of the company. Security and reliability in the conduct of business are increasingly important today. An extended value chain means that breakdowns can occur at many points of the chain, affecting an entire firm, including, of course, the core. Experience learned from recent failures, such as Enron and Andersen, makes it evident that problems, which start out small and trivial at the periphery, end up big and nasty at the core.

In some cases, the strategy of *outsourcing* is reversed into a strategy of *insourcing*. Some companies, such as banks, are heavily dependent on the reliability of their IT systems. No financial institution can afford a breakdown of its IT system, even for a limited amount of time. As a consequence, many banks have decided to bring IT management back into the core company. They believe that the firm takes too great a risk by having such a key competence managed from outside, while retaining little internal knowledge. Whether to insource or not can be a very difficult decision to take. Outsourcing, as a business strategy, is easy to explain – it can be shown that it results in cost savings and asset reductions. Insourcing, on the other hand, generally implies additional costs, more employees on the payroll, and, probably, an increase in assets. It is not easy for managers to argue in favour of such a policy on the grounds of intangible benefits, such as reducing vulnerability or maintaining customer loyalty. However, insourcing is an additional alternative for the future competitiveness of the firm, and can very well take place in parallel to outsourcing activities (Figure 4.7).

Outsourcing strategies, especially when they affect employment, have created significant tension between companies and nations. In many cases, the transfer of assets to a partner means a loss of jobs in the core firm, and less advantageous working conditions for transferred employees. If the partner is overseas, jobs could disappear from the home country. Outsourcing policies have thus forced employees to become more mobile and flexible. Companies have requested more freedom to

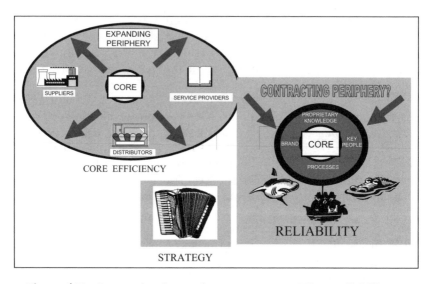

**Figure 4.7 – Insourcing is an alternate strategy. When reliability or
customer satisfaction becomes a concern, many companies revert to
insourcing. When the periphery around the core company has
expanded so much that a loss of control occurs, companies can bring
some vital activities back to, or closer to, the core, and contract the
periphery. Many banks are bringing back IT, and some call centres are
also being insourced as a result of customer backlash. Insourcing
remains, however, exceptional, and will not entirely replace
outsourcing. Like an accordion, both strategies occur simultaneously,
allowing the company to expand and contract its periphery according
to market conditions.**

hire and fire, in line with the Anglo-Saxon Model. Firms have also developed new approaches to work, such as part-time jobs and job-sharing
– as we shall see in the next chapter.

Outsourcing has often damaged the image of a firm in the eyes of the
public. People already have difficulty accepting that a company reduces
employment when it is confronted with an economic crisis. They defi-
nitely do not understand when a firm lays off jobs just to increase efficiency and profits. In these circumstances, senior management has a
hard time convincing employees, and public opinion at large, that it
could be a matter of survival for the future.

4.1.2 The Extended Enterprise Model in pursuit of efficiency

The most significant gains in productivity achieved during recent years have been because of the special attention paid to supply-chain management. Such management involves attaining a long-term relationship with partners, who, in turn, provide access to their assets, processes, and knowledge. Two revolutions took place: process-based competitiveness and value-chain linkages via technology.

Process-based competitiveness

Process-based competitiveness originates in quality management. In Western enterprises after World War II, improvements in quality have traditionally been seen as costly for the firm, and as leading to higher consumer prices. The legendary father of quality management, the American Edward Deming, demonstrated that the contrary was, in fact, true – *more* attention to quality means fewer defects, less rework, and therefore reductions in cost and prices [5, 6]. Edward Deming was not a prophet in his own land, and had to go to Japan to find a receptive ear for his theories, where, today, the Deming Award is the most famous quality award. Quality management theory returned in force to the US and Europe in the early 1980s, as a result of the outstanding performance achieved by Japanese companies, particularly in the automobile industry.

Some of the fundamental principles of quality as they relate to competitiveness are reviewed in Figure 4.8. These principles are some of the most powerful guidelines in modern management and have changed the way of doing business. Asian firms, in particular the Japanese, have adopted them eagerly. In many Asian factories, a sign saying "*Do it right the first time*" is posted on walls. These principles not only apply to manufacturing, they can be applied to all business sectors – even services. For example, airlines have learned to measure quality as the time it takes to board or disembark passengers from a plane. American and European firms were latecomers in adopting these principles, since they were entrenched in the belief that quality is expensive. During the Reagan administration, Malcolm Baldridge, Secretary of Commerce, mobilised US business to adopt quality standards. Now a quality award in the US bears his name. In Europe, such an award is given by the EFQM (European Foundation for Quality Management).

The management of quality laid the groundwork for the development of process competitiveness on the basis of these principles, as well as the works of Edward Deming, Joseph Juran, Armand Feigenbaum, and

1. DO IT RIGHT THE FIRST TIME

2. CUSTOMERS SET SUCCESS STANDARDS
   (FOCUS ON CUSTOMER SATISFACTION)

3. FOCUS ON PROCESSES

4. MEASURE

5. IMPROVE CONTINUOUSLY

6. INVOLVE EVERYONE

Figure 4.8 – The simple and fundamental rules of quality.

Philip B. Crosby, among others [7–9]. A process is a series of actions, which are identifiable, planned, measurable, repeatable, improved permanently, and that have an owner. Product development, procurement, manufacturing, order fulfilment, order-to-cash and customer support are all processes that can be identified and managed within a firm.

A firm can increase its competitiveness by first identifying the best way of performing a process; it can then reorganise itself around its processes if necessary. In 1993, in their book *Reengineering the Corporation: A Manifesto for Business Revolution*, Michael Hammer and James Champy were the first to put forth the notion of reorganising a firm around key processes [10]. Quality management is an ongoing, linear process, which requires time. In contrast, reengineering is an *abrupt shift away* from the past. Reengineering is a fundamental rethinking and a radical redesigning of business processes to achieve dramatic improvements in critical measures of performance, such as cost, quality, speed, and service. As Michael Hammer once put it nicely: ". . . it is all about breaking legs . . .".

Reengineering forces an enterprise to reorganise around processes, and to rethink the company as if it were being created from scratch today. This is a very powerful process and many enterprises have dropped their conventional approach. Instead, they have reorganised along processes such as product development, procurement, value chain, or order fulfilment, providing new managerial roles and titles, which imply the control over a single process throughout the entire firm.

Quality, and more generally process management, is an essential part of the Extended Enterprise Model – it provides a common "language" among partnering firms, and a similar platform for sharing processes and information. Separate value chains cannot be linked if different enterprises cannot interface their processes seamlessly. Quality certification, mainly through standards such as ISO 9000, creates a system allowing companies, which have never worked together before, to benchmark their processes and link with each other in relative ease.

The result of reorganising the supply chain around the specific comparative advantages of the various partners has been huge gains in productivity. However, this management revolution could not have been implemented without a parallel "technological" revolution, which has acted as a formidable enabler for firms' competitiveness: the Internet.

Linking value chains through technology

The biggest business impact of the Internet revolution has been in the development of business-to-business (B2B) and business-to-consumer (B2C) activities. The development of a seamless and standardised technology based on the TCP/IP protocol has enhanced greatly the extension of the firm towards its suppliers and customers (Figure 4.9). It is now possible for a firm to manage and to integrate three levels of activities within a single platform:

- *intranet*, for exchanging sensitive internal information within the core enterprise;
- *extranet*, for exchanging secure information between the core and the firm's partner network;
- *internet*, for interacting with the wider public, as well as serving as a corporate communication and promotion tool.

The connectivity, which is ensured throughout the system, links:

- people with people, through email or voice mail;
- people with machines, through servers and remote connections;
- machines with machines, for the management of inventories and production systems;
- value chains with value chains, through a data interchange network.

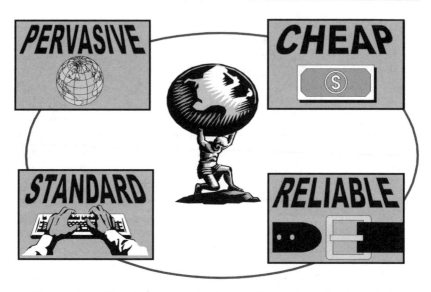

Figure 4.9 – The Internet is the key technological platform. As a technology, an Internet-based technological platform is quite unique, combining the qualities of being (so far) pervasive, cheap, standardised, reliable, and secure enough even for payments. Today, however, viruses and spam hamper its development. In 2003, 10.4 million spam emails were sent via the Internet, every minute, worldwide! If the security of the platform is not improved in future, and the cost of vulnerability increases, new approaches may be implemented, such as a parallel Internet, which would be more restricted in access.

When linked through an Internet technology platform, most devices are identifiable through their IP address. In 2000, there were 60 million IP addresses in operation, reaching 400 million in 2005.

---

e-business

The Internet has opened the floodgates to new businesses such as Amazon and eBay, and greatly expanded others, such as Dell. The Internet reduces transaction costs, inventories, and physical assets, while increasing flexibility (Figure 4.10). Such innovation fuelled the so-called Internet bubble in the late 1990s – as this was what the financial markets wanted. Today, the challenge is to converge the old "bricks and mortar" model with the advantages of e-business – most companies provide both. However, the motto: "e-do or e-die!" still stands!

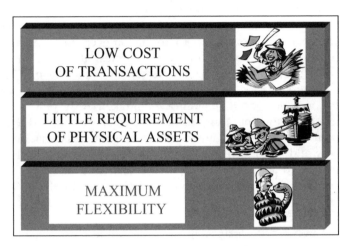

Figure 4.10 – The advantages of e-business.

The combination of networks, machinery, and even people, all operating under a single technological platform, is managed under the heading of Enterprise Resources Planning (ERP) – a service provided by companies like SAP, Oracle, which recently acquired PeopleSoft, or Baan. Originally, these firms operated within the periphery of a core company and offered services targeted to a single specific part of the value chain, such as payroll management or inventory control. Increasingly, these periphery service providers are moving closer to the core, by offering their clients a more complete and integrated approach to the management of resources (such as order to cash management). Being widely available and standardised, ERP is very flexible because it allows customers to follow directly online the various steps of their order – from completion through to delivery. Nonetheless, problems can occur:

- The extension of a firm's technology platform to its network of partners and clients increases the vulnerability of the system, and raises the issue of preserving the confidentiality of the transferred information. In addition, linking value chains increases the interdependence of companies – making it difficult for them to find alternatives when problems arise, or to change partners.

- Linking value chains generates a huge amount of information. To the contrary of emails, a traditional letter, many years ago, would not contain attachments with colour graphs, nor would it be copied and sent to a large number of people. In 2003, it was estimated that the world generates 12 exabytes of information every three years, which would represent a pile of computer diskettes 38 million km high – the same amount of information created since the dawn of civilisation. One reason for such exponential growth in information is the explosion of images: 80 billion of them taken every year.
- Once a huge amount of information is created, storing and retrieving it becomes a problem. Again in 2003, it was estimated that only 10 % of the world's information is stored on a computer. Of the 18 trillion pages printed annually, only 4 % are digital. Most of the information that is created, in enterprises or in society, is irretrievable or lost.

Moving the periphery offshore

The latest trend in the management of the value chain extends every one of its segments internationally. At first, considerable gains in productivity were obtained through quality, reengineering, and the management of business processes. Then, the rolling out of technology from the core enterprise and through the extended value chain amplified productivity gains. Today, offshoring brings an additional dimension to the pursuit of productivity gains, as it merges business processes, technology, and globalisation to expand the periphery of the firm worldwide (Figure 4.11).

Offshoring thus provides a new boost in productivity for enterprises, through the relocation of various segments of the value chain to countries that benefit from a unique comparative advantage. For example, companies can gain significant costsavings when they offshore their manufacturing activities to China, their assembling operations to Mexico, and their service and back-office operations to India.

Most of the time, this advantage is perceived as essentially a saving on labour costs. However, access to skills is also a significant factor. Companies that locate software development centres in Bangalore in India, or banks that are using Russian scientists to develop financial instruments, gain access to an untapped pool of sophisticated knowledge. In 2003, in India alone, GE capital services employed 16 000 back-office staff and 1800 in product R&D; IBM had a staff of 10 000 developing IT services and software, and Oracle 6000. EDS had 3500 on

Figure 4.11 – Offshoring: the third revolution. Offshoring is the third
revolution, following those in business processes (quality,
reengineering) and outsourcing. If outsourcing can be described as a
contraction of the core and the expansion of the periphery, offshoring
is then a contraction of the domestic base and the worldwide
expansion of the periphery. Offshoring thrives on the globalisation of
markets, and the huge differences in operating costs existing between
countries.

its payroll to supply IT services, while Intel employed 1700 conducting
activities in software and chip design. Research by Deloitte shows that,
of the estimated 13 million jobs in financial services in mature industrial
economies in the West (and also in Asia), some 2 million will probably
go to India by 2008! [11]

Offshoring is not just about the relocation of activities to the developing world. European companies have a long tradition of investment
in Silicon Valley in order to have access to the latest developments in
IT. Medical companies, such as Novartis, have invested heavily in New
England to be close to the latest innovations in health sciences. Today,
even Chinese enterprises are locating research centres in Sweden to have
access to skilled engineers, especially in the field of telecommunications.

Nonetheless, differences in labour costs remain the key issue (Figure
4.12). For example, the offshoring of IT activities to India is said to have
had a negative impact on the wages of US-based software programmers.

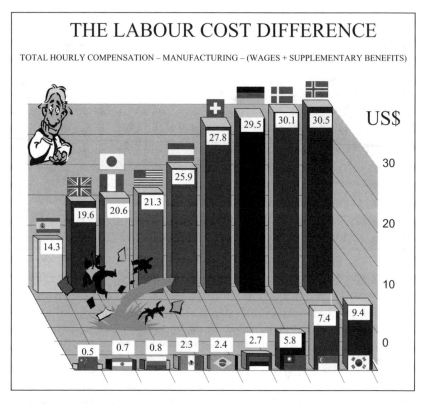

Figure 4.12 – A new, global labour landscape. In 2004, several nations, mostly from the former Eastern bloc, joined the European Union. Unlike previous enlargements, which had seen countries of a relatively similar standard of living joining Europe, the newcomers are, this time, significantly poorer, as reflected in their wage levels: on average, 5–10 times lower than those of their Western European counterparts. Some shift in investment from West to East will occur in Europe, affecting not only the wealthiest EU nations, but also others, such as Ireland and Portugal, that have built their attractiveness on cheap operating costs. Similar differences occur worldwide and produce similar effects. Competitiveness lesson: having a cheap operating base is never a long-term comparative advantage – sooner or later an even cheaper location will open up in the world and take away your competitiveness. *Source:* [12].

The labour-cost differences are indeed striking. In 2003, an IT professional with five years' experience would be paid $75000 in the US, and $95000 in Britain. The same function, with similar experience and skills in India would be paid $26000 [13]. Larger differences exist in manufacturing costs. Also in 2003, a worker earned, on average, $24.07 per hour in Germany, and $20.32 in the US. In China, the average salary of workers was a mere $0.59. Although it could be argued that productivity differences explain such wage differentials, it is hard to imagine that German workers can be up to 50 times more productive than the Chinese. The advantage in labour costs is magnified by the fact that FDIs generally transfer the latest business processes and technology to their foreign affiliates, thus providing productivity levels similar to their Western counterparts.

Offshoring is not a simple strategy to manage. Dealing with a partner located close to the firm is already a complex job; monitoring the activities of a partner on the other side of the world, with a different culture, can turn out to be a daunting and time-consuming task. Because of these challenges, offshoring will remain a big-company option for some time. In addition, partners in countries like China and India are learning fast. Offshoring will breed the creation of many local companies and brands, which will emerge rapidly as tough competitors on global markets. In competitiveness, allies are not allies forever . . .

4.2 A key challenge for the model: keeping in touch with customers

During the past two decades, the greatest improvements in management practice have focused on fulfilling an order. Process management and technology have increased the efficiency of firms in getting the right product to the right customer at the right time and at the right price.

Currently, however, the productivity challenge is twofold. First, firms want to generate not only more orders, but more valuable orders, and fulfil them at a lower cost, and second, firms want to know their customers better to secure an enduring relationship with them. While technology extends the reach of the company towards its customers, new relationship management processes are still in the making.

Companies have two ways to reach customers – either through direct or indirect channels. A direct channel is when the firm relies on its own sales force or distribution system, comprised of employees on the payroll of the firm. An indirect channel is when the firm relies on partners on its periphery, such as when it develops a distribution system comprised of dealers, wholesalers, value-added resellers, and so on.

4.2.1   From order fulfilment to order generation

Companies must balance carefully the management of the two distribution channels – direct and indirect – and the impact on final customers. Hewlett-Packard was a pioneer in developing an effective channel strategy. Today, more than 80 % of its sales come from indirect channels. Dell, on the other hand, is very effective at using technology to create a "direct model," which bypasses distributors and sells directly to the end-user. Migrating from one channel to the other is not easy – it can lead to the "cannibalisation" of sales of existing channels, as well as raising serious tension with partners if they lose profitable business. Most companies develop a strategy using both channels in parallel, but are confronted with the dilemma of defining which types of sales are best done by which channel.

Technology has increased the choice of available channels for reaching customers, as new business models emerge.

- *Disintermediation* endeavours to do away with as many intermediaries as possible between the original vendor and the end-user. Companies as diverse as Dell for PCs, Easyjet for air transport, and Schwab for banking, pursue this type of simplification strategy. It reduces distribution costs significantly, and passes savings on to customers by bypassing distribution services.
- *Reintermediation* is when a service provider is wedged-in between the vendor and the buyer. A firm involved in this strategy intervenes between the core enterprise, or traditional distributors, and the end-user to provide an added-value service. Companies such as Amazon.com, Yahoo!, eBay, and lastminute.com are examples of such

---

Room for improvement

Thanks to the revolution in business processes and in technology, the management of the supply chain is extremely efficient. When a company gets an order, it generally knows what to do with it, and can fulfil it efficiently. The same level of efficiency does not hold for another part of the model – much more could be done to obtain similar productivity gains in generating new and repeat orders, as well as improving customer relations (Figure 4.13). In many companies, the difference in sophistication in managing both parts of the model is striking – while supply chain management is often quite advanced, customer management still lags behind.

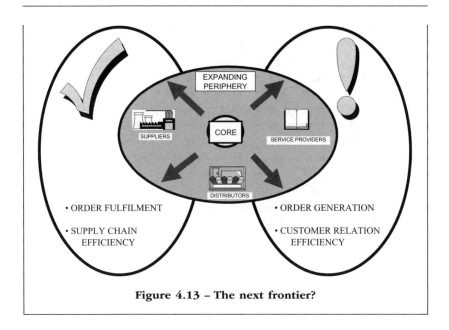

Figure 4.13 – The next frontier?

firms – they provide services from multiple partners on a common platform to consumers.

- *Reverse auctioning* reverses the sale process. In traditional sales, a vendor quotes a price to the buyer and, perhaps after some negotiation, a sale is made. In reverse auctioning, the buyer states his maximum price for a particular product or service and invites vendors to compete to fulfil the order at the lowest price possible below the one stated. Reverse auction sales are increasingly prevailing in the procurement of large quantities of standardised products, such as commodities, raw materials, and/or technology, especially through business-to-business (B2B) platforms.

4.2.2 Locking customers into a relationship

It is one thing to reach customers; it is quite another, and much more important, to retain them within a long-term relationship. Repeat orders are cheaper to obtain and fulfil than those from a new customer. Therefore, the extended enterprise forges closer relationships between the core enterprise and the customer, while abiding by three golden rules. The extended enterprise:

1. Understands the customer's business model and how to interface its own value chain with that of the customer.

2. Identifies the most profitable customers by determining which ones bring the most value to the firm.
3. Locks its customers into long-term relationships to benefit from repeat business.

As we have mentioned, the supply chain dimension of the model is far more productive than the customer relationship part – processes such as order fulfilment are much more efficient than others, such as order generation. The most successful firms, however, are those that excel at both. In the Dell direct-sales model, 40 % of the calls generate an order. However, in 60 % of the calls that resulted in an order, the final order was different to the one customers had in mind when they initiated contact. Dell actively manages the sales process – its operators are encouraged to understand the motivation of the customer, and then advise and guide his choice efficiently, probably to higher margin products if they are suitable.

Technology allows the identification of individual customers better than ever. The objective is to recognise a pattern of behaviour and a buying profile. "One-to-one" marketing, as it is called, allows a company to target their key customers better and exploit their potential fully. The aim is also to escape from bad customers, that is, those on whom much money is spent, but little revenue is generated (Figure 4.14). In this case,

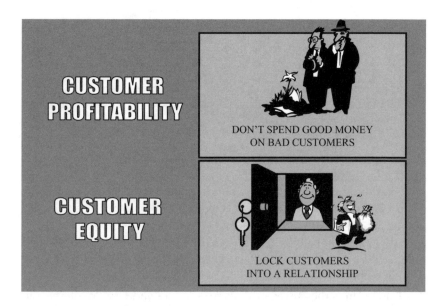

Figure 4.14 – Fundamental objectives in customer management.

the 80–20 principle applies: 80 % of sales are generally generated by 20 % of customers.

Being competitive requires developing "customer equity": a portfolio of dedicated and loyal customers that have a long-standing relationship with the firm. Firms should manage their customer base with care. They should remain in contact with them, even when not working on a specific deal, thus maintaining an open relationship and increasing the possibility of repeat sales. Repeat business is far more profitable than "cold" sales [14].

Not just a product

Few sell a stand-alone product any more. A product always comes wrapped in a service (Figure 4.15). The key components of customer satisfaction today are the product itself, and the services that come bundled with it. The system has to be managed as a whole. The product itself needs to comply with the imperatives of quality and cost efficiency. The wrapping, in other words the service around the product, needs to deliver a rewarding experience to the customer, such as customisation. Most customer dissatisfaction today comes, not from defective products, but from defective service around the product.

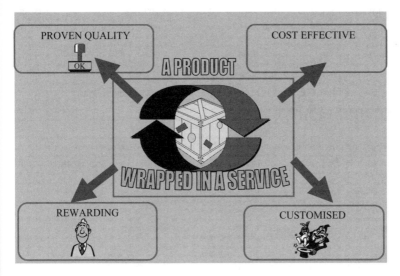

Figure 4.15 – Efficiency is not all!

Such close relationships form the basis of the private banking industry. Asset managers develop a trusted and privileged relationship with their customers over the years. They know everything about their businesses, their families, their tax situations, and their private lives. They become business partners and, often, personal confidants. When bankers leave one bank for another, their customers usually follow them. Hiring firms recognise their added value by not only paying incoming bankers a salary, but also offering a fee for the wealth under management, or the number of loyal customers, they can bring along.

Technology enables companies to have far better knowledge of customers, leading to a "one-to-one marketing" strategy, which targets promotions to the precise needs of an individual. For example, Amazon.com keeps track of the sales made to each customer and actively promotes particular products that match a customer's buying profile. For example, if a customer has recently bought a jazz CD by Oscar Peterson, she will be informed of a new release by, say, jazz singer Diana Krall. Companies are not just accumulating huge quantities of information about their customers, they are also screening the data in search of patterns of customer behaviour, and, ultimately, the development of customer profiles. This is called *data mining*. Food retailers are quite active in this field – electronic tills and loyalty membership cards gather valuable and up-to-date information on their clients' purchasing patterns. The industry estimates, however, that less than 5 % of the total information collected is actually used for customising marketing efforts. Once again, management processes have not yet been able to cope with the speed of technological advancement!

4.3. The new frontiers in the Extended Enterprise Model

When the value chain is extended fully towards suppliers and customers, it not only becomes *leaner*, but also *longer*. Such developments lead to new challenges (Figure 4.16).

4.3.1 Vulnerability

The vulnerability of the system is in direct proportion to the vulnerability of the weakest partner – just like the anchor chain mooring a ship: the chain's overall strength depends upon its weakest link. The

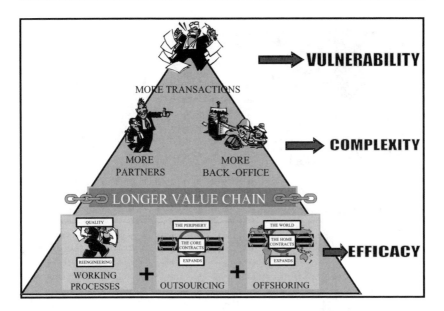

Figure 4.16 – The hidden cost of the model. The revolutions in
working processes – *outsourcing* and *offshoring* – are creating great
gains in efficiency. Although the value chain is increasingly focused, it
has become longer, requiring the monitoring of more partners, and
more back-office functions to manage the entire system – all
increasing complexity. In addition, the model implies more
transactions, which are traditionally a source of inefficiencies and
breakdowns.

proliferation of partners, especially if they are smaller in size than the
core enterprise, can significantly increase the risk that a breakdown will
occur somewhere along the chain, in which case, the entire extended
enterprise could stop functioning effectively (Figure 4.17).

The automobile industry, for example, has been very exposed to such
weak-link vulnerability. Strikes by suppliers, or in the delivery system,
have stopped assembly lines across North America and Europe more
than once, especially since "just-in-time" manufacturing does not allow
any buffer for such occurrences. In 1997, the UPS labour strike forced
companies all over America to stop delivering products to customers, or
to find more expensive supply routing to meet production deadlines. In
May 2001, Ford Motor Company decided to replace voluntarily 13 million
defective Firestone tyres, as the explosion of these tyres may have caused

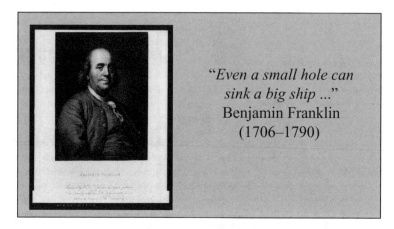

"Even a small hole can sink a big ship ..."
Benjamin Franklin
(1706–1790)

Figure 4.17 – The vulnerability effect.

rollover accidents that resulted in 174 deaths and 700 injuries. In retaliation, Firestone ended a 100-year-old business cooperation with Ford. Furthermore, a few months later, after September 11, Ford had to close its factories for seven days because of significant delays in getting parts coming across the Canadian border.

Breakdowns resulting from natural disasters are even less predictable, and can be very damaging for companies. The 1995 earthquake in Japan forced the closure of Kobe harbour for 26 months – thousands of firms had to alter their production plans. The four largest Japanese automobile companies had to downscale their production and exports significantly. On 21 September 1999, another severe earthquake, reaching 7.6 on the Richter scale, hit Taiwan. This time, the computer industry worldwide was affected – production of PCs was disrupted completely in the US and Europe, because the supply of chips from Taiwan had ceased.

Vulnerability can also result from inappropriate skills, or the lack of competence of partners in the value chain. Large global companies have developed a level of management sophistication which smaller firms may find hard to match, especially if their size limits the amount of management resources at their disposal. Training, or assisting partners in their business endeavours, is fundamental to reducing vulnerability. Such integration raises dilemmas regarding the confidentiality of information within the network of partners. While sharing information and best practices guarantees a smooth functioning of the value chain, there is the very real risk that proprietary knowledge could become commoditised and further disseminated. What happens if a partner leaves the network? How much should the core firm intervene in the management of partner companies? Answers to these questions remain unclear, while vulnerability increases day by day.

4.3.2 Complexity

The Extended Enterprise Model can become complex and sometimes unmanageable very quickly. Very sophisticated managers are needed to run such operations. They have to be highly skilled at process management, and very capable of managing relationships with a network of business partners – not an easy set of competencies to find in any one person. The logical sharpness needed to implement a set of processes is not always compatible with the sense of intuition and sensitivity required to manage partners. To a certain extent, a large company can train its management to adapt to these different functions. For smaller enterprises it is more difficult.

A system that is complex to manage is, in all likelihood, a system that is even more complex for customers to deal with. A purchase order, for example, used to be a simple process – a phone call, a letter, or an email was enough. Today, since a wider community of partners must be kept informed, a purchase order has turned out to be a highly complex technological process that can be time consuming, and frustrating for the customer. The same can be said for customer service – getting in touch with the right person in the voice mail maze of a company can easily turn out to be a real nightmare for customers (Figure 4.18).

For the extended enterprise, simplifying business procedures is a priority. Partners in this model of business relationships want a common system, which is transparent and easy to operate, allowing decisions to be implemented quickly, and that reduces the risk of a breakdown. Customers, ultimately, want a simple and rewarding experience when they buy a product or use a service. Amazon.com, Dell, and easyJet have well-known business models, whose success factors stem from their availability, speed, and low cost. They have also been successful because customers find their business models easy to understand and operate. Purchasing a book or CD on Amazon, getting a customised PC from Dell, or buying a ticket at easyJet is relatively straightforward.

Simplicity can be a significant competitive advantage. Albert Einstein summarised the issue perfectly: "Everything should be made as simple as possible, but not simpler . . ."

PHONE CALLS	LESS THAN 60% ANSWERED IN 10 SEC.
VOICE MAIL	9-HOUR WAIT FOR A CALL BACK
ELECTRONIC MAIL	RESPONSE IN 22.2 HOURS

Figure 4.18 – A worldwide wait! Call-centre operations, which are increasingly outsourced and offshored, show how quickly the complexity of the system can get out of hand. From a cost reduction point of view, an outsourcing decision is best for the company. However, call-centres often generate customer dissatisfaction. Employees working in third-party call-centres may not have the same dedication and commitment to customers as employees in the core enterprise. The company, so efficient at order fulfilment, becomes "unreachable" in the eyes of the customer, thus damaging customer loyalty. *Source:* [15].

4.3.3 Transaction inefficiencies

The Extended Enterprise Model hinges on transactions, which, as we have noted, are not what management is most efficient at overseeing. In Europe, the order fulfilment cycle for a car (i.e. the time taken from order to delivery) lasts, on average, 42 days. In all that time, only two days are devoted to the actual production of the car, and five days are spent on delivery to the dealer. The remainder, an astounding 35 days, is consumed by administration, back-office activities, and paperwork, before and after the sale [16]. The challenge of modern management is less in the making of a product, than in managing the inflated number of transactions generated to fulfil that order.

For the extended enterprise, it is sensible to outsource activities to partners, to link value chains among enterprises, and to offshore production and services. Modern technology, especially in IT and telecommunications, has made such a business model possible. Some transactions can now be automated fully. Systems such as EPOS link the inventory on the shelves of a retailer, or the warehouse of a customer, directly to their respective suppliers. Vulnerability develops from the fact that there is still a human element in many transactions.

Transactions have inflated back-office operations and administration in most large and international companies. An extended enterprise business model needs to be managed and controlled by the core. Since transactions are often the source of inefficiencies and breakdowns, most companies monitor them carefully and create built-in back-up systems. As a result, firms incur new costs, such as the numerous auditors, controllers, accountants, and compliance officers that infiltrate the system. In addition, governments have increased the complexity of transactions by the sheer number of laws, regulations, and procedures by which companies must now abide.

Jeff Immelt, CEO of General Electric, first voiced concern about these developments several years ago: "40 % of the company is now administration, finance, and backroom functions; over the next three years I want to shrink that by 75 %!" Of course, this is probably a "stretch goal" for a large and extended company like GE. However, Jeff Immelt is absolutely right: one of the biggest reserves of productivity and competitiveness in the firm can be untapped by tackling excessive internal administration.

In summary, firms operating according to the principles of the Extended Enterprise Model have unleashed considerable productivity gains for themselves. The model was based originally on increasing productivity through better working methods, such as quality and outsourcing. The model enhanced itself further by coupling better working techniques with the cost-saving opportunities offered by globalisation. In an open world, locating activities wisely can lead to significant cost advantages.

We must note, however, that the Extended Enterprise Model is much more refined "upstream" – when it refers to dealing with procurement of supplies and/or manufacturing – than "downstream" – when it concerns sales, order generation, customer satisfaction, or after-sales service. In addition, the model depends on transactions, which can always be a source of vulnerability, and sometimes inefficiency. Thus, complexity, and the risk of becoming "overstretched," remain shortcomings of the model that are yet to be resolved.

Alteration of the business model will have deep consequences for the other constituents of the competitiveness of a nation – the State and the people. Enterprises, as a primary source of competitiveness, create shock waves throughout the social system whenever they change their operating models. Extended enterprises have changed work structures drastically and expect people to accommodate them, as we shall see in the next chapter. Such enterprises are also compelling nations to review their competitiveness policies, in light of the requirements of their new practices.

4.4. How can nations cope with the Extended Enterprise Model?

Nations must provide an environment that supports the Extended Enterprise Model. Nations can also use this model as a tool to increase their own prosperity. Globalisation works because developing nations can use their low-cost structure to attract investments, and at the same time, gain access to technology and knowledge. Even remote countries have a place in the global business environment, since "distances" have been reduced enormously by transportation and communications. In such a world, even perishable products, such as freshly cut flowers or vegetables, can be delivered daily from Latin America or Africa to shopping malls in the US and Europe.

One of the major risks of the model is that if a breakdown occurs in the value chain of a firm somewhere in the world, it can spread quickly and have devastating effects on the entire organisation. Companies are thus very careful to balance the cost advantages that multiple investments provide, against the risk that a single local collapse could disrupt operations severely.

To cope with the requirements of the Extended Enterprise Model, nations should follow ten golden rules:

1. *One standard of excellence for investments worldwide.* A low-cost operation is never an excuse for low quality – there can be no trade-offs and no compromises in the quality of international investments. A "black sheep" investment can infect the rest of a value chain. Nations must thus provide an environment which supports the standards required for international-grade investments.

2. *One worldwide standard of speed and efficiency.* Delays are just as damaging as low quality. Administrative procedures need to be speedy and transparent in order to avoid bottlenecks in operations, which, in turn, hurt the worldwide profitability of firms. Nations should pay special attention to speed and efficiency in their legislative and administrative processes.

3. *Zero tolerance of corruption and improper practices.* Many companies refuse to tolerate such unethical practices, as they are against their corporate culture, and even their national legislation. Practically speaking, most companies cannot operate in an opaque environment. They lack the resources, time, and skills to handle things

in this manner. Leaders in many developing nations sometimes fail to realise that for many large global companies, prices are non-negotiable and commissions have to be provided transparently. Firms have difficulty in balancing the regulatory rigidity imposed by their home nation (perhaps even excessive) with the regulatory fluidity of the host nation (perhaps also excessive), thus creating major misunderstandings.

4. *A predictable framework for policies.* Large investments, such as sites for the manufacturing of chips or automobiles, are multi-billion dollar investments. A firm cannot commit to such a level of invest-ment, especially if it is critical within its value chain, if the local environment could become excessively capricious, volatile, and unpredictable. Firms are adaptive and can operate within almost any kind of environment, as long as the rules of the game are clear and stable, so they can plan ahead their operations.

5. *Special attention to infrastructure.* Goods need to be shipped, by means of an efficient network of roads, railways, harbours, and air-ports. Russia's development has been hampered during the past decade because of infrastructure deficiencies. Many Russian regions offered generous investment incentives to foreign companies, but they were deterred from taking advantage of such incentives because goods could not be shipped out of the country easily. The necessity of infrastructure explains why, in many instances, the early development of a nation takes place in the coastal regions, which provide easy access to shipping facilities. China has taken advantage of such circumstances in the creation of Special Eco-nomic Zones in the eastern coastal part of the country. The creation of such zones is efficient, in that it allows a nation to concentrate limited resources for infrastructure development efforts on a targeted part of its territory for maximum benefit.

6. *Efficiency of transactions.* Transaction efficiency is built upon an advanced technological infrastructure, which supports the flow of information. New management techniques, such as ERP (enterprise resource planning) or CRM (customer relationship management), depend on the existence of sophisticated communication infra-structure. Call and service centres, as well as outsourced back-office operations, can only work properly if information can flow easily and at a low cost from one part of the company to another. India has recently made tremendous efforts to ensure that the latest com-munication facilities are available, at low cost, to companies invest-ing in the country. When investing, firms want to make sure that they can count on efficient, fast, and integrated transactions with official government channels, such as those that relate to tax, finance, customs, and immigration clearance.

7. *Protection of intellectual property.* A network of partners only functions efficiently if all its members can count on sharing a similar level of knowledge, technology, and management. Proprietary knowledge, owned by one or more of the partners, flows into the system, and the rights of the originator have to be protected. Countries that have failed to maintain data confidentiality, and/or protect intellectual property, have lost numerous investment opportunities. As already mentioned, during the 1960s and 1970s, the Andean Pact agreement did not protect foreign intellectual property sufficiently. Similarly, Brazil became infamous for regulations on foreign IT and pharmaceutical investments that required the transfer of technology to local enterprises. All of these measures effectively deterred many foreign investments in countries in the region.

8. *Security of foreign assets and individuals.* The assets and installations of foreign firms are increasingly the target of politically motivated assaults, especially if the brand is associated closely with the home country. McDonald's, Coca-Cola, and HSBC assets abroad have more than once been targeted by local extremist groups when they wanted to express political dissension with US or British policy. Companies are increasingly reluctant to send employees and their families to countries they deem unsafe, because, as expatriates, they can also be the targets of violence. There are postings in places such as Nigeria and Colombia, which are increasingly difficult to fill because of the security factor. Such issues become extreme in war zones like Iraq or Afghanistan, where the kidnapping of foreigners has become endemic. In contrast, China, Japan, and Singapore have stressed the protection of foreign business and individuals. Salt Lake City in the US, and Switzerland in Europe have, in part, built their attractiveness on their extremely low rates of violent crime.

9. *Support for local small and medium-size enterprises.* Such promotion and support should encourage local SMEs to build the skills necessary and enter into the global network of enterprises. In the Extended Enterprise Model, local firms play a significant role in the supply, distribution, and customisation of goods and services, acquiring valuable knowledge and technology from larger global companies. Such acquisitions can be disseminated further within the local business environment, bringing it to global standards of competitiveness.

10. *Emphasis on education.* The Extended Enterprise Model requires sophisticated and talented people at all levels of the organisation. Global companies spend a significant amount – between 3 and 5 % of their payroll – on the training and development of their

workforce. Yet employers cannot do it all on their own. Nations have to provide an educational system accessible to the great majority of the population, and which cultivates the basic skills that make people economically employable, so that later on, employers can build upon a basic level of literacy and numeracy. Recently, Ireland has been able to attract several high-level investments in information and health science as a result of the strong efforts conducted by the Irish government to raise the general level of education of the population in these areas. However, the latest PISA Study on Achievement in Education, published by the OECD, underlines that industrialised nations should not take their educational excellence for granted.

Nations are not alone in being affected by the extended enterprise revolution. People are also experiencing a profound change in their working environments. In a world without boundaries, of scattered and floating assets, daily working life in the extended enterprise is very different. Job security is increasingly a vanishing concept – loyalty and leadership do not have the same meaning as two decades ago. The purpose of work has changed.

Some question whether competitiveness, as it is promoted in the Extended Enterprise Model, is really a source of prosperity for people. Restructuring firms, reengineering processes, or relocating assets and activities abroad are not perceived necessarily as enhancing the prosperity of the people who live in the home market. For many, globalisation has become a bad word. The biggest intellectual divide today is no longer between capitalism and communism; it is between the supporters and foes of globalisation.

People are less affected by grand theories than by changes in their direct work environment. Individuals have a personal, direct, and even emotional connection to their work, and to where it is performed. Understanding the strategy of a firm remains a theoretical exercise for most employees, they do not care much about it, until it affects their work.

In the extended enterprise, the nature and the structure of work have changed drastically. Employees realise that they are more exposed and at risk than before. Because they do not always understand the reasons, they feel helpless in the face of these changes. In addition, the value systems of modern society are shifting, placing more emphasis on work–life balance, on diversity, on empowerment, and more simply on the quality of life. The coupling of a new business model and changing values leads to a situation in which work is now different to what it used to be – work is being reinvented! In the next chapter, we shall investigate why and how.

Competitiveness and Work: A Love–Hate Relationship

5

*"There is an enormous number of managers who have retired **on** the job."*

Peter Drucker 1909–2005

In his book *The Age of Unreason*, published in 1991, Charles Handy wrote: "In ten years, less than half of the workforce will be holding conventional full time jobs . . . Full-timers or insiders will be the new minority." Ten years later, while the prediction has not materialized fully, the nature and structure of work has certainly evolved in that direction [1]. The implementation of the Extended Enterprise Model has led to new kinds of work relationships.

In the last chapter, we saw how the location of physical and human assets controlled by the core enterprise defines the extended enterprise. The aim of most firms, particularly those quoted on the stock exchange, is to maximise profits by using as few physical or human assets as possible. Taken to the extreme, the model suggests firms can use physical assets, as long as they are not recorded in the firm's financial statements. The approach is similar with regard to human resources – it's fine to use as much labour as necessary, as long as they do not appear on the firm's own payroll. When operating this way, it is imperative that the firm defines what its proprietary knowledge is, and what it is not (Figure 5.1).

5.1 The Extended Work Model

Job structure has evolved into three concentric circles, determined by *where* the work is done, *how* it is performed, and its relationship with the core enterprise. This new structure of work is complex and vaguely defined, as it is evolving continuously. Companies make adjustments to the model, correcting mistakes and shortcomings as they show up. But still, in today's modern life, work is not the same as it used to be. Below, we will review, from the point of view of the core

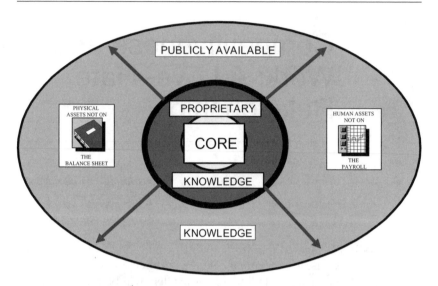

Figure 5.1 – The management of knowledge and assets. In the extended enterprise, the core of the firm manages the proprietary knowledge unique to the firm's core – technology, key processes, brands, and so forth. Proprietary knowledge differentiates the company in relation to its value chain partners. On the other hand, nonproprietary knowledge can be shared with partners at the periphery. As a consequence, physical and human assets, which do not directly involve proprietary knowledge, can be outsourced, and, thus, taken off the books and off the payroll.

enterprise, the main features of the new Extended Work Model and its consequences.

5.1.1   The uncertain glory of work at the centre

Conventional, full-time jobs are more likely to be found in the core enterprise than on its periphery – even if some are part-time, they are still core enterprise jobs (Figure 5.2). Employees within the core enterprise identify themselves closely with the enterprise's objectives and corporate culture, and are more likely to commit their careers long-term to the firm. Jobs in the core enterprise tend to follow the model described below:

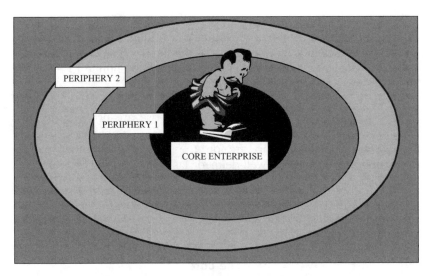

Figure 5.2 – Work at the core enterprise. Full-time jobs – those of senior employees and their support staff – occur mainly in the core enterprise. Today, however, this is less and less the case. In terms of jobs, the tendency has been to shrink at the core and expand at the periphery.

Job attributes	Senior positions and their support staff. Full-time employment (some ad hoc temporary or part-time, depending on the assignment or project).
Contractual relationship	Open-ended contract, permanent position.
Earnings	Salary (for senior staff) and/or wages (support staff); performance incentives (bonus, profit-sharing, options, etc.).
Location	Within the premises of the core enterprise or in the immediate vicinity; supervised and monitored closely.
Benefits and allowances	Provided by the core enterprise, either free or cost-shared, including health care, retirement benefits, sometimes housing and education contributions.
Sense of belonging	Very strong identity link with, and commitment to, the core enterprise.

Such was the one and only work structure in the "good old days." Having a job meant full-time devotion to working within the premises of the firm – whether in an office or at the factory – receiving a regular salary, and having a safety net. Today, such jobs continue to exist, but there are fewer and fewer of them.

Recently, we have seen a very interesting development – the employees on the premises of the core enterprise are not only its *own* employees, but, increasingly, also somebody else's employees. The core firm hosts employees who are on the payroll of another partner company, performing a well-defined task or project for the core enterprise.

The core

"Outsource the work and retain the knowledge" could be the motto of the core enterprise (Figure 5.3). Employees at the core manage the overall network of activities – whether in the core or in the periphery of the firm. These employees set the objectives, monitor activities, and thus control outcomes – in short, they pull the strings. The types of activities to be performed at the core need to be considered carefully – otherwise, one could very well outsource the knowledge and retain the work!

OUTSOURCE THE WORK | RETAIN THE KNOWLEDGE

Figure 5.3 – A magic formula?

Employees of an external service provider (EDS, IBM, etc.), on the payroll of this provider, manage the IT of the core enterprise on-site through outsourcing contracts. Within some manufacturing sites, the proliferation of such work structures is well documented. On the same site, multiple employees, all on the payrolls of different companies, perform interlinked tasks, such as product assembly, transportation, shipping administration, or after-sales service. Sometimes, awkward situations can arise on a business site where the conventional, full-time employees of the core company – those of the company whose name is outside the door – are actually a minority, leading to conflicts of corporate cultures and the development of a multi-tier pecking order among employees.

Companies like HP have recognised the awkwardness of such situations and are trying to eliminate them. HP has pioneered the implementation of the Extended Enterprise Model. As the periphery widens, there has been an increase in "non-HP" employees – on HP premises – whether in offices or manufacturing plants. These non-HP employees, however, perform many critical tasks for the firm, and, often, are in direct contact with key HP suppliers or customers. Despite the fact that they contact outsiders on behalf of HP, at first their email addresses were of the form name@nonhp.com, thus giving the impression that they were some kind of second-class employees. Partners and customers only want to deal with a "real" HP employee. Because of the detrimental image this policy promoted, HP has now provided key individuals working on its behalf, whether "real HP" or "non-HP," with a nondiscriminatory email address.

Some permanent jobs do not need to be performed on-site at the core enterprise – these are mobile jobs. Sales employees are the paramount example of this type of job. A sales employee spends a considerable amount of time each day not selling – time spent travelling, in traffic jams, or filling out paperwork. To increase their sales time, companies have redesigned the working structures of the sales employee. Such employees do not need to check into the office in the morning before sales calls, or return in the evening to report their deals after a working day. Modern technology has made it possible to have access to sales information wherever they are. Sales employees can receive sales leads electronically early in the morning, and then later in the day, report exchanges and closed deals through a central database hosted by the firm. The job of such an employee is completely mobile, leading to the rise of the so-called "road warriors," always on the move and always connected.

The job structure at the core of the firm has been endangered greatly over the past decade, as firms have significantly reduced assets – both physical and human – in the core enterprise. Many jobs have disappeared altogether, or been transferred to the periphery. Some employees, particularly younger ones, don't mind the excitement of a nonconventional full-time job, away from a 9 to 5 routine in the same office, day in, day out. However, most often, employees continue to prefer a conventional full-time job, within the core company, in a "real" work environment and with full benefits. Today, there is even a certain prestige associated with having one of these full-time jobs. Employees with such jobs are perceived as more important, and thus, more indispensable, to the success of the enterprise.

Those who remain at the core of the model, however, do not have a really easy life – cuts in resources and staffing have increased work pressure dramatically. Stress is omnipresent, especially since employees realise that a permanent, full-time job is not necessarily an insurance policy against being made redundant suddenly. The business saying "At the centre, employ half as many people full time, pay them twice as much, work them three times as hard . . ." is no longer a laughing matter!

5.1.2   The first periphery: who is your boss?

The new job structure results from the changing relationship among several companies as they outsource parts of the value chain beyond the enterprise's core. Suddenly, people in different geographical places are part of the same value chain, doing their jobs at the sites of suppliers, distributors, or customers – either on the payroll of the core or a partner firm. Employees in the periphery of the extended enterprise (Figure 5.4)

Job attributes	Middle management and project-driven experts, reporting directly to the core enterprise.
Contractual relationship	Open-ended contract, permanent (full or part-time) position, on the payroll of the partner enterprise.
Earnings	Regular salary and wages with a strong variable compensation component.
Location	Generally at the premises of the partner firm; at times at the core enterprise.
Benefits and allowances	Covered by the employing partner firm.
Sense of belonging	Diminishing for the core enterprise, moving to the partner firm.

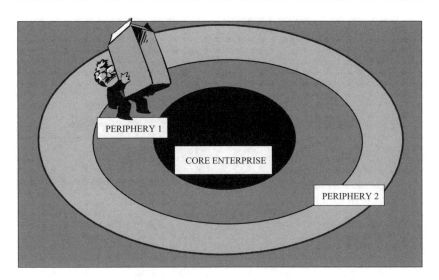

**Figure 5.4 – Work in the first periphery. The functions performed in
the periphery of the core enterprise are just as important as those
at the core, they are part of the uniqueness that drives the
competitiveness of the core firm. Tasks are outsourced to the
periphery when it is better at performing them than the core firm.
Work at the periphery should not be considered as "second class."**

report to two supervisors: those of the company of employment, and
those of the company where the task is to be performed. The sense of
commitment to the core enterprise is somewhat diluted. Jobs in the first
periphery of the core enterprise tend to follow the model described
below.

A full-time employee from a core enterprise can also work in the
premises of a partner enterprise when managing part of an extended
value chain. For example, a core firm can dispatch some of its core
employees to install a manufacturing operation at a partner site, which
needs to be integrated into the operating standards of their common
value chain. Such employees could also be seconded and transferred to
the payroll of the partner firm, while receiving their training and instructions from the core enterprise.

The proliferation of reporting relationships with employers – with
those who pay and with those for whom the work is done – makes the
work structure ambiguous, and even destabilising for the employee.
Splitting time between working on the premises of the core company
and at the periphery doesn't foster attachment to one or the other,
leading to questions about the employees' primary loyalty (Figure 5.5).
The partner firm will wonder whether they are drifting away ("they are

WHO ARE YOUR FRIENDS? YOUR ENEMIES?

Figure 5.5 – The key question. Defining who works for whom, and who competes with whom, is one of the key issues in the periphery: for people, and for companies. An environment of shared knowledge, where efficiency is always questioned, is, by definition, very volatile. Partnerships can be tangled and untangled easily. Under these circumstances, it is difficult to judge how much each can be trusted, and for how long. In addition, large, global companies have many different relationships with partner companies. The same company, or rather its divisions, can be a supplier, a distributor, and a competitor at the same time. It can be hard to manage, and is sometimes destabilising for employees.

really working for my client, not for me anymore"), just as the core enterprise may think: "their first loyalty is to my partner firm – where they get their paycheque." In the end, such employees generally leave both, a situation aggravated by the fact that such jobs tend to be project-driven, and therefore have a temporary dimension.

The proliferation of outsourcing agreements has led to work structures in the periphery that might seem like anarchy to outsiders. Since most outsourcing agreements are not long-term, they have led to very flexible working relationships. While cost-efficient for both the partner and core enterprise, such working relationships can lead to significant challenges in melding corporate cultures and work habits. Job satisfaction and motivation are harder to maintain for both firms, making it difficult to retain employees.

5.1.3 Work in the second periphery: a world of mercenaries?

The working relationships between the firm and individuals in the second periphery – independent experts, who are external providers of a service or task directly to the core enterprise – are perhaps the most fluid and the most volatile (Figure 5.6). Individuals in the second periphery do not belong, or have a sense of belonging, to any single company infrastructure. Very often, the working relationship exists for a defined task and period of time, and disappears once the task is completed. Jobs in the second periphery of the core enterprise tend to follow the model described below:

Job attributes	Knowledge worker, expert or specialist in a well-defined field or task.
Contractual relationship	Temporary, ends with task completion.
Earnings	Based on a business contract between independent parties.
Location	Can be anywhere – virtual office, core enterprise, home office, on the road. Always in close contact with the core enterprise for the duration of the assignment.
Benefits and allowances	The independent contractors assume all insurance costs. The core firm only reimburses job-related, out-of-pocket expenses.
Sense of belonging	Low – only loyal because the firm is a client and they expect repeat business.

Such is the job structure for "mercenaries," who do not wish to be part of, or need, a permanent work structure, and who are perhaps in the process of creating their own firm. These mercenaries do not assume high levels of responsibility inside the core enterprise, since firms hesitate to share their most confidential information – they might perform another assignment for a competitor. The task to be performed is well defined through a series of milestones and deadlines. The timing of the relationship is limited, and will be terminated when the task is

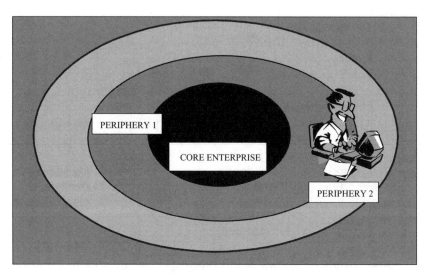

Figure 5.6 – The second periphery. The newest type of working relationship is found in the second periphery of the core firm, as the work actually takes place outside the conventional configuration of work. Knowledge workers are the best examples, since they are stand-alone entities. Sometimes they are former employees of the firm, who almost act as independent professionals, and indeed, as entrepreneurs, while retaining a relationship with the core enterprise. Some people need the formal structure provided by an enterprise and cannot function within such an uncertain status.

completed. Remuneration is somewhat higher than for employees in the first periphery, to compensate for the absence of employment benefits and allowances, as well as the volatility of the job.

In recent years, this job structure no longer affects only people who are complete "outsiders" to the core enterprise. Full-time employees of a core enterprise may, willingly or unwillingly, leave their jobs and be guaranteed a consulting agreement with their former employer. Employees are often offered such package deals during times of business restructuring. If employees are still willing to work and wish to create their own firm, the former employer can choose to guarantee a certain amount of independent work to its departing employee, ensuring a smoother transition to the labour market.

Such arrangements can be positive, both for the company and the employee. The firm benefits, as it maintains access to expertise accumulated over the years, and the employee does not feel "let down." In addition, governments are always keen to lengthen the period of time between the loss of permanent employment and the complete absence of work. It is easier to find another job when one has some sort of employment activity than none at all.

The Extended Work Model corresponds to the rise of new value systems in society. Many people, especially those in younger generations, find it difficult to enter the mould of a rigid corporate structure. Many are eager to try out their entrepreneurial skills by launching their own firms, even if for many years, they are their sole employees (Figure 5.7). Indeed, modern technology has made the *home office*, as well as the *home company*, widespread realities. Nowadays, it is perfectly possible to run a significant business operation single-handedly from one's home, when, just a few years ago, this business would have required a significant labour force and facilities. Services, trading, wealth management and software customisation are all prime examples of this revolution.

The growth of such independent jobs – whether as freelancers, contractors, consultants, or advisers – is extremely positive for the development of a nation's competitiveness, as it brings a touch of the Schumpeterian approach. This type of work arrangement provides great dynamism in the economy of proximity described earlier. The windfall of such jobs is that they have shown that the economy of proximity need not only be comprised of traditional occupations or unskilled activities. Independent jobs in the second periphery can be highly skilled and bring a lot of added value. Further, the right legislative and taxation framework supporting this type of work structure can unleash a lot of inventiveness and economic vitality. Some of the most dynamic places in the world, such as Silicon Valley, or Bangalore in India, thrive on the widespread existence and ready acceptance of this type of working relationship within the immediate vicinity of large firms.

5.2 Work in the age of anxiety

Work is not something that can be moved freely here or there without consequences for the firm and society. Any changes to work structures and relationships have to be decided and implemented carefully, since those transformations can have a significant psychological impact – not only on employees, but also on organisations. A strategy of cost-cutting at all costs is not always the best way of achieving a work structure that actually increases the competitiveness of the firm. It can open a Pandora's box: destabilising people and processes, and leading to a very real, deep impact on the minds of employees – those leaving and those staying – and on the company's soul.

ENTREPRENEURSHIP

		2005
	Entrepreneurship of managers	
is not widespread in your economy		is widespread in your economy

Ranking		
1	HONG KONG	7.91
2	ISRAEL	7.56
3	USA	7.29
4	ZHEJIANG	7.19
5	CHILE	6.99
6	TAIWAN	6.95
7	SAO PAULO	6.94
8	BRAZIL	6.80
8	ICELAND	6.80
10	TURKEY	6.61
11	ESTONIA	6.61
12	CANADA	6.57
13	NEW ZEALAND	6.40
14	AUSTRALIA	6.39
15	SLOVENIA	6.34
16	IRELAND	6.33
17	PHILIPPINES	6.29
18	HUNGARY	6.27
19	COLOMBIA	6.26
20	RHONE-ALPS	6.24
21	SWITZERLAND	6.11
22	THAILAND	6.04
23	FINLAND	6.00
23	MAHARASHTRA	6.00
25	DENMARK	5.97
26	BELGIUM	5.97
27	AUSTRIA	5.96
28	KOREA	5.93
29	BAVARIA	5.84
30	SLOVAK REPUBLIC	5.83
31	LOMBARDY	5.80
32	INDIA	5.78
33	MALAYSIA	5.74
34	SWEDEN	5.58
35	CZECH REPUBLIC	5.54
36	RUSSIA	5.45
37	SINGAPORE	5.38
38	NETHERLANDS	5.33
39	FRANCE	5.29
40	VENEZUELA	5.25
41	ILE-DE-FRANCE	5.23
42	GREECE	5.21
43	POLAND	5.18
44	LUXEMBOURG	5.13
45	ITALY	5.12
46	JORDAN	5.09
47	CHINA MAINLAND	5.04
48	NORWAY	4.98
49	GERMANY	4.97
50	CATALONIA	4.91
51	SPAIN	4.91
52	MEXICO	4.89
53	UNITED KINGDOM	4.88
54	ROMANIA	4.82
55	SOUTH AFRICA	4.81
56	ARGENTINA	4.67
57	INDONESIA	4.29
58	SCOTLAND	4.26
59	JAPAN	4.23
60	PORTUGAL	4.08

Figure 5.7 – The emergence of entrepreneurs. Entrepreneurship is a key factor for increasing the competitiveness of a nation. While the United States is widely known to be a hotbed of entrepreneurship, emerging economies, such as Brazil, Russia, India and China, have some quite remarkable entrepreneurs too. These represent, however, a smaller proportion of the population than would be the case in Anglo-Saxon countries. (Reproduced from [2] by permission of IMD.)

5.2.1 The loss of the office as a status symbol

There is no other symbol as powerful in communicating status as the office. In most organisations, the location and size of office space is directly proportional to the level of seniority of an executive. The top job gets the top office, often a corner one. As your office gets closer to that of a powerful executive, it reverberates a strong message to your colleagues and the rest of the firm. Some firms even have a so-called *executive floor*, where they pack their most senior executives. In a firm, no other process is as charged with emotion and subtle signals as the allocation of offices.

The first attempt to break the traditional office mould came from the United States, with the notion of open-plan offices with no, or mid-height, partitions designating a specific "work-space" for each employee. The only enclosed areas are conference rooms. Proponents of such environments claim they favour communication and an egalitarian culture. Everybody can see everybody and talk to everybody. You can pop in and see if the most senior managers are available. Open-plans can be enhanced by a frequent rotation of offices, so that employees change neighbourhood and routines regularly.

In the beginning, some people suffer from the lack of privacy. Some periods of the day are not as efficient as they should be; some phone calls are not as business-oriented as they should be. Nobody really feels happy about having his or her private life exposed to office colleagues. But everyone realises quickly that they are in the same boat. At the end of the day, all employees learn that everyone else in the company is "human" too, and has a personal life.

The new business world means extensive travel for executives, especially in an extended enterprise environment. In reality, at any moment

---

Flexibility of the workforce

There is a strong cultural element in the willingness of people to accept new challenges and new work structures (Figure 5.8). People in Anglo-Saxon nations seem to be more willing to accept new experiments than traditional Continental European countries, such as France and Germany. However, people in Nordic countries are also quite adventurous, maybe because their relationship with work has less "emotional" content than in other, more traditional societies.

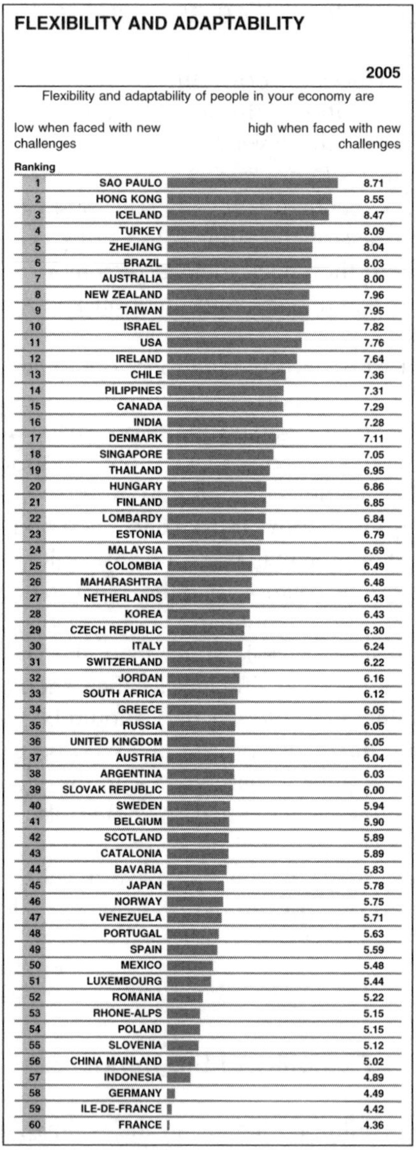

FLEXIBILITY AND ADAPTABILITY

2005

Flexibility and adaptability of people in your economy are

low when faced with new
challenges

high when faced with new
challenges

Ranking

Ranking	Country		Score
1	SAO PAULO		8.71
2	HONG KONG		8.55
3	ICELAND		8.47
4	TURKEY		8.09
5	ZHEJIANG		8.04
6	BRAZIL		8.03
7	AUSTRALIA		8.00
8	NEW ZEALAND		7.96
9	TAIWAN		7.95
10	ISRAEL		7.82
11	USA		7.76
12	IRELAND		7.64
13	CHILE		7.36
14	PILIPPINES		7.31
15	CANADA		7.29
16	INDIA		7.28
17	DENMARK		7.11
18	SINGAPORE		7.05
19	THAILAND		6.95
20	HUNGARY		6.86
21	FINLAND		6.85
22	LOMBARDY		6.84
23	ESTONIA		6.79
24	MALAYSIA		6.69
25	COLOMBIA		6.49
26	MAHARASHTRA		6.48
27	NETHERLANDS		6.43
28	KOREA		6.43
29	CZECH REPUBLIC		6.30
30	ITALY		6.24
31	SWITZERLAND		6.22
32	JORDAN		6.16
33	SOUTH AFRICA		6.12
34	GREECE		6.05
35	RUSSIA		6.05
36	UNITED KINGDOM		6.05
37	AUSTRIA		6.04
38	ARGENTINA		6.03
39	SLOVAK REPUBLIC		6.00
40	SWEDEN		5.94
41	BELGIUM		5.90
42	SCOTLAND		5.89
43	CATALONIA		5.89
44	BAVARIA		5.83
45	JAPAN		5.78
46	NORWAY		5.75
47	VENEZUELA		5.71
48	PORTUGAL		5.63
49	SPAIN		5.59
50	MEXICO		5.48
51	LUXEMBOURG		5.44
52	ROMANIA		5.22
53	RHONE-ALPS		5.15
54	POLAND		5.15
55	SLOVENIA		5.12
56	CHINA MAINLAND		5.02
57	INDONESIA		4.89
58	GERMANY		4.49
59	ILE-DE-FRANCE		4.42
60	FRANCE		4.36

**Figure 5.8 – There is a cultural element in flexibility.
(Reproduced from [2] by permission of IMD.)**

of the day, about one-third of workspaces are vacant. It is a telling experience to walk into the headquarters of a large global company midweek. Most of the time, the only people around are the staff assistants, who are actually the only people left who know where everybody is, and what they are up to. Realising that few are actually making use of their space, many companies have asked their executives to make their workspace available to visiting colleagues while they are away. Sharing one's precious workspace can be difficult from a psychological point of view. The office must be kept tidy, and personal items have to be easily removable. One's relationship to the office becomes more impersonal.

After the breakthrough of open-plan offices, the next revolutionary concept arrived – *hotelling*. In hotelling, office space is considered a standard facility, just like a hotel room. Upon arrival at a hotel, the traveller expects to find certain standard amenities – a bed, a bathroom, a phone, a TV, a computer connection, etc. Analogously, upon arriving at a company premises, a business traveller expects to find a workspace with the typical amenities of an office – a direct telephone line, a high-speed computer connection, storage facilities, a desk, and a chair. In some enterprises, executives can "book" an office in advance before they visit a company's location. Companies such as the World Trade Centers Group make it their business to offer consistent business facilities globally to executives, on a short- or medium-term basis.

Oticon, a Danish hearing-aid company, takes "hotelling" even a step further. Employees are provided with a caddy that serves as a wheeled storage facility. When employees arrive, they "check-in" at the reception, collect "their" caddy containing all of their company files, communication devices, and personal belongings. They move around the office floors and take possession of any available office space. After a few days of work, or before leaving for a trip, they pack their belongings into the caddy and leave it at the reception. The office space they were occupying is then free to be used by another employee [3].

The loss of an office is often perceived as a demotion or a loss of status, especially for sales employees, who, as we have seen earlier, may no longer be expected to come into the office every day. These physical rearrangements of the workforce create some tricky situations, such as when a customer calls the company to speak to the office of their sales representative, and learns that he has no office, and, of course, no assistant. Negotiations and visits take place increasingly at dedicated conference rooms in the core enterprise, void of all elements of personalisation. Taking away the office and the identity of the employee from the workspace also means diminishing the pride of belonging to an organisation.

5.2.2   Working from home: a mixed blessing?

A number of companies have tried to get employees, mostly part-timers, to work from home. After all, several jobs, such as researchers, software programmers, and research analysts, need not always be performed at the firm's core office. Companies ask employees to telecommute – the firm equips the homes of employees with communication devices so that they can work from home easily and stay in touch with "the office." Such a strategy is not pursued because it is cheaper to do so than to provide a normal office space, but because it increases the flexibility of working hours, and, thus, the motivation of employees. The results of these experiments have been mixed.

During the first six months, productivity increases because the employee feels greatly empowered. However, after a certain period of time, the employee begins to feel "cut off" from the core office, and, thus, out of the loop. Because information flow is not as constant as before, one feels forgotten because one is not seen in the office. More-over, a lot of the information flow within an enterprise is unstructured and according to unwritten rules – the rumours around the coffee machine, or the fortuitous encounter in a hallway with a colleague, who "drops" valuable information.

The most striking drawback of telecommuting is that employees lose touch with the corporate culture of a company while away from the office. Corporate culture is composed of dynamic values and principles, which evolve over time, and is not necessarily found in the company brochure. A telecommuting employee can quickly miss some important changes in the corporate culture or strategy by being "out of the loop." To tackle this issue, many companies institute a policy whereby em-ployees must come to the office regularly, at least for a day a week. Such policies recognise the importance of informal information flows, and encourage employees to intermingle, and thus become aligned with current policies and values.

Cultural background is another influencing factor. In California or the Nordic countries, it is not considered a "demotion" to work from home, or to be a mobile worker outside the core enterprise office. People recog-nise and accept that it may be a fact of life or a personal choice. In some countries, harsh weather conditions (like those in Canada), or traffic congestion (like in The Netherlands or greater London), have been natural incentives to work away from the office. However, in many Latin countries, for example, it is considered a demotion not to have to leave home every morning to go to the office. The neighbours may ask the spouse: "Why is your partner still at home?" – "He is working from home." – "Ah, he does not have a real job . . ." Cultural traditions explain why working away from the office can be a success in certain countries and a dismal failure in others.

5.2.3   Can part-time work be a real alternative?

Competitiveness thrives on the flexibility of a nation's workforce; as such, flexibility is increasingly in demand by firms. At the same time, the entry of large numbers of women into the labour force has increased the demand for working relationships that are more in tune with work–life balance. The combination of these two factors – labour flexibility and work–life balance – has led to the development of a permanent market for part-time or temporary positions (Figure 5.9).

In Sweden, Finland, Russia, Norway, Slovenia, and the US, women compose more than 46 % of the total labour force. In Spain, it is only 40 %, followed by Mexico at 39 %, and then Italy and Indonesia with 38 % each. It seems cultural traditions, as well as historical factors, play some role in explaining such differences across countries – in former communist countries, women were as represented in the overall labour force as men.

The Netherlands has created the essential infrastructure for an efficient part-time and temporary labour market. The Dutch have passed the necessary legislation for protecting part-time and temporary workers adequately, and have also actively supported firms willing to engage in this new approach to employment. Today, one can find all sorts of qualifications on the Dutch part-time and temporary employment market: from low-skilled jobs to engineers and even senior managers.

Part-time employment provides considerable flexibility to the firm and to employees – for example, it allows more women to be involved in economic life, especially while raising children. Part-time employment suffers, however, from a legislative vacuum in many countries – often, it is still considered as a part of a parallel, underground labour force, with few social benefits and official protection. Those seeking a full-time job consider part-time employment only a temporary and nonpermanent solution – yet, it need not be the case that part-time work is only temporary. A sophisticated infrastructure for permanent part-time employment, as has been put in place in The Netherlands, can "oil" the labour market, ensuring that more individuals are either employed and/or employable within the economy.

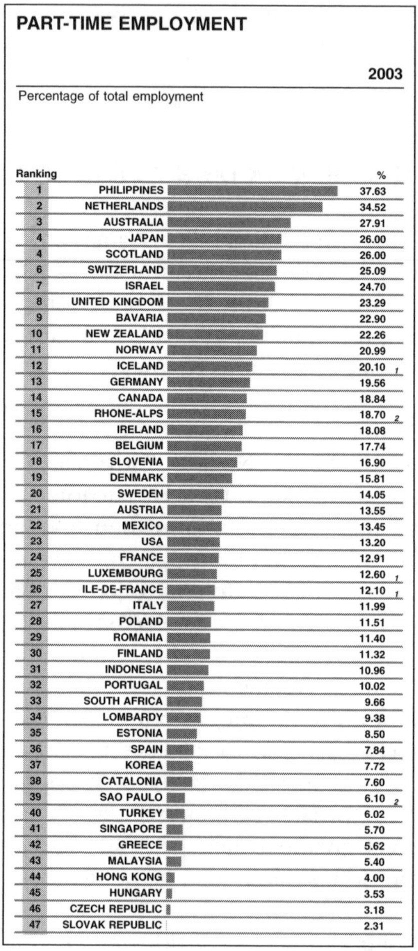

PART-TIME EMPLOYMENT

2003

Percentage of total employment

Ranking		%
1	PHILIPPINES	37.63
2	NETHERLANDS	34.52
3	AUSTRALIA	27.91
4	JAPAN	26.00
4	SCOTLAND	26.00
6	SWITZERLAND	25.09
7	ISRAEL	24.70
8	UNITED KINGDOM	23.29
9	BAVARIA	22.90
10	NEW ZEALAND	22.26
11	NORWAY	20.99
12	ICELAND	20.10
13	GERMANY	19.56
14	CANADA	18.84
15	RHONE-ALPS	18.70
16	IRELAND	18.08
17	BELGIUM	17.74
18	SLOVENIA	16.90
19	DENMARK	15.81
20	SWEDEN	14.05
21	AUSTRIA	13.55
22	MEXICO	13.45
23	USA	13.20
24	FRANCE	12.91
25	LUXEMBOURG	12.60
26	ILE-DE-FRANCE	12.10
27	ITALY	11.99
28	POLAND	11.51
29	ROMANIA	11.40
30	FINLAND	11.32
31	INDONESIA	10.96
32	PORTUGAL	10.02
33	SOUTH AFRICA	9.66
34	LOMBARDY	9.38
35	ESTONIA	8.50
36	SPAIN	7.84
37	KOREA	7.72
38	CATALONIA	7.60
39	SAO PAULO	6.10
40	TURKEY	6.02
41	SINGAPORE	5.70
42	GREECE	5.62
43	MALAYSIA	5.40
44	HONG KONG	4.00
45	HUNGARY	3.53
46	CZECH REPUBLIC	3.18
47	SLOVAK REPUBLIC	2.31

Figure 5.9 – Part-time employment. (Reproduced from [2] by permission of IMD.)

5.3 The disappearance of work, really?

The "utopian" writers of the 19th century dreamed of an ideal society, where work would disappear to be replaced totally by a life of leisure. Machines would perform the hard, boring, repetitive work that has plagued human society. For them, the ultimate goal of the Industrial Revolution would thus be to replace humans with machines in order to free the humans.

5.3.1 Working less . . . or more?

On Friday 3 August 1923, an article in the *New York Times* broke the news that the directors of the American Iron and Steel Institute, during a meeting at the Metropolitan Club, had approved a major agreement, hailed as a breakthrough. The president, Judge Elbert H. Gary, announced that all members of the Institute had agreed to end the 12-hour day in the steel industry without delay. Workers would be paid a higher wage but earn less, and labour costs would increase by 15 %. US President Harding had been lobbying for these measures.

Those times seem so near to us, and yet so very far away. Since Judge Gary's announcement, the average working week in the industrialised nations has been gradually, but constantly, reduced. Pre-World War II, employees worked, on average, between 60 and 70 hours a week, with little or no paid holidays or vacations. Today's France (and it could be an extreme case) is down to a mere 35 hours a week – with up to six weeks' vacation and 11 holidays per year. Increases in productivity (Figure 5.10) have led to more time off for employees. In this case, at least, competitiveness has played its role as a creator of prosperity, assuming that leisure is something people value.

However, many differences still exist today between nations. Malaysia, Chile, and The Philippines still work slightly more than 2200 hours a year. In 2002, the US employee was working 1918 hours on average, compared to 1864 hours in Japan, 1833 hours in the UK, 1688 hours in Germany, and a mere 1587 in France!

These numbers are only averages. Many employees working in companies outside manufacturing would probably have the feeling that they are working more today than ten years ago – and it is probably true. Such feelings are reinforced by the fact that the working time of a knowledge worker is not determined by the time spent at their working place – these workers do not turn "off" after leaving the office. While a steel worker needs to be in the mill to perform his task, a knowledge worker can work any time, anywhere – in the office, at home, or on the road. Modern technology, such as email and voice mail, allows the knowledge worker to be connected permanently with work. Under these conditions, calculating working time becomes meaningless.

Knowledge workers are thus like the ancient farmers. Farmers would tend their farms 24 hours a day and 7 days a week. If hail fell on the crops, or an animal was sick, there was no excuse not to work simply because it was time off! Today, in enterprises, the same applies, but with two additional dimensions. First, the globalisation of business, with activities spanning different time zones, can result in really long working days. By the time Asian markets are closing, European ones are just opening. In addition, contrary to farmers, knowledge workers are highly

LABOUR PRODUCTIVITY (PPP)

2004

Estimates: GDP (PPP) per person employed per hour. US$

		US$	
1	ILE-DE-FRANCE	56.44	p
2	LUXEMBOURG	54.56	
3	IRELAND	48.73	
4	NORWAY	46.06	
5	FRANCE	44.53	
6	LOMBARDY	43.50	p
7	USA	43.22	
8	BAVARIA	42.22	p
9	BELGIUM	42.06	
10	ITALY	40.04	
11	RHONE-ALPS	39.42	pl
12	AUSTRIA	39.22	
13	DENMARK	38.45	
14	FINLAND	36.83	
15	CATALONIA	36.31	pl
16	GERMANY	36.17	
17	AUSTRALIA	35.90	
18	NETHERLANDS	35.01	
19	ICELAND	34.51	
20	CANADA	33.46	
21	UNITED KINGDOM	33.23	
22	SWEDEN	32.24	
23	SPAIN	31.32	
24	JAPAN	31.03	
25	GREECE	30.50	
26	ISRAEL	29.44	
27	SWITZERLAND	29.02	
28	SINGAPORE	26.54	
29	SCOTLAND	26.46	p
30	NONG KONG	25.38	
31	TAIWAN	24.59	
32	SLOVENIA	24.00	
33	NEW ZEALAND	23.22	
34	SOUTH AFRICA	21.48	
35	PORTUGAL	20.95	
36	HUNGARY	19.58	
37	CZECH REPUBLIC	18.95	
38	SLOVAK REPUBLIC	18.79	
39	ARGENTINA	18.35	
40	POLAND	17.65	
41	KOREA	17.59	
42	ESTONIA	17.25	
43	CHILE	13.80	
44	SAO PAULO	13.36	pl
45	MALAYSIA	12.06	
46	RUSSIA	11.98	
47	TURKEY	11.14	
48	MEXICO	10.21	
49	ZHEJIANG	10.10	p
50	JORDAN	10.08	l
51	BRAZIL	9.23	
52	ROMANIA	9.15	
53	COLOMBIA	8.86	
54	VENEZUELA	7.27	
55	THAILAND	6.56	
56	PHILIPPINES	5.14	
57	CHINA MAINLAND	4.78	
58	MAHARASHTRA	3.95	pl
59	INDONESIA	3.64	l
60	INDIA	3.10	l

Figure 5.10 – Disparities in labour productivity remain high in the world. Yet, many developing nations are "pockets of productivity," where efficiency is as high as in industrial nations, often because of the presence of foreign investments. (Reproduced from [2] by permission of IMD.)

mobile, and, given the right technology, their "office" can be wherever they are. Knowledge workers are highly efficient, but they can no longer escape the pressure of work.

The profound shifts in the nature and structure of work, and the skills that are demanded by today's employers have led to the creation of structural unemployment in both industrialised and developing nations. The formidable explosion of productivity in manufacturing – thanks to increased automation and technology – has shifted labour demand from manufacturing to services. Those who have the skills, abilities, and flexibility can shift into a service job; but many do not have these competencies and become the structurally unemployed.

5.3.2 Manufacturing jobs are indeed disappearing

Today, yet another revolution has occurred in the American steel industry. While in the past 20 years, production of steel has surged from 75 to 105 million tons, productivity increases have meant that the total number of American steel workers has fallen – from 289 000 to 74 000 in the same period. The US steel industry has boosted its production by half, while employing one-quarter of the workers!

Productivity is shifting employment – from manufacturing to service jobs. Even China, now considered to be the locomotive of world manufacturing, is being affected. In today's China, industry still accounts for 52 % of GDP; services for 34 %. By comparison, in the US, industry accounts for 27 % of GDP; services for 72 %. However, between 1995 and 2002, China lost some 15 million jobs in manufacturing, which corresponds to about 15 % of its total workforce in the industry sector – despite an average GDP growth in excess of 8 %. During the same period of time, worldwide, some 31 million jobs were lost in the manufacturing sector (Figure 5.11). Jeremy Rifkin, the author of *The End of Work* in 1995, estimates that if the present rate of job destruction continues, some 164 million jobs will have been lost in industry by 2040 [4].

The initial objective of the "utopians" has been perverted. Some people are, indeed, working less and more efficiently, such as in manufacturing – but they are fewer and fewer in number, and their jobs are threatened constantly by automation and productivity increases. As a result, structural unemployment – not just leisure – has increased all over the world. Others, especially those in service positions, are working more hours, and more intensively than ever before. The overall *quantity* of jobs is increasing, yet their nature and the structure of the job is changing constantly, demanding more mobility, more flexibility, and more skills to survive in the labour market.

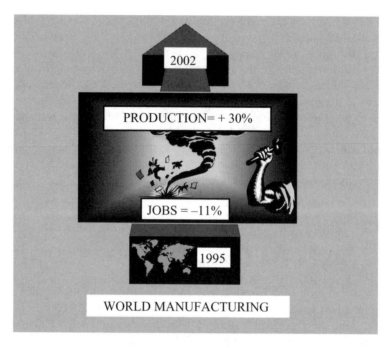

Figure 5.11 – The productivity trap. Productivity is a double-edged sword. Despite increasing production everywhere, manufacturing jobs are disappearing worldwide. In just seven years, between 1995 and 2002, notwithstanding an economic slowdown during part of that period, world manufacturing production jumped by 30 %, while jobs were reduced by 11 %.

In her book, *When Giants Learn to Dance*, Rosabeth Moss Kanter of Harvard Business School argues that the "new" corporate balance is to achieve *more* with *fewer* resources [5]. The pressure of work has increased considerably, and working relationships have become more complex. Stress and uncertainty prevail in the modern corporate world. As a result, employees are ever more destabilised, and, thus, demotivated, wondering often what is the *purpose* of the work they do.

5.4   A market value for work?

The labour market today in many countries is characterised by the parallel existence of a level of unemployment impossible to reduce, and a shortage of qualified employees.

5.4.1 The employability of the labour force

This situation is the result of a mismatch between the skills requirement for competitiveness, and the skills available in the pool of the unemployed. It is no longer unusual (more often in Europe than in the US) to observe this apparent contradiction. In 2004, the Spanish economy only employed 40 % of its population, compared to 47 % in the US and 57 % in Switzerland. In spite of a greater theoretical potential for the Spanish population to be active, the unemployment rate in Spain was 11 % of the workforce for that same year, compared to 4.4 % in Switzerland, and 5.5 % in the US – high numbers for both countries by historical standards. Clearly, there is a mismatch between the skills available in the Spanish potential labour force, and those needed by enterprises to operate competitively in Spain. In other words, there are proportionately fewer "employable" people in Spain than in the US or Switzerland.

As described earlier, sound competitiveness policy balances the economy of globalisation with that of proximity. From a work perspective, a parallel can be drawn between the global economy, which flourishes on an Anglo-Saxon Model, and the economy of proximity, which functions on the more protective Continental European Model. During the past two decades, the global economy has favoured the Anglo-Saxon Model, building international operations on the basis of a flexible and adaptable workforce that can be hired and fired freely – the "rough and tough" model. This model, through its drive for privatisation and the liberalisation of markets, poses a direct threat to the "cosiness" characterising the economy of proximity.

However, many governments, and probably most people, are now seeking a softer model – a third way. This "third way" does not require firms to preserve employment at all costs, but expects companies to demonstrate greater social commitment in cases of restructuring. Most companies try to soften redundancy with accompanying measures, such as pre-retirement plans, or an outplacement service, and work closely with local employment authorities.

Another strategy to help staff overcome the personal impact of restructuring consists of lengthening the period of time that exists between the formal loss of a job and a situation of total inactivity for the job seeker. It is easier for a person *in* the labour force to find another job than for one who has lost most contact with the working world. Scandinavian nations, especially Sweden, have pioneered the development of vocational training and education. Their employment offices effectively assist people in bridging between two jobs – the transition period is used to update and diversify skills that will, in turn, increase the future employability of a person.

Rigid labour markets can, however, dampen the best of intentions. In Europe, on average, 45 % of unemployed people have been out of work for more than one year. In the US, depending on the economic situation, the vast majority of unemployed people find a new job within six weeks. In Europe, losing one's job is often perceived as a life tragedy. In the US, it is often regarded as a new challenge and an opportunity to move upward and ahead.

5.4.2 Corporate value and market value for work

Individuals must take charge of their lives and monitor closely the evolution of their "market value." Individuals who only have "corporate value," i.e. a set of skills and competencies only valuable for the present employer, are increasingly vulnerable. The division of labour in very large companies leads to very narrow job descriptions, which may only exist within the context of the present employer. Employees should always keep an eye on their "market value" and make sure they build a set of skills and competencies that are *also* valuable for other companies (Figure 5.12).

Figure 5.12 – What is your value? There is a difference between having a value for the corporation that employs you, and having a market value. People who have left a large company, willingly or not, are often shocked when they discover their value was derived exclusively from the company for which they worked. Very often, they had been led into a highly-specialised job that had no duplicate on the job market. Developing a market value, beyond the company of present employment, is a survival priority today.

Companies also have an interest in developing the market value of their employees. Employees who know that they can find another job on the market easily, because they have the right set of skills, will be more flexible, motivated, and willing to take greater risks in their current job. Alternatively, employees with a limited market appeal are aware of their inherently limited employability outside their current job and will, thus, oppose anything that threatens their position.

I was once involved in a company project that tried to increase the market value of its employees. The company conducted a study with its employees to help them define their sets of skills. To guarantee the process's objectivity and confidentiality, outplacement agencies and work experts conducted the interviews. The market value of the employees in the study was assessed, thus determining their level of employability.

Bearing in mind employees with high market value are more "open-minded" than others, the company agreed to help all employees taking part in the study to update and diversify their skills. It was a remarkable idea – and a resolute failure. Most employees felt depressed after the process had taken place. In spite of all the reassurances given by the company as to the objectives of the study, instead of motivating people, everyone became convinced that they had been placed next on the redundancy list. The result was to destabilise and worry people. When it comes to revising working structures and relationships, sometimes even the best ideas can backfire!

5.5 Work structures: a point of no return for competitiveness?

Management should take utmost care and caution with any attempt to alter the structure of work and relationships in the company. A cost–benefit analysis may not be the only yardstick. When managers have a low cost/low importance attitude toward workers, they demotivate their employees and damage the trust the workforce might have in the company. Situations in which employees no longer believe what management says are the most difficult to remedy.

Training people is obviously a good way to develop employability and market value. Good training programmes strive for labour employability – they develop the skills and competencies of people *per se*, and not necessarily those for a specific job in the company. Expanding employability means broadening, while diversifying, the skills of the workforce, and not only deepening them. Surprisingly, many companies do not realise the benefits they could gain by investing in employability. There are two reasons for this. First, for most enterprises, training is seen as an investment that must have a measurable return for the firm. If training is not linked to a specific part of the job, or does not increase job productivity, it is hard to justify the expense. Second, enterprises fear that better trained employees will ask for a better job, a better salary, and a promotion, and, if the expectation is not met, they will leave.

Employability is one thing; *respect* for employability is another. The skills and competencies of an employee also need to be respected. People hate to feel like pawns, which can be displaced back and forth within the organisation, according to changes in strategy. Greater flexibility in workforce attitudes, and more employability, should not be used as an excuse for taking restructuring decisions lightly and without proper preparation, or for moving people around without thinking. An enterprise can only develop employability if the skills and talent of employees are respected and valued within the organisation.

However, companies face formidable pressure to react quickly to market forces, and reacting at the speed of business can sometimes lead to ill-conceived decisions. A wrong decision that affects physical assets can eventually be corrected. A bad decision affecting human assets is far more complex to amend – it takes time, and involves dealing with human emotions. People have long memories.

Furthermore, top management tend to concentrate more on taking strategic decisions, rather than on mapping the consequences of those decisions fully. In particular, top management rarely give due attention to the full impact of their decisions on work structures and people. Decisions are taken based on tangible facts – they must be rational. While cost–benefit analysis can be a very powerful tool, decisions regarding work structure cannot be based purely on cost. Work is an investment – management needs to take into account the amount of money and effort the company has invested over the years to educate, train, and motivate people.

To attract the best employees, work structures, and companies in general, have to be aligned with the value systems of collaborators, whether they are in the core enterprise or on the periphery. Individualism, sensitivity to environmental issues, a concern for ethics, and the desire to balance work and lifestyles are becoming important values for employees. People want to work in companies, and in work structures, that are aligned with these new values. Companies that fail to realise this will have increasing difficulty in attracting the best talent, even if they are successful in business. Modern employees want to be proud of their employers (Figure 5.13).

If accounting standards treated labour as true "assets," and not as "expenditures," people would rightly become the most valuable asset

Figure 5.13 – Being an employer of choice.

in the company. Redundancy measures, as announced by companies, are seen as "cost-saving" measures. Strictly speaking, they are indeed. However, if a true valuation had been considered, such measures would account for a loss of assets and a corresponding impoverishment of the company.

Changing the work structure, or moving people from the core to the periphery, are sometimes needed to gain competitiveness – their effects on people are seen as collateral damage. Such a view is short-sighted. There might be good reasons for moving people across the value chain – the same employee, with the same set of skills, will perform dramatically differently in an alternate place within the value chain. A demotivated employee at the core can become energetic and entrepreneurial as a partner in the periphery. But, altering work structures to increase competitiveness is a strategy of no return. In contrast to most other management decisions, mistakes are extremely difficult to correct, forgive, or forget. The price of a mistake is a great loss of credibility. And, without credibility, there is no leadership, and thus, no competitiveness.

Competitiveness and Value Systems

6

> *"Perfection of means and confusion of goals characterise our age."*
>
> Albert Einstein (1879–1955)

The competitiveness of a firm hinges on two key factors: first, on the efficiency of its intangible assets (brand, loyalty of customers), and second, as we have seen in the preceding chapter, on the levels of commitment and motivation of employees. To best manage intangible assets, it becomes crucial to understand the value system that operates in the background. Cross-cultural management is a recent field of research, which analyses the differences in value systems and attitudes facing global companies. Intuitively, we all know that Japanese employees should not be treated in the same way as Arab or Latin American employees. The issue is not only *how*, but also *why*? Is there a relationship between value systems and competitiveness? And if there is, what does it mean for the management of global organisations?

In Chapter 2, our brief description of Max Weber's early 20th century work underlined how religious and philosophical beliefs can have an impact on economic development. Later, we established distinctions across three specific models – the Southern, Continental European, and Anglo-Saxon.

There is, thus, a strong link between value systems and competitiveness. In addition, companies have to cope with not one, but multiple, value systems, both at home and abroad. Over time, value systems evolve, either while adapting to prevalent conditions, or preceding major changes in society – today's employee may not respond to the same beliefs and motivations as an employee of a decade or two ago.

The theory of competitiveness brings together the two value systems – society's and the firm's – confronting an employee. While these two value systems are often congruent, it can be the case that some of their elements are incompatible; a person may follow a set of values inside the company that is not entirely the same as the one he would follow at home. For example, this person might be hard working and dedicated

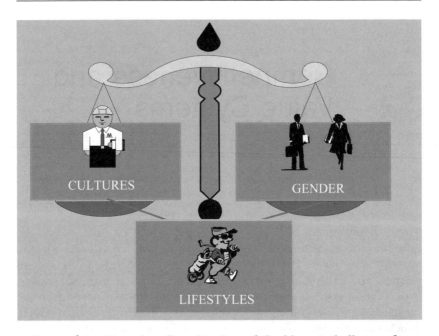

Figure 6.1 – Managing diversity. One of the biggest challenges for global companies today is managing the diverse cultures, gender, and lifestyles represented across an organisation. Corporate culture strives to balance competing aspirations, preventing the fragmentation of the company – it is the "invisible glue" holding people together more than any organisational chart could. In a volatile world filled with uncertainty, corporate culture serves as a fundamental stabiliser for the company.

to tough business goals in the office, while practising a quieter, gentler life at home. Some Japanese executives act, for example, like "Samurai" during the week, but are keen adepts of Zen meditation during the weekend.

When developing its corporate culture, a firm must bear in mind the beliefs of employees, and the values established by the society under which it operates (Figure 6.1). Competitive companies spend a considerable amount of time and energy aligning their corporate objectives with the value systems of their employees, their customers, and the public at large.

Figure 6.2 – The favourite words of the Japanese. *Source*: **[1].**

6.1   When the East meets the West

6.1.1   Japan: the land of hard work?

In 1979, the Dentsu Institute for Human Studies carried out a comprehensive survey of the ten favourite words used by the Japanese. These words would, it hoped, provide some indication of the value system of Japan. The result, shown in Figure 6.2, might be surprising for a Westerner.

The favourite words of the Japanese revealed by the study can be divided into two categories: those relating to *effort*, such as perseverance, loyalty, and tenacity, and those relating to *consensus*, such as love, harmony, and friendship.

The hard-working lifestyle of the Japanese people is notorious – similar attitudes are found in most Asian nations. Neither the desire to contribute to the economic growth of the nation, nor the desire to gain personal wealth, fully explains such a dedicated approach to work. In the background, deep cultural beliefs drive and sustain these attitudes. Most Asian value systems today are rooted profoundly in Confucianism. Five words can summarise the influence of the philosophy and teachings of Confucius in these value systems: loyalty, discipline, education, saving, and hard work (Figure 6.3).

A very strict work ethic (it was said, jokingly, that in Korea, workers used to sleep on factory sites in order not to lose time commuting),

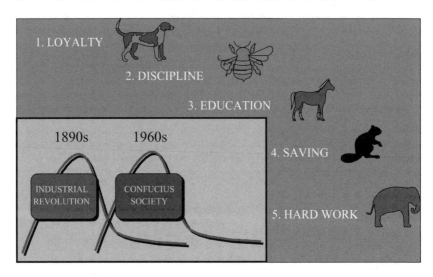

Figure 6.3 – Confucianism and Protestantism: a similar impact on industrialisation? Max Weber's description of Calvinism and Protestant values is similar to the Confucian value system encapsulated in the five words stated above (see Chapter 2). The value systems that flourish under Confucianism and Protestantism foster the earlier stages of economic development. To a great extent, Protestant values drove the industrial revolutions in Britain and Germany in the 19th century, just as the Confucian value system has propelled the industrial development of many Asian nations since the 1960s.

when combined with frugality and an appetite for education, laid the foundations for economic development in Asia. All of these factors meld together into a value system that is supportive of the industrial development of a nation, helping Asia sustain high economic growth rates, and ultimately, the rise of a middle class. The value systems that have driven and supported economic development in Asia are not very different from those prevalent in Europe and in the United States more than a century ago.

The discipline and frugality espoused by Asian value systems have had concrete economic consequences. For example, the rate of personal saving is high all over Asia (Figure 6.4). As a percentage of GDP, Singapore saves 44.92 %, Malaysia 42.93 %, and China 40.49 %. By comparison, savings in Britain account for only 13.25 % of GDP, and in the US, for 14.87 %. Although saving rates in Asia have declined slightly as prosperity has increased, Asian countries still have high savings that

GROSS DOMESTIC SAVING RATES		
Percentage of GDP		*2003*
1	ZHEJIANG	52.01 *ₗ*
2	SINGAPORE	44.92
3	MALAYSIA	42.93
4	CHINA MAINLAND	40.49 *ₗ*
5	IRELAND	39.98
6	LUXEMBOURG	39.52
7	RUSSIA	33.23 *ₗ*
8	THAILAND	33.14
9	KOREA	32.82
10	HONG KONG	32.32
11	LOMBARDY	31.76 *₂*
12	NORWAY	31.58
13	BAVARIA	31.24 *₂*
14	CATALONIA	30.04 *ₗ*
15	CANADA	27.19
16	ARGENTINA	26.78
17	VENEZUELA	26.59 *ₗ*
18	DENMARK	26.20
19	SLOVENIA	26.09
20	FINLAND	25.70
21	JAPAN	25.57
22	NETHERLANDS	25.50
23	CZECH REPUBLIC	25.24
24	CHILE	24.91
25	TAIWAN	24.37
26	AUSTRIA	24.35
27	SWITZERLAND	24.16 *ₗ*
28	SPAIN	24.14
29	ESTONIA	24.05
30	BRAZIL	23.80
31	SLOVAK REPUBLIC	23.26
32	AUSTRALIA	23.11 *ₗ*
33	BELGIUM	22.71
34	SWEDEN	22.70
35	NEW ZEALAND	22.56
36	HUNDGARY	22.17
37	GERMANY	22.13
38	INDONESIA	21.50
39	RHONE-ALPS	21.39 *ₚₗ*
40	MEXICO	20.95
41	FRANCE	20.21 *ₚ*
41	ILE-DE-FRANCE	20.21
43	ITALY	20.09
44	PHILIPPINES	20.08
45	SAO PAULO	19.78 *ₚₗ*
46	TURKEY	19.29 *ₗ*
47	SOUTH AFRICA	18.93
48	PORTUGAL	18.34 *ₗ*
49	ICELAND	18.09
50	GREECE	18.02
51	POLAND	16.74 *ₗ*
52	ROMANIA	16.73
53	INDIA	15.54 *ₗ*
54	MAHARASHTRA	14.95 *ₚ₂*
55	USA	14.87 *ₗ*
56	SCOTLAND	13.61 *ₚₗ*
57	UNITED KINGDOM	13.25
58	COLOMBIA	12.17 *ₗ*
59	ISRAEL	7.97
60	JORDAN	-4.44 *₂*

Figure 6.4 – Gross domestic saving rates. Although the situation has evolved somewhat over the years, Asian nations are still showing a high level of saving as a percentage of GDP – Confucian cultural values encourage people to save. In addition, the very high saving rates in Singapore and Malaysia are also the result of compulsory saving schemes. (Reproduced from [2] by permission of IMD.)

support the industrialisation of the region. According to fundamental economics, $I = S$, investment equals savings. Thus, Asia's high level of savings provided for high levels of investment, which, in turn, fuelled the industrialisation of the region.

6.1.2   Europe and the US were there before . . .

During their early economic development, Western nations were just as impressively hard working as Asian nations are today. Western industrialisation was also built on the basis of very long working hours and harsh labour conditions – socialism and trade unions rose to counteract such difficult situations. Nevertheless, it was through the ruthlessness of the hard-work ethic of the time that Western nations were able to accumulate great amounts of physical and intellectual capital, providing the basis for their future prosperity. Such historical circumstances have led to similar outcomes in Europe, North America, and Asia – an industrial revolution, capital accumulation, and most significantly from the point of view of competitiveness, the rise of a middle class.

Value systems, however, are not static – they evolve over time, and, in a global world, they have a tendency to converge. The Dentsu Institute for Human Studies mentioned earlier, repeated the study of the most favoured words of the Japanese 13 years later, in 1992. The results showed significant changes in the Japanese social value system (Figure 6.5).

If we were to divide the words according to the two categories we used in analysing the 1979 results, we find that the only word remaining that relates to the work ethic is "effort." All of the other words of the 1992 results fall into the category of "consensus": love, harmony, and friendship. Yet there is more to what the study's results tell us about changes in Japanese values. Many of the words introduced in the 1992 results, words such as "freedom," "health," and "dreams," reflect a shift of the value system towards more individualism.

Between the two studies, Japanese society has changed priorities, partly as a result of economic success and the accumulation of household wealth. The era when Japanese employees would only take a few days vacation a year, and would totally devote a hard-working life to a single employer, is slowly, but surely, disappearing. While the younger generation is still eager to succeed, their definition of success balances work with time to enjoy life, and they cultivate their sense of individuality. Opponents of these developments believe Japanese society has been influenced for the worse by Western values, inducing the current economic and social woes of Japan. In their view, Japan should revert to its traditional value system.

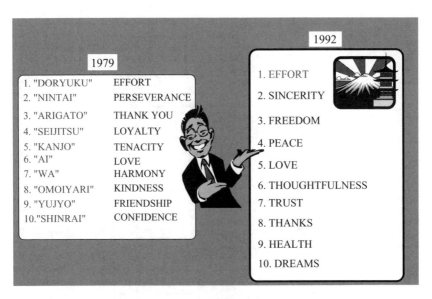

Figure 6.5 – The favourite words of the Japanese in 1992. In little over a decade, the priorities of the Japanese had changed. While the pace of change has been fast, and the changes themselves have been profound, they are not reflected in the same way across generations. Younger generations are more pliable and likely to change their value systems than older ones. We thus see within a nation, and for an extended period of time, two parallel value systems, giving rise to a conflict of generations. The shifting of Japanese priorities perhaps foretells what may happen in other Asian nations. *Source*: **[1].**

Political leaders in different countries advance similar arguments – the leadership of China, Singapore, Malaysia, and Saudi Arabia warn their populations repeatedly against the negative impact of Western culture. Some countries have tried to limit information access through censorship of the media, or the strict monitoring of Internet activities. Similar developments are occurring in industrialised Western nations – many political parties in Europe and the US advocate a "return to the good old value system of our parents" (Figure 6.6).

It is quite likely that Western values influence other value systems. The globalisation of business, and the instantaneous availability of information worldwide through global media networks, certainly tend to homogenise cultural values among nations. However, the main source of change is time – value systems evolve.

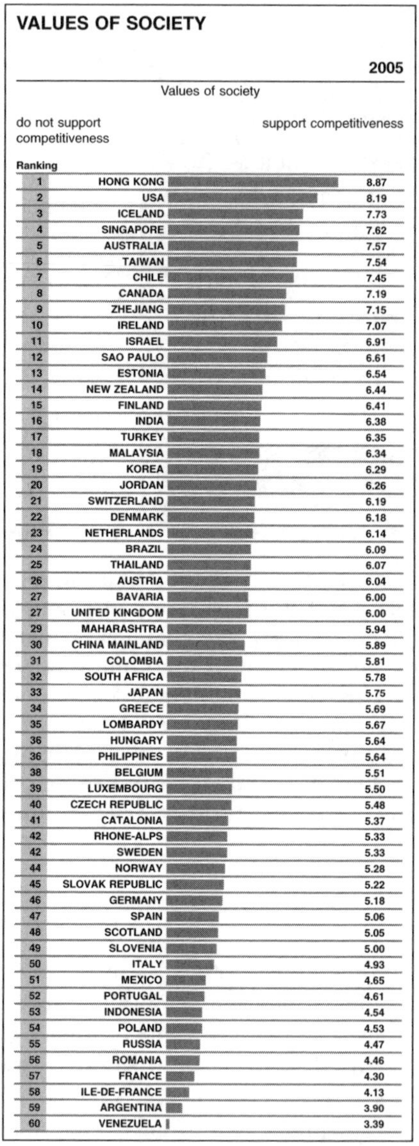

VALUES OF SOCIETY

		2005

Values of society

do not support   support competitiveness
competitiveness

Ranking		
1	HONG KONG	8.87
2	USA	8.19
3	ICELAND	7.73
4	SINGAPORE	7.62
5	AUSTRALIA	7.57
6	TAIWAN	7.54
7	CHILE	7.45
8	CANADA	7.19
9	ZHEJIANG	7.15
10	IRELAND	7.07
11	ISRAEL	6.91
12	SAO PAULO	6.61
13	ESTONIA	6.54
14	NEW ZEALAND	6.44
15	FINLAND	6.41
16	INDIA	6.38
17	TURKEY	6.35
18	MALAYSIA	6.34
19	KOREA	6.29
20	JORDAN	6.26
21	SWITZERLAND	6.19
22	DENMARK	6.18
23	NETHERLANDS	6.14
24	BRAZIL	6.09
25	THAILAND	6.07
26	AUSTRIA	6.04
27	BAVARIA	6.00
27	UNITED KINGDOM	6.00
29	MAHARASHTRA	5.94
30	CHINA MAINLAND	5.89
31	COLOMBIA	5.81
32	SOUTH AFRICA	5.78
33	JAPAN	5.75
34	GREECE	5.69
35	LOMBARDY	5.67
36	HUNGARY	5.64
36	PHILIPPINES	5.64
38	BELGIUM	5.51
39	LUXEMBOURG	5.50
40	CZECH REPUBLIC	5.48
41	CATALONIA	5.37
42	RHONE-ALPS	5.33
42	SWEDEN	5.33
44	NORWAY	5.28
45	SLOVAK REPUBLIC	5.22
46	GERMANY	5.18
47	SPAIN	5.06
48	SCOTLAND	5.05
49	SLOVENIA	5.00
50	ITALY	4.93
51	MEXICO	4.65
52	PORTUGAL	4.61
53	INDONESIA	4.54
54	POLAND	4.53
55	RUSSIA	4.47
56	ROMANIA	4.46
57	FRANCE	4.30
58	ILE-DE-FRANCE	4.13
59	ARGENTINA	3.90
60	VENEZUELA	3.39

Figure 6.6 – Do national value systems support competitiveness?
A value system's cohesiveness – such as that of Asia – or the
dynamism it fosters – such as in the US – is an important driver for
competitiveness. Great leaders pay attention to managing and
influencing the value system underpinning their nation and/or their
enterprise. A deteriorating value system seriously hampers
competitiveness, even if such decline does not lead, at first sight, to
direct economic consequences. (Reproduced from [2] by permission of
IMD.)

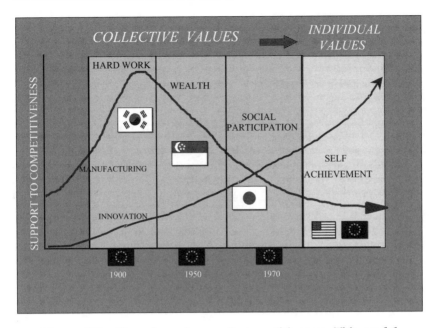

Figure 6.7 – Changing values and competitiveness. This model illustrates how value systems evolve over time, and how they influence competitiveness. The four phases indicate the dominant element within a value system. Before these phases, a nation may have a group of beliefs, but not necessarily melded into a cohesive system – the case in some African countries today. Over time, the three phases related to a more collective value system – hard work, wealth, and social participation – give way to a more individualistic value system based on self-achievement. Different value systems have a differentiated impact on the competitiveness of either manufacturing or innovation. Dates below the chart illustrate how fast systems evolve, using Europe as a reference.

6.2 Value systems change over time

One of the most stable pillars of a society – its value system – changes as new values emerge and disappear with time (Figure 6.7). Since such evolution takes place over long periods of time, documenting and analysing the evolution of value systems has traditionally been the domain of historians, philosophers, and theologians. Individuals would hardly notice such changes, unless they happened to live at crucial moments in history, such as revolutions. More recently, however, the speed at which a value system can evolve has increased, leading to noticeable changes in prosperity and, hence, it has become a concern for economists.

Globalisation and economic development have accelerated shifts within value systems considerably. Today, individuals can witness, and be fully aware of, value system evolutions that occur within their lifetimes. Industrial and technological revolutions have displaced political ones as catalysts for change within value systems.

Models of product lifecycles can be used to describe the evolution of value systems, and their relationship to competitiveness. Just like in product lifecycle theory, the evolution of a value system has phases of growth, maturity, and decline. While each phase can be extended, such extension is only temporary – with time, its importance diminishes, and its elements are replaced by those of the next phase. Thus, a nation's value system is always the result of history, and represents a juxtaposition of values inherited from the past. Nevertheless, at any one point in time, one set of values is always dominant. Value systems develop in four phases.

6.2.1   First phase: hard work

During this phase, people dedicate themselves totally to achieving the country's economic objectives. They are willing to work long hours, not necessarily well paid, in their zeal to attain economic success. Labour force cohesion is very high, whether imposed by a strong system, as in the former communist world, or as a result of cultural attitudes, as is the case in Confucian societies today. In this phase, we find a strong sense of hierarchy. People live for their work and the prosperity of their country (Figure 6.8).

A value system based on hard work is to be found at the beginning of a development process, as was the case for Korea, where, for many years, the working week averaged 54 hours. As seen earlier, an attitude of hard work similarly prevailed during the early stages of the Industrial Revolution in Europe and the US.

6.2.2   Second phase: wealth

The second phase occurs when a nation can be counted upon to deliver consistent economic growth. Households start to accumulate savings and assets, giving rise to a middle class. The sense of hierarchy begins to

Figure 6.8 – What do Chinese people want? A poll conducted in 1995 shows the eagerness of the Chinese to work hard and succeed as the "Open Door" policy was enacted. Today, the same hard work and success-driven society can be found in other emerging nations, such as the Baltic States in Europe.

weaken; although dedication to the country's economic objective and commitment to the firm remain strong. In this phase, the accumulation of personal wealth motivates people – they accept the need to work hard, provided that they are compensated properly (Figure 6.9).

Several years of economic success with a steady growth pattern give rise to a phase focusing on wealth accumulation – people start thinking about their own individual wellbeing. Such is the case today with nations like Singapore and Ireland. Complementary goals, such as the prosperity of the nation and the desire for personal wealth, tend to be balanced in the mind of the individual.

6.2.3 Third phase: social participation

In the third phase, people strive for greater social participation and inclusion (Figure 6.10). The phase arises when a nation's economic development is well under way, and there is no longer a sense of urgency

GDP (PPP) PER CAPITA

2004

Estimates: US$ per capita at purchasing power parity

Ranking		US$	
1	LUXEMBOURG	64,626	
2	ILE-DE-FRANCE	42,156	p
3	IRELAND	39,397	
4	NORWAY	38,484	
5	USA	38,360	
6	BAVARIA	33,138	p
7	LOMBARDY	33,087	p
8	ICELAND	32,419	
9	DENMARK	32,135	
10	CANADA	31,260	
11	SWITZERLAND	30,968	
12	AUSTRIA	30,639	
13	AUSTRALIA	30,348	
14	NETHERLANDS	29,716	
15	HONG KONG	29,107	
16	BELGIUM	29,016	
17	JAPAN	28,670	
18	FINLAND	28,510	
19	GERMANY	28,159	
20	FRANCE	28,118	
21	UNITED KINGDOM	27,872	
22	CATALONIA	27,586	pi
23	ITALY	27,496	
24	SWEDEN	27,463	
25	RHONE-ALPS	26,705	pi
26	SINGAPORE	26,601	
27	SCOTLAND	25,984	p
28	TAIWAN	24,676	
29	NEW ZEALAND	23,155	
30	SPAIN	21,877	
31	GREECE	20,528	
32	ISRAEL	20,371	
33	SLOVENIA	19,790	
34	KOREA	18,686	
35	PORTUGAL	18,266	
36	CZECH REPUBLIC	17,073	
37	HUNGARY	15,209	
38	ESTONIA	14,421	
39	SLOVAK REPUBLIC	14,270	
40	ARGENTINA	12,417	
41	ZHEJIANG	12,317	p
42	POLAND	12,000	
43	SAO PAULO	11,827	p
44	CHILE	10,774	
45	SOUTH AFRICA	10,553	
46	MALAYSIA	9,867	
47	RUSSIA	9,832	
48	MEXICO	9,281	
49	BRAZIL	7,969	
50	ROMANIA	7,908	
51	THAILAND	7,675	
52	TURKEY	7,358	
53	COLOMBIA	6,830	
54	VENEZUELA	5,669	
55	CHINA MAINLAND	5,430	
56	JORDAN	4,607	
57	PHILIPPINES	4,438	
58	MAHARASHTRA	4,038	pi
59	INDONESIA	3,505	
60	INDIA	3,013	

Figure 6.9 – GDP per capita at purchasing power parity. The
adjustment of the GDP to purchasing power parity gives a clearer
picture of what money can really buy in a country. Despite the
shortcomings of GDP already discussed, it is the best available
indicator of household wealth, and documents the rise of the middle
class. (Reproduced from [2] by permission of IMD.)

SOCIAL RESPONSIBILITY

		2005

Social responsibility of business leaders is

low towards society   high towards society

Ranking		
1	DENMARK	7.51
2	AUSTRIA	7.43
3	ZHEJIANG	7.37
4	FINLAND	7.08
5	SWEDEN	7.05
6	ICELAND	6.87
7	NORWAY	6.81
8	SOUTH AFRICA	6.80
9	NEW ZEALAND	6.67
10	NETHERLANDS	6.58
11	AUSTRALIA	6.56
12	SWITZERLAND	6.55
13	CANADA	6.55
14	LUXEMBOURG	6.44
15	THAILAND	6.25
16	BELGIUM	6.13
17	TAIWAN	6.12
18	CHILE	6.12
19	FRANCE	6.11
20	BAVARIA	6.08
21	SINGAPORE	6.05
22	HONG KONG	6.04
23	GERMANY	6.02
24	SAO PAULO	6.00
25	BRAZIL	5.97
26	ILE-DE-FRANCE	5.96
27	JAPAN	5.95
28	USA	5.95
29	MALAYSIA	5.94
30	KOREA	5.89
31	IRELAND	5.85
32	RHONE-ALPS	5.69
33	SCOTLAND	5.63
34	TURKEY	5.57
35	PHILIPPINES	5.53
36	ISRAEL	5.52
37	CATALONIA	5.49
38	CZECH REPUBLIC	5.48
39	COLOMBIA	5.31
40	UNITED KINGDOM	5.24
41	SLOVENIA	5.14
42	MAHARASHTRA	4.97
43	INDIA	4.94
44	LOMBARDY	4.86
45	CHINA MAINLAND	4.81
46	SPAIN	4.63
47	JORDAN	4.62
48	SLOVAK REPUBLIC	4.61
49	MEXICO	4.56
50	GREECE	4.47
51	ESTONIA	4.46
52	VENEZUELA	4.38
53	ITALY	4.32
54	PORTUGAL	4.29
55	HUNGARY	4.23
56	INDONESIA	4.18
57	ROMANIA	3.69
58	ARGENTINA	3.30
59	POLAND	3.18
60	RUSSIA	2.84

Figure 6.10 – Social responsibility attitude of business leaders. The Nordic European countries have a long tradition of social inclusion and participation. During the rise of the social participation phase, leaders in business and government pay careful attention to social demands. If not, then social unrest may occur, such as in 1968 across Europe. (Reproduced from [2] by permission of IMD.)

that demands great sacrifice. By now, households have accumulated significant amounts of savings and capital. Middle and upper classes co-exist and devote some of their attention to noneconomic pursuits – leisure, quality, and purpose of life, as well as their social standing.

By this stage, the society is one of affluence – making money is no longer the main, or the only, motivation of people. They aspire to a better quality of life, which could be fewer working hours, or simply, a better work–life balance. Citizens want to be involved actively in the decision-making of the nation, and have their voices heard within their firms. The sense of hierarchy weakens even further than in the previous phase, as society becomes ever more participatory. Japanese society has also been moving through this phase; the shift in preferred key words described earlier points to this conclusion.

6.2.4 Fourth phase: self-achievement

During the fourth phase, the focus shifts to the needs and desires of the individual, over and above those of society. It occurs when economic development is taken for granted, and is no longer a driving national issue. In some cases, individuals might even perceive the imperatives of economic development to be in conflict with their own personal goals. The objectives of the individual centre around the self – "I am more important than the country in which I live, I am more important than the company for which I work." The objective of work is to enlighten one's life – it is thus considered a means of personal self-achievement, not just for subsistence. Hierarchy is widely rejected as a form of oppression.

The fourth phase, focusing on self-achievement, arrives when economic development is attained, and when prosperity is a given. This is the pervasive "Me" society of Europe and the US today (Figure 6.11). For example, employees no longer say: "I *work* for company X or Y," but rather: "I *am* a financial analyst (or a marketing manager . . .)." The relationship between the State, society, and the individual is often at odds. To remain competitive, firms find they must adapt their management structures and their corporate cultures to remain in tune with the changing lifestyles and aspirations of their employees.

6.3 From collective to individual values

The model underlines the evolution from a collective set of values, shared by most of the population, to an individual set of values, which

Figure 6.11 – Values for the younger generations? For a younger generation, the concept of working hard and getting rich is simply unattractive, and even sometimes irrelevant. An affluent society has produced a generation that has the choice of its value system. For some, it means having the life they really want. Self-achievement is the real motivator. "Me-ism" (me first) prevails.

is, by definition, very diverse, as it is centred on the individual. This evolution is gradual, and moves in tandem with economic development. In the model, the first and final stages – hard work and self-achievement, respectively – are recognized quite easily. However, delineating the transitions from a collective set of values to an individual set is much more difficult. Such transitions tend to occur when individuals have accumulated a certain level of personal wealth, that empowers them to move to the next motivational phase – self-achievement. In a nation, a wealthy middle and upper class drives this last phase.

The great leap forward

The well-known British historian Angus Maddison has estimated the evolution of purchasing power since year 1 AD. The evolution of GDP per capita for Africa, India, and China is very telling. In the extreme case of China, for example, no additional personal wealth was created for almost 2000 years. The GDP per capita of

China even dropped slightly to $439 in 1950, compared to $450 in year 1 (Figure 6.12). However, during the following 50 years, the GDP per capita of China increased 8-fold to $3583 in 2001. Meanwhile, India has tripled its GDP per capita. Such formidable increases in personal wealth have a considerable impact on our world. The rise of a sizeable middle class, for example in China, will move the dominant value system towards more individualism, challenging the communist system.

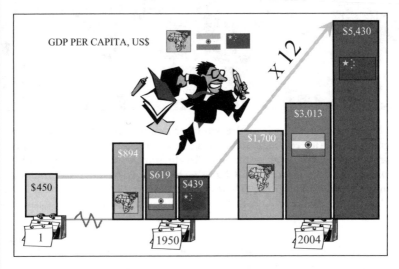

Figure 6.12 – The great leap forward. *Source*: **[3]**.

Japan is today arriving at this fourth phase. Over the past decade, Japanese society has not only endured a prolonged period of economic stagnation, but also a transition within its value system. Japan is entering the phase of self-achievement, while most of the country's structures – social, political, and business – continue to operate as if a collective value system still motivated the Japanese. Slowly, but surely, the Japanese are moving toward a different set of values for their society: they want it to be more transparent, more open to new ideas; a society that expects more accountability from its leaders, and provides greater opportunity to women. Such a society would reward personal success, and would be more tolerant of a greater diversity in lifestyles.

However, evolution within a value system can give rise to tension. Old structures within Japanese society are stretched to the limit, and the relationships between the older and the younger Japanese are strained. Different communication channels influence generations; the power of the media, especially television, music, and the Internet, is prevalent among the young. The rise of a globalised world exposes people to the same products, behavioural patterns, and styles, inciting an individualistic attitude, influenced by the pervasive Anglo-Saxon cultural model.

It is highly likely that such a transitionary phase is inescapable – its roots are not political or cultural, but driven by economic prosperity. The more a nation's economy develops, the wealthier society becomes, the more people tend to move towards a set of values centred on the individual. While the transition cannot be stopped, it can be resisted. Certain nations try to keep out new value systems in their efforts to preserve their ancestral culture: Saudi Arabia does so to preserve an Islamic society, Iran to maintain the primacy of religion in state affairs, China limits Internet access to control the flow of information entering the country, and Dr Mahatir, the former long-term prime minister of Malaysia, became famous for his virulent attacks against Western values.

The law can be used as a tool to counteract influences deemed negative to existing social norms. Again in Malaysia, the "Bumi Putra" law (the law of the sons of the earth) aims at preserving the ownership of business by ethnic Malay. In France, media legislation tries to contain the invasion of a global culture by imposing quotas, protecting and encouraging the production of Francophone music, film, drama, and so on.

In the end, while changes in value systems can be delayed, they can rarely be stopped. The wisest policy, therefore, is to *manage* such shifts

---

Politics and economics

The "economic literacy" of political leaders is a key challenge in many nations – politicians need to have a minimum understanding of economic issues to be able to identify changes and implement new policies. Many politicians do not have the necessary economic policy-making knowledge (Figure 6.13). For example, it would make sense to oblige elected members of legislative bodies to follow a short and basic training in economics and competitiveness of nations, before they legislate. Unfortunately, for many politicians, politics is only about politics, not economics. (Reproduced from [2] by permission of IMD.)

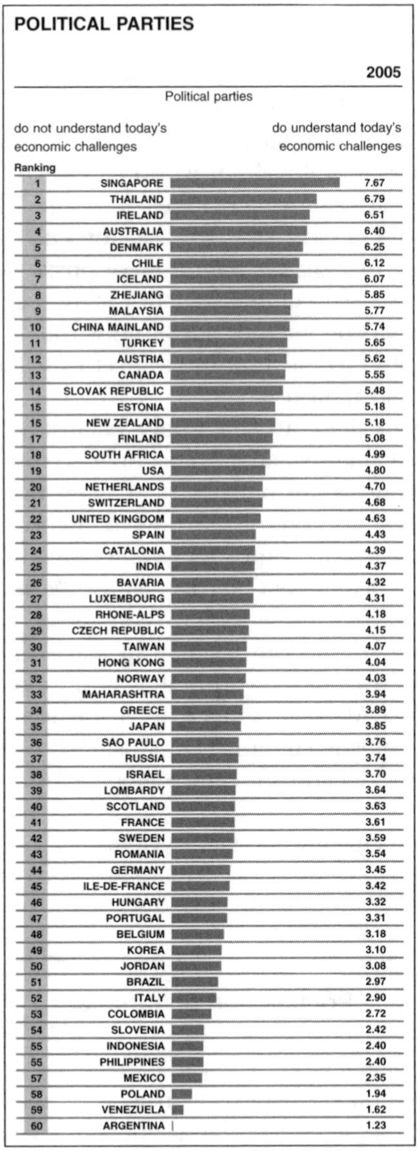

POLITICAL PARTIES

2005

Political parties

do not understand today's economic challenges   do understand today's economic challenges

Ranking		
1	SINGAPORE	7.67
2	THAILAND	6.79
3	IRELAND	6.51
4	AUSTRALIA	6.40
5	DENMARK	6.25
6	CHILE	6.12
7	ICELAND	6.07
8	ZHEJIANG	5.85
9	MALAYSIA	5.77
10	CHINA MAINLAND	5.74
11	TURKEY	5.65
12	AUSTRIA	5.62
13	CANADA	5.55
14	SLOVAK REPUBLIC	5.48
15	ESTONIA	5.18
15	NEW ZEALAND	5.18
17	FINLAND	5.08
18	SOUTH AFRICA	4.99
19	USA	4.80
20	NETHERLANDS	4.70
21	SWITZERLAND	4.68
22	UNITED KINGDOM	4.63
23	SPAIN	4.43
24	CATALONIA	4.39
25	INDIA	4.37
26	BAVARIA	4.32
27	LUXEMBOURG	4.31
28	RHONE-ALPS	4.18
29	CZECH REPUBLIC	4.15
30	TAIWAN	4.07
31	HONG KONG	4.04
32	NORWAY	4.03
33	MAHARASHTRA	3.94
34	GREECE	3.89
35	JAPAN	3.85
36	SAO PAULO	3.76
37	RUSSIA	3.74
38	ISRAEL	3.70
39	LOMBARDY	3.64
40	SCOTLAND	3.63
41	FRANCE	3.61
42	SWEDEN	3.59
43	ROMANIA	3.54
44	GERMANY	3.45
45	ILE-DE-FRANCE	3.42
46	HUNGARY	3.32
47	PORTUGAL	3.31
48	BELGIUM	3.18
49	KOREA	3.10
50	JORDAN	3.08
51	BRAZIL	2.97
52	ITALY	2.90
53	COLOMBIA	2.72
54	SLOVENIA	2.42
55	INDONESIA	2.40
55	PHILIPPINES	2.40
57	MEXICO	2.35
58	POLAND	1.94
59	VENEZUELA	1.62
60	ARGENTINA	1.23

Figure 6.13 – Do political parties understand economic challenges?

in values. If a nation recognises that value systems evolve along the path described in the model, it should introduce the measures needed to adapt to the change. Such measures include not only the modernisation of laws and regulations, but also adjustments in the national leaders' behaviour, so that they are sensitive toward these changes. Indeed, the respect for principles such as accountability, transparency, and so on, mentioned earlier for Japan, apply to all other nations. A failure to adopt measures for increasing accountability and transparency can seriously undermine a nation's competitiveness, since such a failure could result in social unrest.

Value systems within a nation can also be influenced and altered through the globalisation of business operations. Today's global firms can originate in countries operating under different models – when firms move, they take their home value systems abroad. More importantly, firms are generally accountable at home for their actions abroad – if not to the law, then at least to public opinion. For example, legislation passed against corruption, bribery, or money laundering in many countries is not just about business. By imposing strict rules of behaviour on companies, legislators have "exported" their country's values overseas. The extraterritoriality of the law is also a principle that applies to value systems.

6.4   How long do value systems take to evolve?

In our model, nations go through the four phases, though their specific circumstances determine the pace at which they do so. In the case of North America and Western Europe, we can trace the following timeline:

1. The *hard work* phase corresponds with the 19th century Industrial Revolution and the rapid industrial and urban expansion that took place during the early parts of the 20th century. The period after WWI, and during the Great Depression, marks a transition period from the hard-work phase to one stressing wealth accumulation.
2. The emphasis on *wealth* begins in the mid-1930s, and peaks after WWII with the baby-boom generation. Households focused on accumulating private assets and personal wealth, partly to rebuild wealth lost during the Great Depression, and to reconstruct after the damage caused by WWII. This catch-up mentality also exists in Central Europe and China – places that were once relatively wealthy and would like to return to that state of affairs.

3. The *social participation* phase occurred in the US after the Vietnam War, and in Europe after 1968 as a revolt against the established set of values: the focus on hard work and the accumulation of wealth at the expense of individual interests and desires. Both regions experienced demonstrations and civil unrest on a scale unusual for these regions, forcing significant changes in the priorities of the value system. Although the objective of the demonstrations may have been more linked to the immediate concerns of the time – war, racism, sexism, unemployment – at the core, people's value systems had shifted. The 1970s were the transition period to the new value system.

4. The *self-achievement* phase is the name of the game today – but it is quite difficult to predict how long it will last. It began with the phenomenon of the "yuppie" during the Reagan and Thatcher administrations, when achieving personal wealth and doing whatever made you happy became widely acceptable. During this era, different lifestyle options became increasingly accepted within nations, societies, and firms – tolerance became a buzzword.

It took over a century for Europe and North America to pass through the four phases of the model; nations today don't have as much time. Japan, for example, has had to move from hard work to social participation in little more than 50 years. Germany has had to move even faster, and has already reached the stage of self-achievement during the same timeframe. Nations such as Korea, India, and China will follow the same path as other nations through the system, but most likely will do it faster – economic expansion has been very brisk in these regions, and they are exposed increasingly to the value systems of other parts of the world.

6.5 Managing value systems for competitiveness

Intuitively, one could imagine that the more people shift away from a hard working, frugal attitude, the less the model supports competitiveness. This would be true if the competitiveness of a nation depended upon mass manufacturing and repetitive operations. In such cases, motivated, hard working, and cheap labour drives competitiveness – it is why South East Asia and China today are such attractive places for assembling and manufacturing.

However, at a later stage of competitiveness, a nation relies more on innovation and added value than on low labour costs. Collective value systems are not fertile ground for fundamental innovation resulting in new technologies. An individual-driven value system is more amenable to innovation and entrepreneurship – two key drivers of an advanced industrial nation's competitiveness.

In contrast to the innovation of individualistic systems, collective systems are more likely to excel at process, rather than product, innovation, as the case of Japan illustrates. Although it is the second largest patent holder in the world after the US, Japan's patents are not fundamentally for new products (Figure 6.14). A closer look at Japanese patents shows that most of them deal with processes. Japan remains an outstanding implementer of technology, but its value system prizes consensus, and thus deters breakaway innovation that requires the questioning of deeply ingrained ways of thinking.

In contrast, an individual set of values supports breakaway innovation by encouraging people to think, and act, differently – it does not penalise lateral thinking, thereby promoting the freedom to try new things. The tolerance for a diversity of approaches and values, which need not be in line with the commonly accepted values of conventional society, unleashes a huge amount of innovative energy in countries where self-achievement prevails. As a result, in the past two decades, most of the fundamental technological breakthroughs have taken place in the US and in Europe.

The drawback of such an individualistic system is perhaps greater social instability. A mosaic of individual value systems does not necessarily constitute, when aggregated, a national value system. In a self-achievement society, the sense of the common good and solidarity tends to weaken. Laws, regulations, and established practices are often perceived as restrictions on the development of the individual.

6.6 Diversity as the next phase for value systems?

Prior to the four phases, there is no dominant value system. The nation is at a stage of economic development characterised mainly by a multitude of small private businesses, such as craftsmen and street shops. The main objective of most citizens is mere survival. Such a nation is in the early stages of development – real economic take-off has not yet occurred. Political powers have created little adequate infrastructure to promote the economy, and have not succeeded in aligning the country's population behind a common objective. Political instability often prevails – such is the situation we see, even today, in many developing countries.

PATENTS GRANTED TO RESIDENTS

2002

Number of patents granted to residents (average 2000–2002)

Ranking		number
1	JAPAN	110,053
2	USA	86,551
3	TAIWAN	26,964
4	KOREA	24,984
5	GERMANY	19,593
6	RUSSIA	14,454
7	FRANCE	10,737
8	CHINA MAINLAND	5,913
9	ILE-DE-FRANCE	5,077
10	UNITED KINGDOM	4,452
11	NETHERLANDS	2,929
12	BAVARIA	2,923 *p*
13	ITALY	2,298
14	SWEDEN	1,795
15	SWITZERLAND	1,746
16	SPAIN	1,564
17	AUSTRALIA	1,415
18	AUSTRIA	1,349
19	CANADA	1,193
20	RHONE-ALPS	1,038 *p*
21	POLAND	875
22	BELGIUM	783
23	CATALONIA	734
24	ROMANIA	696
25	BRAZIL	680
26	INDIA	537 *1*
27	NORWAY	442 *1*
28	DENMARK	381
29	LOMBARDY	365 *p*
30	NEW ZEALAND	361
31	ISRAEL	346
32	IRELAND	294
33	CZECH REPUBLIC	251
34	ZHEJIANG	214 *p*
35	SLOVENIA	208
36	ARGENTINA	202 *2*
37	HUNGARY	189
38	SINGAPORE	174
39	SAO PAULO	147 *p*
40	SCOTLAND	137
41	MEXICO	123
42	GREECE	114
43	THAILAND	98 *2*
44	FINLAND	96
45	LUXEMBOURG	83
46	SLOVAK REPUBLIC	80
47	MAHARASHTRA	50 *pl*
48	PORTUGAL	44
49	TURKEY	44
50	HONG KONG	27
51	MALAYSIA	25
52	CHILE	21 *2*
53	COLOMBIA	15
54	VENEZUELA	14 *2*
55	ESTONIA	9
56	PHILIPPINES	6 *2*
57	ICELAND	3

Figure 6.14 – Patents and innovation. The absolute number of patents granted to Japanese residents is remarkable and could, at first sight, indicate a high level of innovation. However, most of these patents are linked to processes, or the development of products invented elsewhere. For example, most of the fundamental products that have served as a basis for the formidable expansion of Japanese enterprises come from non-Japanese firms: the transistor was invented by Western Electric, the industrial robot by Unimation, the video recorder by Ampex, the CD by Philips, the photocopier by Xerox. Japanese enterprises have excelled at producing and marketing products – often licensed to them – faster and better than Western counterparts. The value system of Japan supports this type of competitiveness, rather than basic research. (Reproduced from [2] by permission of IMD.)

After the fourth phase, the evolution of the system is a matter of conjecture. First, it is quite unlikely that the system would go backward, which would mean forcing people who are in a self-achievement mode to return to the hard-working phase. The exception to this rule may be the case of war, or extreme catastrophic natural disasters. People, if confronted with such a massive and sudden destruction of wealth, might very well revert to an earlier phase in the system, such as hard work, but probably for a limited period of time. Germany after World War II exemplifies just such a situation.

Nevertheless, in all likelihood, the system only moves forward. So, what could happen after the self-achievement phase? Some would say decadence, using the example of the rise and fall of the Roman Empire, and arguing that the proliferation of self-interests would bring the end of society. While such an outcome cannot be ruled out, there may be another possibility. The system could evolve into a phase called *diversity*, where several layers of the different value systems could coexist.

In the diversity phase, society would accommodate a proliferation of diverse value systems, some collective, some individual, and each of them composed of many disparate subgroups (Figure 6.15). Modern value systems will not necessarily turn into a wild jungle of individualised self-interest – there will always be a contingent of individuals caring for the local community, education, the older generation, culture, or young people at risk. Other individuals will turn their attention to more global issues, such as environmental protection, assisting the development of poor nations, or the fight against global epidemics. The rise in the number and notoriety of nongovernmental organisations (NGOs) is a sign of this trend. The strengthening of a "civil society" may well mitigate the excesses of an all-powerful "self-achievement" society in the future.

6.7   Combining national and corporate value systems

Choice, indeed, characterises the last phase in our model of value systems. The younger generation today have many more choices for their working lives than their forebears. Younger people can be more selective in the work they choose, in the life they want, and in the prosperity level they aspire to, than were their parents and grandparents. For today's parents and grandparents, work was often a question of sheer survival – it provided for the basic necessities, such as food, shelter, and education. In contrast, most of the younger generation in the industrialised world do not need to worry about whether their basic needs will

DISCRIMINATION

2005

Discrimination (race, gender, etc.)

poses a handicap in society   does not pose a handicap
in society

Ranking		
1	ICELAND	8.33
2	BAVARIA	8.16
3	FINLAND	8.03
4	CANADA	8.03
5	AUSTRALIA	7.77
6	THAILAND	7.69
7	AUSTRIA	7.66
8	LUXEMBOURG	7.63
9	GERMANY	7.55
10	PORTUGAL	7.55
11	ESTONIA	7.50
12	ZHEJIANG	7.45
13	PHILIPPINES	7.42
14	TURKEY	7.26
15	SWITZERLAND	7.21
16	LOMBARDY	7.16
17	SINGAPORE	7.05
18	SLOVAK REPUBLIC	6.96
19	HONG KONG	6.94
20	DENMARK	6.88
21	CHINA MAINLAND	6.81
22	GREECE	6.79
23	SWEDEN	6.79
24	NEW ZEALAND	6.75
25	CZECH REPUBLIC	6.74
26	NORWAY	6.65
27	CHILE	6.61
28	ITALY	6.51
29	TAIWAN	6.44
30	SLOVENIA	6.40
31	COLOMBIA	6.38
32	SAO PAULO	6.36
33	UNITED KINGDOM	6.26
34	BRAZIL	6.26
35	BELGIUM	6.23
36	JORDAN	6.21
37	CATALONIA	6.00
38	IRELAND	5.97
39	ISRAEL	5.94
40	NETHERLANDS	5.91
41	SPAIN	5.90
42	HUNGARY	5.86
43	FRANCE	5.73
44	USA	5.69
45	RHONE-ALPS	5.63
46	MAHARASHTRA	5.58
47	MEXICO	5.48
48	ARGENTINA	5.45
49	ILE-DE-FRANCE	5.33
50	MALAYSIA	5.12
51	INDIA	5.11
52	RUSSIA	5.10
53	SCOTLAND	5.05
54	KOREA	4.99
55	JAPAN	4.90
56	POLAND	4.88
57	INDONESIA	4.86
58	VENEZUELA	4.81
59	ROMANIA	4.08
60	SOUTH AFRICA	3.88

Figure 6.15 – Discrimination (race, gender, etc.) and society. A society tolerant of diversity is most likely the next phase of the model. In such societies, cultural and historical backgrounds matter as much as economic development. (Reproduced from [2] by permission of IMD.)

be covered. They have, thus, more freedom to choose their work as a function of their lifestyle, and less because of the income work provides.

Companies need to realise the changes that have occurred in the value system of their employees. Within a firm, the corporate culture is the counterpart of a nation's value system. Corporate culture, therefore, changes over time, as does a nation's value system. In addition, part of the evolution of an individual's value system corresponds with their movement along their career path – various stages in corporate life induce reprioritising within a value system. Companies have to manage the changes in the value system phases of employees just as carefully as a nation must with citizens.

6.7.1 The Tiger, Cat, Bear Model

Three animals – the tiger, the cat, and the bear – serve to model and illustrate the three evolutionary phases of an employee's priorities as they progress through their career. The "tigers" are obviously characterised by aggressiveness and mobility, the "cats" strive for a more balanced life, while "bears" are self-centred and indolent.

The tigers

These are the hard-working, success-driven employees, usually at the beginning of their corporate careers. They are industrious, working more than 60 hours a week, and are dedicated totally to achieving corporate goals (Figure 6.16).

They know that they have to be mobile and willingly accept postings all over the world at regular intervals. They are expert at moving house, and adapt to the life of an expatriate in remote countries. Their career is driven by their ambition: they want to reach the top of the hierarchy quickly, and are willing to do whatever it takes, constantly seeking new prey (hence the name "tigers"). Their family life, if any, is secondary at this stage of their career – they are dedicated totally to the company's future, and corporate recognition is what matters most to them.

The cats

After a certain period of time, the tigers develop into "cats" The success-driven executive gets married, has children, buys a house, gets a mortgage, discovers the maze of his/her children's education system, and so on.

The corporation is no longer at centre stage of the former tiger's pre-occupations: they realise that there is a life beyond the company, and take the time to deal with it. Family becomes more important; so does

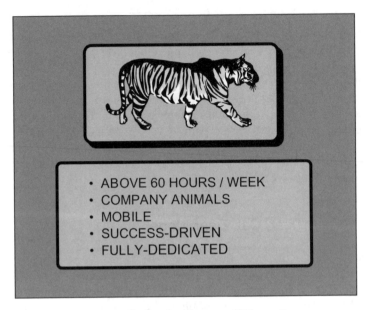

Figure 6.16 – Attributes of "tigers."

quality of life. As a consequence, a cat's working week falls to between 40 and 60 hours, to allow some extra time for the "other life" (Figure 6.17).

Cats are still very mobile, but not in the same way as tigers. They will still accept relocation, but only for longer time intervals. After a certain period, especially when their children approach secondary school, their mobility diminishes drastically. Extensive travelling can take place during the week, but the weekend has to be spent back home with the family. Just like a real cat, corporate cats are also wandering animals, but they need a home base, and are very attached to it.

Cats have a different sense of loyalty to the company. They remain dedicated to the success of their work, and to the objectives of the company, but this is not a complete surrender of loyalty. Cats expect their companies to understand their different needs, their new priorities, and to accommodate their lifestyles. A subtle mix of corporate and personal recognition motivates cats. The corporate value system has to mould to the individual's value system – this is essential for cats to remain high performers in the company.

Cats thrive on the balance of work and life. Until two decades ago, corporate "professionalism" demanded a thick wall between the

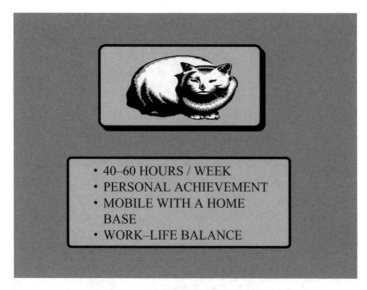

Figure 6.17 – Attributes of "cats."

company and the personal lives of employees. Sometimes, the corporate value system would impose itself on the private sphere. For many years at DuPont, for example, employees had to abide strictly by security measures at home to avoid any sort of accident. Disney imposes a dress and behavioural code on its employees (no beard, long hair, etc.). In addition, abiding by the "dress code" was imposed as a sign of corporate loyalty: a blue or dark grey suit, white shirt, and conservative tie were a "must" for men in many companies.

Today, cats want recognition and acceptance of their private lives and choices. Corporate value systems accept more differences in lifestyle, religious values, and sexual orientation than ever before. Personal problems, such as divorce, anxiety, substance abuse, stress, or health problems, can also be addressed in the corporate environment. Such sensitivity to the life of employees is important to attract and retain cats. Employers of choice have all implemented the necessary policies, recognising that they would not attract the best talent with obsolete corporate values – they admit that the vast majority of employees today are probably cats.

The bears

In the latter part of a working life, cats could turn into bears. Bears believe they have given enough to the company over the years. They

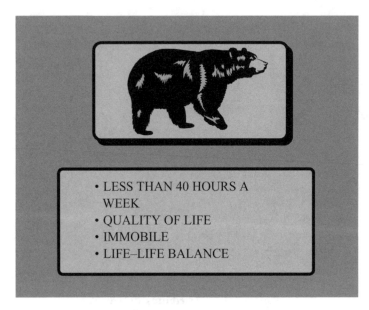

Figure 6.18 – Attributes of "bears."

are now reflecting, not only about their life *outside* the company – when they leave the office at the end of the day – but also about their life *beyond* the company – when they retire.

Gradually, bears shift into low gear. A bear might want to reduce his working week to less than 40 hours, even it means becoming a part-timer. Bears are no longer company-centred: corporate life does not excite them any more. They just cannot get enthusiastic any more for the latest grand strategy, for the results of the next quarter, or for "killing" the competition. They have seen it all, and even the latest reorganisation fails to produce hope or fear for the future. Bears are also less focused on their family, which has grown up and probably left home (Figure 6.18).

Bears now have time for their own lives. Their priority is themselves. For many bears, the main objective is to leave the company at 5 pm and forget everything about it after that until the next day. They no longer care about promotions or new assignments, and are now completely immobile. They want to be left alone. They are interested in *life–life balance*.

Despite this rather unappealing profile, it is in a company's best interests to manage and retain at least some bears. At higher levels in the hierarchy, such employees are often the living memory of the corporation. They have lived the history of the company, its successes, and its failures. They know why and how things work. Such repositories of institutional knowledge are extremely valuable in a corporate world characterised by high turnover in management, and a short-term perspective.

Bears are also found in the lower corporate levels, where employees are involved in repetitive or harsh tasks, for example on a manufacturing site. They can, understandably, be less motivated by grand strategic considerations. In this case, adapting the motivational approach to their objectives is fundamental. A "management by walking around" approach makes management seem accessible and "human" to all levels of the hierarchy. Providing good working conditions (a new cafeteria, facilities for sport or training, etc.) is far more appreciated by bears than a motivational speech on how to kill the competition.

6.7.2 Moving through the Tiger, Cat, Bear Model

The Tiger, Cat, Bear Model (Figure 6.19) has important implications on how a firm should deal with the mobility of its employees. For example, it will become more and more difficult to promote someone abroad who has already settled into the "cat" phase. The firm may have to provide a job for the expatriate spouse – in this phase of their lives, many families are dual-income households. The house mortgage and adjustments in the children's education can also be deterrents to a move. Cats expect a guaranteed, clear return path home.

In the case of senior regional responsibilities, some companies are dealing with this issue by moving the job to the person, and not the person to the job. National executives can gain regional (Europe, Americas, Asia, etc.) responsibility, without having to leave their countries of current residence. In return, the company will probably expect such executives to spend several days a month at the company headquarters. Such flexible approaches have made it possible to retain and promote talent in enterprises, while accommodating the executive "cat" value system.

The model also reveals that enterprises need to have several different layers in corporate values to be able to adapt to distinct employee value systems. A tiger, needs to be nurtured constantly and reassured by the company. Continuous attention needs to be paid to those likely to constitute the next generation of the firm's leadership. Senior executives can act as mentors and guide them as they perfect their job and career skills. Tigers are disappointed easily, and may lose their drive and motivation if they do not get expected promotions or other benefits. In an organisation with few opportunities to rise because it has a flat hierarchy,

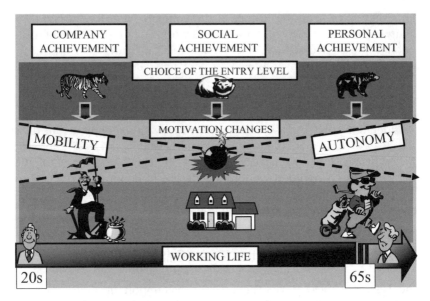

Figure 6.19 – The Tiger, Cat, Bear Model. The model represents the three phases in the evolution of the value system of employees as they move along their career paths – building from company achievement to social achievement and finally, personal achievement. Along this path, mobility diminishes as desire for autonomy increases. Midway, there is a breaking point, indicating an overturn in the value system. If a company fails to pinpoint that moment, a crisis occurs and the employee often leaves.

demoralised tigers do not turn into cats – they generally go elsewhere. Only a few will remain tigers throughout their entire careers and reach the top.

The normal evolution path from tigers to cats to bears does not always hold today. Because of the changes in value systems, some at the early stages of their careers may very well want to shortcut the system, starting their professional careers immediately as either a cat or a bear, with little or no interest in corporate life. Certain types of activity are predisposed to those with an inclination for a certain value system. It is difficult to find a tiger on a factory floor.

6.7.3 Aligning national and corporate value systems

In Figure 6.20, the evolutionary phases in the national value systems are in parallel with those of the corporate value systems (although the

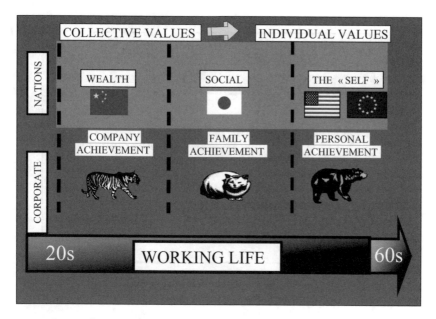

Figure 6.20 – Value systems in nations and in corporate life.

working life time dimension only applies to individuals). Such a paral-lel theoretical approach emphasises the interaction between the national value systems and the corporate culture developed by a company.

In the first phase, this parallel approach highlights the fact that the value system of today's China tends to breed more tigers – people eager to succeed at work. In the second phase, value systems such as the Japanese yield more and more cats – people increasingly interested in social participation and work–life balance. Finally, in the third phase, the Western North American and European model allows more respect for the individual, for his/her interest in self-achievement, and in diversity in general, leading to a high acceptance of bears. Wherever a company operates around the world, it has to take these various stages of devel-opment into account, and, if possible, incorporate them into its own value system.

6.8 Managing the proliferation of cultures in global companies

Howard Perlmutter, a former professor at Wharton Business School, many years ago recognised that national value systems could influence

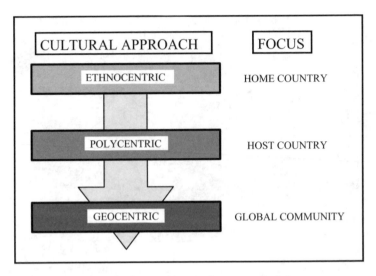

Figure 6.21 – The Perlmutter Model.

how global corporations would select and promote their executives [4]. He has shown that companies can be categorised into three broad types, according to their values and attitude in selecting their managers abroad. These are shown in Figure 6.21.

6.8.1   The ethnocentric approach

In this category of Perlmutter's model, executives abroad are selected mainly from a pool of home country nationals. In general, such a system exists when a company begins its internationalisation process. The heavy reliance on nationals from home reflects a desire to maintain tight control over international operations, which are still perceived as insecure. In addition, it also often reflects a lack of international competencies within the firm. Finally, there may be a cultural element – some nations are less at ease working with other nationalities than others – some corporate cultures are less integrative than others.

Such an ethnocentric approach dominates in many European and US corporations during their early stages of internationalisation. Japanese and Korean companies also have a reputation of remaining very Japanese or Korean, even when they have become big international players with extensive overseas operations. Some Northern European corporations – for example, Tetra Pak, Ericsson, and Nokia – used to be very ethnocentric, at least in their top management.

The advantage of ethnocentrism is the greater unity in corporate value systems it produces. National pride is not totally absent from competitiveness. On the other hand, this is a corporate culture where non-nationals feel left out, or less important. They know that they will never reach the top of the company, because they have the "wrong" nationality. Such feelings of rejection can trigger excessive management turnover.

Ethnocentrism is not necessarily negative. Many foreign employees actually enjoy and appreciate features of a strong home culture. For example, high-tech companies from California carry their aura when they go abroad – people enjoy the less formal Californian atmosphere, the strong entrepreneurial spirit, respect for diversity, a more relaxed dress code. Disney, Coca-Cola, McDonald's and Ikea carry with them elements of their home culture – that is part of their employer brand. It would probably be wrong not to capitalise on it.

6.8.2   The polycentric approach

In this part of the model, executives posted abroad are selected mostly on the basis of citizenship of the host country. For example, an overseas operation in the UK would be headed by a Briton, one in Mexico by a Mexican, and one in India by an Indian. Having a local heading a country's operation reinforces the local image of the foreign firm – it is a strong message of commitment to the local community. In addition, from a legal viewpoint, operations that are incorporated abroad, especially if they are a direct investment, have the nationality of the country of residence. It is usually well perceived when, for example, a "French company of American parentage," (read: the subsidiary of an American company in France) is headed by a French citizen.

For the parent company, polycentrism provides a way to gain greater sensitivity toward local cultures – a local manager might be more aware of taking local differences into account. Local managers can more easily foster close relationships with local customers – if you really want to sell in places such as Spain or Japan, it is advantageous to have a local, well-regarded manager at the head of the affiliate. A more localised approach benefits the customisation and marketing of products, such as cosmetics or food.

On the other hand, polycentrism breeds more complexity – central management has to take cultural diversity into consideration. Polycentrism can also be used, or rather abused, as a means of obstructing instructions from the head office by local managers, weakening corporate alignment: "We just do not do it that way in our country," "People will never accept such a new product."

To maintain corporate alignment and keep an eye out for any centrifugal forces, some companies choose to establish regional corporate headquarters. Such entities oversee the operations in Europe, Asia, or the Americas. These regional headquarters provide a base for polycentric managers to gather, coordinate, and align their policy on a regional basis, before sending it on to country managers and reporting back to central headquarters.

6.8.3 The geocentric approach

The third, geocentric, approach is the most global one – executives abroad are placed on the basis of their competence, not their nationality. The underlying principle is the best person, regardless of nationality, should be selected for the job. In theory, such overseas assignments form part of the firm's meritocracy. In practice, those assigned to these positions have also been recruited to form part of the firm's "fast track." These jobs are given to tigers needing to acquire a diversity of international experiences before being given a more senior, global position back at the company's headquarters. Fast-track executives are highly competent, dynamic, and generally well connected with the top management of the firm. They are also very performance-oriented, knowing their next promotion will depend on the numbers they generate overseas. They are in a rat race for top jobs, and must deliver at all costs.

Yet, the relentless drive for quick success may be precisely the biggest disadvantage of the geocentric approach, as it breeds managers who are more committed to their career in the company, than to the long-term presence of the company in the country to which they have been assigned. Such managers can be short-term in their thinking, appearing "cold-blooded," and end up being resented by customers. Geocentric managers seem always to be preoccupied with their next move. If underperforming, they will leave quickly. If successful, they will also leave quickly. In a geocentric approach, it is very difficult to maintain customer loyalty, or to develop a true bond with employees – there is little commitment to the local dimension on the part of a geocentric manager.

6.9 A new trend: the emergence of the third culture

In today's globalising world, cultural and value systems intermingle, and must find ways of cohabiting. Similar principles apply to corporations, as they have their own particular cultures and values, which form the firm's identity. It would be too much to ask of a company to create a completely different identity and values for each country in which it operates, or to incorporate completely the value system of the local staff. Such measures could compromise the essence of the firm – as well as becoming unmanageable. Therefore, companies strive to get three distinct "cultures" to cohabit in their overseas operations.

1. The *first culture* carries elements brought from the country of origin of the company. An American, a Swedish, or a Japanese company is easily recognised as such abroad – they bring their home values, symbols, and executives to their foreign affiliates. The first culture permeates the firm's local operations, whether to a greater or lesser extent, as we have seen with the ethnocentric approach of Perlmutter's model. No company is entirely global: that is, without trace of a home culture.

2. The *second culture* incorporates elements acquired from the host country. Companies operating abroad cannot ignore the specificities of the culture of the country in which they operate. Their operations must adapt to the local flavour and culture. Business in Saudi Arabia is not conducted exactly as in California.

3. Finally, there is a *third culture* – the global culture developed through interactions across world markets. The third culture is a widely accepted amalgam, bringing together a series of globally accepted values, rituals, symbols, and patterns of behaviour that can no longer be identified as coming from any one culture or nation. In a global world, global people often read the same newspapers, watch the same TV stations, dress alike, speak "international" English, and share a similar vision of success.

The "third culture" is often interlinked to the geocentric approach, and has a profound influence on international companies. Some are even eager to join this third culture as a status symbol, rejecting their home culture in favour of a global one – the yuppies of global business centres, or the rising younger generation of entrepreneurs in former communist countries.

Companies sometimes want to denationalise, distancing themselves from the culture of the country of origin: "We are a global company serving global markets! We have thus a global culture." Erasing home culture links in favour of a one-size-fits-all "global culture" is not always a wise move. The third culture cannot serve as a strong cultural anchor, as it is quite shallow – it is a mix of behaviours and beliefs selected because of their acceptance by a wider community – and not necessarily a guarantee of quality or motivation.

The third culture can only be adopted successfully *on top* of the host and home country cultures. Wholesale adoption of the third culture should not lead to demeaning host or home cultural origins. On the contrary, to be powerful, the third culture needs to be built upon first and second cultures. Companies should not feel compelled to reject either their origins, or the principles of their founders, because they are no longer in vogue, or simply because they want to become global. Roots are essential in business, and should not be considered shameful. Firms should ensure their corporate culture does not include factors of exclusion in a global world – nobody should be ashamed of where he or she comes from.

Managing value systems leads the way to managing people. Individuals have been at the forefront of a revolution in competitiveness, that has so deeply changed the world economic and business landscape during the past decades. The drivers for individual success have changed. The competencies and skills to survive are not the same as before. As we shall see now in the next chapter, *competent people are not necessarily competitive people*.

Competent People and Competitive People: They Are Not The Same . . .

7

> "*We are changing the world faster than we can change ourselves . . .*
> *We are applying to the present the habits of the past . . ."*
>
> Winston Churchill, 1874–1965

While competitiveness and competencies are seemingly related terms, having competencies does not necessarily lead to competitiveness. Education and training certainly can help in developing competitive people – they can provide new competencies, or build upon existing ones. However, highly competent people – those with a high level of competencies – are not automatically high performers. Within academia we find a large concentration of extremely competent people, whose knowledge might be at the top of their field. Yet, a top marketing professor may not necessarily be a good marketing manager. To succeed in the corporate world, one needs more than raw knowledge and intellectual power. Good management transforms *competencies* into *competitiveness* – turning a *resource* into a *result*.

Whether leaders are born or made is debated hotly. Similar debates exist as to whether some managers are competitive inherently, or whether it is a talent that can be acquired. After all, there is clear evidence that some individuals have a seemingly natural aptitude to lead, or to be competitive: they are not afraid of being in the spotlight; many even seek it. To some, competition is an integral part of a way of being – whether in business, life, or sport. Others don't care about competition and being out ahead; they prefer to remain in the background. Some of these can be described as the bears we examined in Chapter 6, who leave the office at the end of the day and forget everything about competitiveness after work. Between these extremes, we find many people who have some level of competitive ability. They are diamonds in the rough – their qualities are not strong enough to surface by themselves, but they can be developed.

The right attitudes reflect the skill of being competitive – successful people and companies show behaviour patterns that set them apart. Competitive companies become icons in the press, to be revered and

Figure 7.1 – How to cope and be competitive. To deal with uncertainty and volatility, companies must develop a broad range of competencies and skills. In parallel, to be competitive at meeting future challenges and increase employability, individuals must possess a vast array of capabilities and experiences.

imitated by other firms. Competitive executives are "shadowed" by their juniors, who wish to learn how to be successful in the corporate world.

Acquiring competitiveness skills requires a hands-on approach to learning; there are no recipes that will produce competitive people with certainty. Instead, it is direct observation, and a compilation of the behaviours and attitudes that have worked in building success, that prove to be the most useful tools in capturing the distinctive features of competitiveness (Figure 7.1). Applying the following principles does not guarantee, but increases, the likelihood of becoming competitive.

7.1 A higher level of energy

> *"Activity is the only means of overcoming adversity."*
>
> Johann Wolfgang von Goethe, 1749–1832

Creating and sustaining a high level of energy throughout an organisation drives its competitiveness. Yet, being in such a high-energy mode is not the steady state of organisations. Entropy – the tendency for a system to become disorderly or randomised – is more likely the norm for an organisation. Individuals, too, aim to reduce their use of energy, while optimising their efforts – "maximum result for minimum effort." With time, individuals become increasingly efficient at performing particular tasks, especially repetitive ones – such changes are referred to as increases in productivity. Firms and other organisations also seek to optimise their efforts. Economies of scale – a fundamental concept in economics – describe how production units are able to increase marginal results, while using less additional effort (or inputs). Henri Fayol (1841–1925) and F.W. Taylor (1856–1915) argued for the "rationalisation" of work – better organisation of the workplace that can lead to better performance. When applied to the production of goods, the results of these principles are increased productivity and an improvement in the cost structure [1].

Such rationalisation and optimisation in the management of energy is part of the effective running of a firm. Nevertheless, to be competitive, tactical injections of higher levels of energy are imperative. During such bursts of energy, maximum effort should be guided and applied at the specific inflection points that will really make a difference for the success of the firm. Gathering energy into outbursts, concentrating on a project, or innovative breakthrough, helps a firm to outpace its rivals. Yet, it doesn't make sense to apply energy all the time – such an undifferentiated approach can be wasteful if the time and place is not chosen carefully.

In addition, employee energy is not managed like a valve that can be opened and closed at will. Managing energy is more like working with a thermostat – if the temperature is either raised too quickly or kept on "high" for too long, people get burned-out. If the energy level is not raised on time or kept on "low" for too long, people can become apathetic or complacent. An important part of an executive's role is to strive to achieve a subtle balance when setting goals for others to meet.

The technique of "stretch goals" can be used to produce such bursts of energy. Their use was quite popular, and indeed effective, during the years when quality breakthroughs were key objectives for companies.

Stretch goals are those that set the performance bar higher than usual, requiring a great deal of energy to achieve. Nevertheless, stretch goals are achievable if energy is focused on their accomplishment. For example, a stretch goal for production would be to move from calculating defect rates in the range of 5 % or 10 % – defective parts per hundred – to calculating defective parts per million (PPM). Such a goal energises employees as they conceive and implement new ways of doing things, and observe their progress toward stated goals. Even if the company does not reach such a level of excellence, it improves its performance considerably by just trying.

Tactical injections of energy at specific moments boost overall performance. Of course, bursts of energy are inherently destabilising, but if well managed and focused on a clear goal, such bursts of energy can motivate and drive higher performance, as they trigger a deep need for action. Periods of the year, such as the general management meeting, or a conference with customers or analysts, can stimulate the company to develop fresh goals, or acquire new attitudes. Energetic firms, or individuals, always try new things, even if they don't have to. They are combative and forward-looking, motivated to be at the leading edge of innovation in ideas, products, and processes, and dread boredom. Energising firms are exciting places in which to work – there is always something interesting going on, to be talked about after hours.

Problems arise with such stretch goals if employees judge them to be unattainable or not "serious." If, after a number of attempts, people are not able to reach the goals, they simply begin to disregard them – they become burned out. If there are too many stretch goals imposed at the same time, people cannot focus their energy into achieving all of them, and they become paralysed. If management's handling of the thermostat is indiscriminate, over time it loses its credibility, and employees their motivation. Finally, if everything is run as if in a state of constant crisis, performance diminishes – it leads to energy-fatigue.

To follow up on Goethe's words, enterprises are organisations created to overcome economic adversity, independent of whether such adversity stems from competition, nonperforming processes, defective products, or demanding customers. A discriminate, high sense of energy gives enterprises the capacity to confront and resolve problems quickly as they occur. Firms and people often lose their competitive edge, not so much because they took the wrong decision, but because they were too late or too slow in implementation. Hence, the second principle.

7.2   A more intense sense of urgency

"We have to be fast enough, and perfect enough."

Carly Fiorina, former chairman and CEO of HP.

The business environment in which companies have to operate today has two main characteristics that affect them deeply:

- business conditions and markets have become open and globalised, and thus can change very fast, building on a *domino effect*;
- volatility prevails, and it has become increasingly difficult to *predict* where market and business trends are headed.

Under such difficult conditions, the business environment influences corporate strategy more than ever. Companies carry out their activities in a world where the "reset button" is pressed at shorter intervals, and it is increasingly difficult to envisage the conditions that they will face at "start-up." Organisations are constantly challenged to keep up with the pace of change.

Yet, preserving a sense of direction, and finding the right balance between what is *urgent* and what is *important*, is not easy. The success of some firms depends precisely on rejecting the pressure to bow to the prevailing environment. Such companies, often privately owned, pride themselves in ignoring the pressures from financial analysts to deliver in the short term, and concentrate on the longer term. Companies operating in niche markets, especially if they have a high degree of differentiation, may also fall into this category. Church, the shoemaker, and Rolls Royce serve as examples of companies that have built their competitiveness by resisting markets fads.

German and Japanese companies have a tradition of emphasising the long term as a key feature of their strategy, while US companies tend to be more focused on delivering immediate results. The legal and regulatory frameworks of these three countries have largely determined the differences in approach. In the German and Japanese model, banks commonly provide a significant part of the capital base of large enterprises – representatives of banks often sit on the boards of these enterprises. Conversely, in the US model, the relationship between banks and firms is more arms-length – in some cases there are even regulations that specifically prohibit banks from serving on the boards of client companies.

An approach such as the German or the Japanese gives firms a higher degree of predictability in preparing their business strategies. Yet, such approaches are also criticised for not pressuring managers into taking painful restructuring steps when business is performing poorly: there is little incentive to act. In contrast, the US model puts pressure on management to deliver good, short-term results, and to change gears as soon as a problem arises: such an approach develops a higher sense of urgency, and an incentive for action.

In the US model, the long-term perspective can sometimes be neglected, because the numbers produced are not acceptable to Wall Street – even when they are caused by a sustained period of investment before better results can be produced (for example, when entering new markets or industry segments).

Such pressure to focus on short-term results, while it has increased in the past decade, should not be seen as entirely negative – it forces companies to restructure quickly when economic slowdowns occur, or when a new business model, such as e-business, emerges. Companies remain agile, and thus can respond quickly to changes in market conditions. As a consequence, management develops a sense of urgency that it instils throughout the firm – it is not only *what* you do that is important, but also *how quickly* you do it.

Dell has turned having such a sense of urgency into a competitive advantage. Michael Dell is quoted as saying: "celebrate [achievements] for a nanosecond, then, move on." Their business model does not rely on a proprietary or unique technology [2]. Rather, it is based on efficiency and speed, thus generating a competitive advantage powerful enough to lure customers away from the competition, even for a product as generic as a computer. Dell recognises that in the modern business environment, customers are not willing to wait, and has structured itself accordingly. Since product information is disseminated online, so that it can be available readily to the customer, order processing and the rest of the value chain needs to be organised accordingly, so that it can operate at matching speed. At Dell, urgency has become a guiding principle for management, and a key determinant of its corporate competitiveness.

Urgency, as a guiding management principle, need not only apply to implementation – it is also a key factor in strategic success. Many strategies fail, not so much because they are ill-conceived, but because management took too long to begin, or complete, implementation. In cases in which firms failed to restructure, it is often striking to see how the remedial actions taken were not necessarily the wrong ones. They were simply implemented too late, or too slowly, or not with enough momentum. Far too often, firms take too long to identify the problem, or to acknowledge a threat to the company, to decide on solutions, or to implement them.

"We study a *good idea*,
until it becomes
a bad one!"

An anonymous CEO

Figure 7.2 – Over kill! The best way to delay making a decision is to ask for one more study about its implications. In fact, it is highly probable that no good idea would pass the test of consecutive studies. Overdoing critical analysis can kill a good idea. It is always easier to say why something will not work, than to say why it will work!

In the mindset of competitiveness, reaction time has to be short, and implementation decisive. Delaying decisions can have a detrimental effect on people and their motivation (Figure 7.2). People prefer it when management deals decisively with events, even if it means some job losses, than when it carries on and ignores the facts. One CEO summarised this dilemma: "we are lousy at firing a few people when needed, but we are good at firing thousands when it's too late." In many cases, a management that cultivates an effective level of urgency as a modus operandi avoids the massive damage that often results from delayed decision-making.

A sense of urgency helps a company to anticipate, and prepare for, market changes. When an organisation thrives on acting and reacting quickly, it needs to have its proverbial finger on the pulse of market trends and customer needs. As a consequence, employees become accustomed to dealing with market conditions, and can identify changes more easily. They pick up the smallest piece of information emitted by the market, and act on it.

Those who question the appropriateness of increasing the sense of urgency as a guiding management principle, raise two objections. First, they point out that people can, and often do, burn out, or at least "switch off," or "tune out." Nothing is more depressing and frustrating in an organisation than managers applying the label "top priority" to every action in the company. It often leads people to question management ability to tell the difference between what is really urgent and what is not! Second, urgency makes people want to do things quickly, and can lead to overall carelessness. Some actions take time, and indeed would suffer from being implemented hastily. Indeed, there are companies that prefer *not* to be a pioneer in a new market, or in innovation. They prefer to observe the pioneer, and learn from their mistakes and successes.

Many large companies employ such a wait-and-see strategy. Rather than entering the market directly and taking the risks such a move would entail, they let others do it for them. Such firms closely follow developments in start-ups of their industry of interest. At just the right moment, such firms tend to buy handpicked start-up companies that have developed successfully, or even launched, a breakthrough product or service. They acquire the firm and its products, and then apply their marketing and distribution power to obtain a competitive advantage. In the IT industry, large companies have developed and launched only a minority of the most important innovations which have, over the past couple of decades, reshaped the market – Internet browsers, electronic spreadsheets, and transaction security. Innovations such as these were developed and launched by smaller firms, later to be bought by the larger IT companies.

A sense of urgency can lead people to devise ways of doing things quickly. It is, however, possible to do things too quickly, breeding carelessness and thereby colliding with the key management goal of quality. Can quality and urgency be reconciled? Many employees would say no, arguing that the pressure to innovate, to market, or to deliver in shorter periods of time, either creates defects or does not allow enough time to address them. Such attitudes are especially ubiquitous in R&D and other "creative" departments. Researchers and engineers and other creative professionals hate being placed under time pressure; they perceive it as an attack on the integrity of their function. They feel that scientific exactitude, innovation, or creativity does not respond well to timetables. This point of view is highly debated in companies today, but increasingly, deadlines also apply for innovation and product launches.

There is a trade-off between quality and urgency; management is there to strike a balance. If the goal is to be 100 % correct, or defect free, it is likely that the company will be 100 % late to market. Of course, the importance placed on quality depends on the critical nature of the product. Some products, like planes, or medical implants, or safety equipment, because their function is critical (malfunctions can be life-threatening), or mission-critical (such as enterprise servers), must aim at being 100 % reliable and defect-free. Other products are not as critical, and hence need not be as dependable. In such cases, it doesn't make economic sense to drive for such a high level of precision – the products' costs could be prohibitive, or they could take too long to develop and reach the market. For the vast majority of products and services offered on market, reaching the six-sigma category (3.4 defects PPM) is superfluous [3].

The driving force created by a sense of urgency is particularly relevant to firms with products with short lifecycles, such as technology companies. In mobile telephony and PCs, products have an average 6 to 12 month lifecycle – the amount of time before a product is rendered obsolete by the following generation. Companies whose products have such short lifecycles have little flexibility in altering the timing or sequence of launching of such products. If a product misses its market window, its arrival on the market might conflict with that of the next product to be launched by the same company, which could be of far greater interest to consumers. When products have such limited lifecycles, companies become their own competitors – they themselves make their products obsolete. There are many examples of products that have been conceived, designed, manufactured, and never launched, simply because it was too late to place them on the market, as they would be cannibalised or compete with the upcoming new version.

Having a sense of urgency also creates within firms the agility necessary to deal with problems effectively as they crop up. The Coca-Cola Company launched *New Coke* in 1985 – the first change in the formula of the popular soft drink in its 99 years of existence. Coca-Cola executives had no idea of the consumer backlash they were about to face. *New Coke* met vehement consumer resistance and even hostility, and even industry experts were surprised. Consumers were simply neither prepared, nor willing to accept, such a bold new initiative. Sales of Coca-Cola collapsed. The firestorm of consumer protest against the company's decision was rooted in how cheated consumers felt. Nobody had anticipated the strength of the bond that existed between customers and "their" brand [4].

Roberto C. Goizueta, then CEO of Coca-Cola, was quick to admit they had made some miscalculations, and changed strategy quickly. He relaunched the original formula as "Classic" Coke. Customers were relieved they were once again able to have "their" product, and sales rebounded immediately. Even The Coca-Cola Company readily identifies the "New Coke" experience as "the marketing blunder of the century." Quick decision-making and effective implementation of

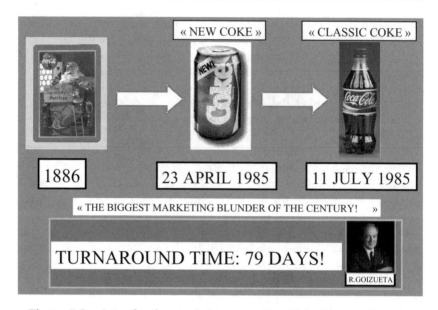

Figure 7.3 – A textbook case in urgency. New Coke serves as a case study illustrating the need for urgency in making decisions that will save a company. Companies can indeed survive the worst situations if they are quick to realise they made a mistake, fast to react, and flawless in implementation. "The biggest marketing blunder" of the century, according to the company itself, is now an example of good management: 79 days to turn the situation around! Roberto Goizueta will be remembered as one of the best US managers.

corrective strategy in the face of an impending crisis, limited the long-term damage for the company and its products (Figure 7.3). Within a few years, Coca-Cola was, once more, one of the most admired companies in the United States.

When analysing the experience ten years later, Goizueta described it as "a prime example of intelligent risk-taking." Such intelligent risk-taking stemmed from the existence of a sense of urgency – urgency to accept the facts, urgency to decide, and urgency to implement. The relatively short time-span involved demonstrates the strength of the sense of urgency – New Coke was launched on 23 April 1985, Classic Coke on 11 July 1985 – a mere 79 days, during which Coca-Cola was saved from the brink of disaster [4]!

7.3   A deeper sense of purpose

> *"If a man does not know to what port he is steering, then no wind is favourable to him."*
>
> Seneca, 5BC–65 AD

To be competitive, leaders must have a strong sense of purpose guiding their internal compass. Numerous books have been written to describe the unique vision that has taken an entrepreneur "from rags to riches," or to competitive success. Every great entrepreneur has been driven by a vision – from Henry Ford, who wanted to afford every American household the opportunity to own a car, to Bill Gates, who aims to put a PC, originally on every desk, but now also in every home. While these individuals had clear visions in mind, they fine-tuned them during the course of business – thus, the key issue is how much of the vision should a visionary have worked out at the onset, and how much of it evolves and is developed over time. One can even stretch it as far as asking whether it is possible to run a business competitively, *without* an overarching vision.

William McKnight, former chairman of 3M, emphasised that he was not driven by any specific, grand vision when he ran the business – he simply wanted an atmosphere where managers "try a lot of stuff and see what works." Dave Packard, the co-founder with Bill Hewlett of HP, expressed a similar sentiment. Back in their garage, at the onset of their enterprise, they were not quite sure what their new company would do – they simply assumed, sooner or later, they would find a product they would be able to sell. It turned out that their first commercial success was their audio oscillator, purchased by Disney for the movie Fantasia. As they expanded, they hired people who shared in their entrepreneurial spirit, without necessarily having a pre-established direction in which they were heading.

There is a difference between *vision* and *purpose*; a difference which is often blurred in the minds of most. A company can indeed prosper if it has a strong sense of purpose, and a weaker vision. Purpose justifies the *existence* of a company; vision justifies a *strategy*. A sense of purpose precedes, and gives *meaning* to, a vision. While a company obviously depends on profits and success for its long-term survival, being solely a profit mercenary is not enough to motivate employees, or attract customers. The purpose gives the company its *raison d'être* beyond making profits, and gives meaning to the work of employees.

William McKnight and Dave Packard had a clear sense of purpose, if not yet a vision, when they started their businesses. Peter Drucker argues that the main purpose of a company is "to create a customer," while

Henry Mintzberg suggests corporations are social institutions: "if they don't serve society, they have no business existing" [5]. Whatever it is, a sense of purpose gives meaning to work *beyond* the work itself.

The Great Depression, and the hardships it caused employees, were formative to the sense of purpose of HP. Bill Hewlett and Dave Packard wanted a firm which reconciled corporate objectives and employee needs constantly. The founders believed a firm should show consideration to both the private lives of employees, and their personal beliefs. Thus, their basic tenet of management is to provide a sense of purpose and the right working environment for employees – under these two conditions, employees *naturally*, without coercion, perform well. Such a stance might have been adopted simply because it seemed to be correct morally to do so. But it also proved itself to be a very powerful business concept.

Just like a competitive leader is guided by a strong sense of purpose, the competitiveness of a firm also needs strong points of reference. In a change-driven environment, employees need at least some enduring statements or principles upon which they can base themselves, like sailors when navigating. If weather conditions change suddenly, or when enveloped by fog in open seas, sailors can lose sight of the coast, or their sense of direction and location. In such circumstances, while there is a sense of apprehension, they turn to the most stable and reliable instrument on-board ship – the compass. Because it provides a way to determine direction, a compass provides comfort.

A compass always points north – it gives one a sense of direction, of where one is headed. Even if you do not know *where you are*, at least you know *where you are heading*. An enterprise also needs some means – usually the corporate culture – of providing a strong sense of direction and purpose. The corporate culture can encompass a set of visions, principles, customs, and practices that prevail, and change very little over time. While resilient strategies adapt to accommodate new circumstances, the sense of purpose needs to be stable, transparent, widely held, and understood across the organisation. Managing is *not* only about change; it is also about providing islands of stability and direction (Figure 7.4). At the end of the day, many employees are worn out by change for the sake of change, especially if they themselves do not understand its purpose.

Its sense of purpose – *for what* a company stands – also dictates the code of conduct of the firm – *how* it goes about its business: the behaviours, attitudes, and ways in which business is conducted within and outside the organisation. A company is not merely a collection of assets, people, products, and processes – it needs something to hold it all together. Corporate culture acts like the glue, providing the institutional memory holding all of the pieces together, especially during turbulent

A SENSE
OF PURPOSE...

LEADERS
SHOULD LEAD THE WAY

(EVEN IF THEY ARE LOST)

**Figure 7.4 – A leader's ultimate responsibility. The ultimate
responsibility of leaders is to lead the way – even if they are lost. The
last thing most want to find out is that their leader has lost the way.
If one is temporarily lost as a leader, it is better to say nothing and
continue, while you figure the way out – as long as you have your
overall sense of purpose, this is only a minor deviation. A sense of
purpose, just like a compass, gives direction – even when you lose
your bearings briefly in the stormiest of weather.**

times when uncertainty prevails. Therefore, having a strong corporate
culture supports competitiveness.

Moreover, firms whose corporate culture contains a strong ethical
component, have a strategic advantage in attracting and retaining the
most talented people in the labour force. How these firms behave in the
marketplace, vis-à-vis competitors, customers, and suppliers, provide
strong indications to employees of how the firm will treat them. To
remain competitive, today's firms need to be recognised as employers
of choice – especially to rising generations of workers and consumers.
If a company has a good reputation, employees easily brag to friends
during cocktails about working there.

More and more, people come to expect a choice in the type of organisation for which they work. Since World War II, sixty years of economic
expansion have created an unprecedented accumulation of capital in
households in the industrialised world, leading to a major shift in
people's views toward work. Especially within the well-educated, upper
echelons of society, work is no longer a means of survival; it is one of
personal fulfilment. Rising generations are increasingly vocal about
expecting corporate acceptance of diverse value systems relating to

environmental protection, ethics, and respect for diversity in lifestyles and cultures. No company can succeed if it ignores the beliefs of its employees, and does not incorporate them into the firm's sense of purpose and corporate culture.

To retain a competitive edge, companies can no longer count on simply being good at business – they should also aim at becoming admirable from a societal point of view. As a consequence, many companies have taken a broader approach, and have deepened their sense of purpose by including responsibility to the communities in which they operate as a corporate value. Shell and BP support environmental programmes beyond those related to energy consumption; the Body Shop is active against product testing in animals [6]; General Mills finances school programmes; Microsoft, through the Bill and Melinda Gates Foundation, fights diseases in the developing world. On the other hand, companies in industries like tobacco, alcohol, or even defence, might at times encounter difficulties in recruitment. Some people shy away from opportunities in such companies, as they would find it difficult to justify themselves to family and friends.

In recent decades, employers have begun to realise that monetary rewards and opportunities for career promotion are decreasing in their ability to motivate employees. In 1959, Frederick Herzberg, in his seminal work *The Motivation to Work*, identified "sense of belonging" as one of the upper levels of motivation. Increasingly, a company's competitiveness is driven by its *cultural attractiveness*, as derived from its sense of purpose [7].

Bill George, CEO of Medtronic, one of the leading medical instrumentation companies in the world, illustrates the importance of culture in career decisions. He was contemplating leaving his position at Honeywell, where he was on the path to becoming CEO, to take a more discreet job at Medtronic. He recalled: "Honeywell was changing *me* more than *I* was changing Honeywell. I wasn't building anything; I wasn't creating anything. Sure, I was leading, but I no longer knew where my leading was leading to . . ." [8]. He left his job at Honeywell to become COO, and then CEO, of Medtronic. The sense of purpose he found Medtronic could give him was more in tune with his own sense of purpose than what Honeywell was able to provide for him. It proved to be a mutually beneficial decision – under his leadership, Medtronic's market capitalisation has risen from $1.1 bn to $60 bn, with a compound return of 35 % a year.

Unfortunately, leaders are not always good at providing a clear sense of purpose to their firm, and/or to the public community at large. Their communication skills are often poor. But leaders lead not only by words, or by strategy, but also by their own attitudes, behaviours, and actions.

Management by walking about is a powerful tool for motivating and leading people. Short, informal, and unplanned meetings with employees in their own workplace serve, not only as opportunities to convey important business and emotional messages, but also as an opportunity to build the communal sense of purpose.

Finally, leaders should make sure to keep in touch with followers. Some leaders are so obsessed with their own sense of purpose, or their vision of the business, that they fail to make sure that others in the firm share their passion. Franklin Delano Roosevelt encapsulated that situation when he said: "A good leader cannot go too far from followers!" Sometimes leaders should indeed turn around and see if anybody is behind them . . .

7.4 A stronger sense of resilience

There are few certainties in economics, but one of them is that cycles do exist – some times are good, other times are not so good. The problem with economic cycles is that nobody knows when they start, for how long they will last, nor when they will end. The only way to survive cycles is to be resilient – to be able to recover quickly from setbacks. Being resilient is not just about being flexible. The term, originating from the physical sciences, implies an ability to bounce back quickly into shape after being subject to stress or strain. Both individuals and firms, as illustrated by the "New Coke" example used earlier, need to be resilient in order to maintain their competitiveness. Keynes identified resilience as one of the major qualities of a competitive economy [9].

*"Success consists
in going
from failure to failure
without loss
of enthusiasm."*

Winston Churchill, 1874–1965

During the Internet bubble, it was not unusual to encounter companies where most of the executives were very young, most likely fresh out of college, with little or no experience. In many such enterprises, especially in telecommunications or the Internet, it was common to find a majority of employees with less than three years' work experience. The exponential development of the economy in the late 1990s led to a frantic need to hire new people as quickly as possible, to be able to cope with ever-expanding business. In some cases, larger companies would acquire smaller ones simply to gain quick access to qualified staff, that it would otherwise take too long to recruit and train. Times were good; there were a number of years with record earnings. Profits exploded. Salaries and stock options followed this exuberant trend. For many, the sky was the limit. Some started to doubt that it could last forever. The latter were right . . .

The markets yielded to a long and painful period of correction. For the first time in their working lives, these young employees were faced with an adverse business environment – their world was falling apart. Many of the "heroes" of the day were found to have committed "accounting irregularities," and if they were not fined and/or jailed, at least most had to resign their lucrative positions. Surviving employees were not exactly in a positive frame of mind.

Besides the business impact, periods of recession have a huge psychological impact on employees. Younger employees, fresh from the Internet bubble, suffered even more, as they had not yet developed coping mechanisms to deal with unemployment and diminished opportunities. In fact, they didn't believe such "corrections" could ever occur. Other employees, some of whom had left their "steady jobs," to jump on the risky bandwagon of a new start-up, felt betrayed. Most of these individuals ended up becoming depressed and in despair – they only knew how to manage themselves in a successful environment. Having no previous experience with business cycles, they didn't have the resilience necessary to deal with a gloomy situation.

Anybody can manage well in a successful streak – an expanding economy is a very forgiving environment. Brisk sales growth can mask many, many mistakes, and even the mismanagement of resources. Conversely, tough times reduce allowances for mistakes considerably – only the best survive. Recessions, thus, can be seen as opportunities to identify the most resilient people and organisations.

Niels Bohr, a noted 20th century Danish scientist, stated: "forecasting is very difficult, especially when it is about the future." All jokes aside, Bohr touches upon a fundamental aspect of life and business – the future never arrives when, where, and how you expect it. The fall of the Berlin

The future never happens when and where you expect it

Figure 7.5 shows The Beatles at the beginning of their careers – who would have thought that the biggest revolution in modern music would have started in a shabby cellar in Liverpool? The future is anything but predictable. Most of the events which have shaped our modern world could not be foretold. The ability to overcome temporary discomfort, to confront adversity, and to be resilient, are important survival qualities.

Figure 7.5 – The Beatles.

Wall, the Internet revolution, terrorism, epidemics, and wars, are some of the most recent major changes in our environment that have affected the way firms operate drastically. Yet, none of these events, or their effects, could ever have been forecast.

Resilience applies to people, to strategies, and to organisational structures. Rather than trying to second-guess the future, which is, by nature, unpredictable, it is much more efficient to develop the capabilities necessary to react faster and better than competitors.

To confront future situations effectively, firms and individuals need to rely upon a broader range of capabilities and competencies. Moreover, one can prepare better by thinking through possible alternative scenarios, identifying and acquiring the skills and resources necessary to manage them. Shell has a long tradition of determining possible scenarios with which it may be confronted in the energy sector, and developing possible strategies to deal with them ahead of time. Such strategic scenario planning serves as an early warning system that allows companies to identify new imbalances in the business environment quickly, and to create pre-made strategies with which to react faster than the competition.

There comes a time when resilience is even more valuable – the half-way syndrome (Figure 7.6). In almost every project or task, there is a

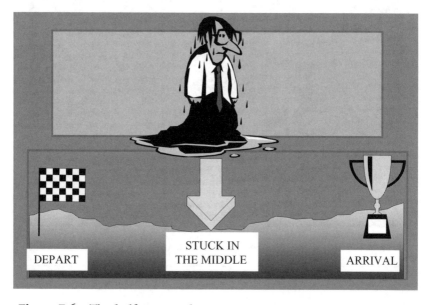

Figure 7.6 – The half-way syndrome. Just as a company's strategy can be "stuck in the middle" between two objectives (for example, between cost leadership and differentiation), people are often in the same situation. In any project, there is a starting point, clearly defined, and a motivating goal. It is easy enough to begin a project, or conclude it. The difficulty arises at the mid-point – where neither the beginning nor the end seems to be in sight. At that point, those involved in the project often feel stuck and abandoned; resilience provides the means and necessary drive for them to forge ahead and finish. Such situations serve as good tests to identify the most competitive individuals or teams in the organisation.

specific moment where one begins to feel stuck. Such feelings arise at the point where one has advanced far enough from the starting point that it would be difficult, or almost impossible, to go back, yet where there is still no end in sight. This middle point is riddled with solitude, intense doubt, and, even at times, despair. There is no light in sight at the end of the tunnel. The middle point is a turning point – it is the point at which it is essential to draw upon one's sources of resilience to continue, rather than staying stuck, or abandoning the project or task.

Those individuals who have the capacity to rebound and find renewed energy "in the middle of nowhere" tend to make the most competitive managers. Some people naturally have a large degree of resilience – they can weather turbulence, manage themselves in uncertainty, and face the possibility of failure. Others might need some help getting started – certain personal development programmes can aid in developing resilience skills. In such programmes, individuals are placed in difficult and stressful physical situations, such as a forest survival trek, mountain climbing, or white-water rafting, and learn to draw upon their inner strengths to overcome the challenges they face. Resilience is a fundamental survival skill for the competitiveness of an individual – it stems from an attitude conducive to always looking for the proverbial silver lining in any situation. Like Thomas Edison, these individuals can say: "I have not failed; I have just found 10 000 ways that don't work . . ."

7.5   A more acute sense of timing

> *"It is very wrong to be right before everyone else."*
>
> Montaigne, 1533–1592

As we have seen, energy, urgency, purpose, and resilience are key ingredients to competitiveness. Timing is also fundamental to success. Being able to do things at just the right moment is essential in management, yet it is one of the most difficult things to achieve – it is all too easy to either procrastinate, or act in haste. A good idea at the wrong moment in time is actually a bad idea! An idea that did not work many years ago is not necessarily a bad idea – it might simply have been an untimely one (Figure 7.7).

In August 1993, Apple introduced *Newton* – the first personal digital assistant (PDA). *Newton* was quite a remarkable technological achievement, intended to revolutionise how people managed their appointments and contacts. Yet it flopped on the market for two reasons: its price was too high, and it failed the "pocket test" – it did not fit into an average

Figure 7.7 – A good idea at the wrong moment. When Apple launched
the Apple Newton Personal Digital Assistant in August 1993, it seemed
to be a good idea. However consumers – as well as the technology –
were not ready for the launch. John Sculley, the then CEO of Apple,
lost his job, in part, because of this mistake. Yet, only a few years
later, the PalmPilot, with the same overall concept, became a huge
success. PDAs are now sold all over the world. However, the lesson
remains: a good idea at the wrong moment is still a bad idea. (Apple
Newton and Apple are trademarks of Apple Computer, Inc., registered
in the US and other countries; PalmPilot is a trademark of Palm Inc.,
registered in the US and other countries.)

shirt pocket. A few years later, in 1996, Palm introduced the PalmPilot
– a very similar product to the Newton – paying special attention to the
marketing strategy: the PalmPilot did fit into a shirt pocket! The second
time around, the PDA concept was a huge success. The market was
ready for it, and today, PDAs are part of the lives of millions of users.

Sometimes, timing is about the convergence of a series of seemingly
unrelated events. In 1973, Fischer Black and Myron Scholes published
their famous theory for the pricing of options – recognition was immediate [10]. A few months earlier, the Chicago Options Exchange had just
opened: Black and Scholes's theory was exactly what the exchange
needed to have a solid foundation for option trading. In addition, Texas
Instruments and Hewlett-Packard were flooding the market with hand-
held financial calculators, allowing traders to calculate the value of

options immediately. In this example, timing was perfect; a convergence of events made the market ready for such new ideas.

Having a good sense of timing is a powerful competence. Business breakthroughs, such as those of McDonald's, Ikea, or Dell, usually contradict the established business model of their time. Yet, no matter how unusual they may appear at the time, they are never totally out of line with the emerging demands of consumers – in fact, they are responding to unmet demands. There is always a small window of opportunity between an old business model and a new market demand, and it is in that space that entrepreneurs thrive, by seizing new opportunities that others have missed.

Nokia's success is underpinned by the fact that it identified just the right moment when mobile phones evolved from being a piece of technology for "techies," and increasingly began to be considered a trendy, fashionable item, appealing to different types of consumers. As a consequence, they asked Italian designer Frank Nuovo to design their famous silver model, the 8810, which was introduced in 1998. Nokia had identified an inflection point, where the market was ready to merge technology and fashion. Swatch serves as a similar example. The CEO, Nicolas Hayek, revived a declining company, then called SMH, by identifying a specific moment in time when people were ready to change their perception of a watch [11].

Hayek believed that people could stop looking at watches as occasional, long-term purchases, and instead think of them as fashion accessories. In his view, people would be willing to buy several low-cost watches a year, and to change them, just as they changed their sweater. A watch would no longer be perceived as a luxury item only, or a precious jewel, or even as a simple timekeeping instrument. A watch could now become an item expressing emotion for a *moment* in time. Again, it was the right idea at the right time, contributing to the revival of the Swiss watch industry.

Maintaining a sense of timing is very subtle, as it implies having the patience necessary to differentiate between what matters most, and what matters less. As mentioned earlier, some executives treat everything as urgent, out of fear they might miss something. They are unable – or unwilling – to prioritise. Such executives cause organisational burnout, and produce sceptical employees.

A sense of timing helps when determining the right moment for injecting a shot of energy and innovation into an organisation. A sense of timing is a soft skill, which comes from the intimate knowledge of the industry sector in which an executive operates – in plain words, it's a gut feeling. After being active for many years in a certain type of activity or environment, individuals develop a kind of *sixth sense*, which alerts them when something should happen and is not happening, or when new phenomena occur in their field. While it is hard to convince colleagues or business partners something should be done simply because you have a "strong gut feeling," very often such intuition proves to be correct.

Total immersion in a business activity sensitises executives to regular patterns of events or behaviours; it also makes them aware, even unintentionally, of subtle clues and signals others might easily miss. These perceptions are not wholly analytical, but rather, form part of a permanent synchronisation and symbiosis with the business environment. Companies are aware of the importance of executive responsiveness to the business environment, and therefore find it useful to devote significant time and resources on "total immersion" experiences for them. Annual industry conferences, or corporate retreats, are tools to help executives get "in sync" with their business and corporate environment. These measures ensure that executives become more sensitive and permeable to changes, and increase the likelihood that they will react intuitively in a timely and appropriate manner.

Looking at issues through the lens of timing reinforces an individual's resilience. Timing (or untimeliness), therefore, provides an acceptable explanation for risk-taking and failure, without jeopardising one's self-esteem: it is not my fault, it was just the wrong moment. In this way, a sense of timing provides a coping mechanism for failures or setbacks, protecting the person's dignity and integrity, and is, thus, very valuable for developing people's self-confidence, and maintaining a high level of motivation. Looking at setbacks as the results of untimeliness means that a second opportunity is possible in the future. Entrepreneurs rely on this aspect to be able to forge ahead through the most trying of circumstances – "I am *always* right, it is just a matter of knowing *when* . . ."

7.6 A stricter sense of alignment

The ability to align corporate objectives, people, and processes is one of the key challenges of today's managers. The internationalisation of business, decentralisation of responsibilities, and a more individualistic culture, have created companies that might look like a patchwork quilt of entities and behaviours to outsiders. In order to operate competitively, the different parts, people, and ideas of an organisation need to be in alignment with overall corporate strategy. Such alignment in business requires the existence of mechanisms and systems that improve relationships, maintain the flow of information, and ensure common agreement about the strategy and its implementation.

Clearly, alignment goes beyond agreement in reach and scope – it requires, not only accepting that the action is worthwhile, but also signals commitment to achieving the result. A pleasant attitude is: "Why don't you do it and tell me if it works . . . ?" To be in alignment, you not only agree with something, but commit yourself to making it happen – "we agree, now, let's do it . . ." While there is lot of agreement in companies today, there tends to be very little alignment – "Yes-men" are more numerous than "doers."

Having spent 28 years of his life in jail, when he was finally released on 11 February 1990, Nelson Mandela owned few possessions. In particular, to continue his political activities, and to travel within South Africa, he needed a car. But how could he get one without savings or a job? Mercedes-Benz workers in South Africa wanted to help him, and approached the management of the company to see what could be done. After discussion, an agreement was reached to get Mandela a car: the workers agreed to provide the labour, while the company provided the parts and the use of the factory, all free of charge. As a result, in 1990, at the Sisa Dukashe Stadium in Mdantsane, the company workers presented Nelson Mandela with the gift of a superb red Mercedes-Benz, which became a legendary item in South Africa.

This story is not just about people caring for Mandela, but also about how motivating forces can help accomplish anything. Mandela's car was produced in record time, and with fewer defects, than the plant had ever managed in a single vehicle. However, there was more than motivation at work here – more importantly, there was a clear alignment of objectives between the company and the workers, and that alignment drove competitiveness.

Alignment as a business imperative first arose during the drives toward standardisation and specialisation of labour in manufacturing, and the development of supply chains across organisations. For the entire system to be able to produce efficiently at the lowest possible cost, meant a number of elements in separate locations had to be kept aligned – they had to each understand their specific role and timing across the entire value chain of production. Further refinements in alignment came with the quality drives – it was no longer about working together, but working with others to produce *better*.

Quality provides a common reference point to build alignment across multiple interconnected value chains. As a consequence, the management of processes within and between enterprises is being streamlined constantly, made more efficient, and, especially, standardised. Once it became possible to align *processes*, within and among organisations, companies could then proceed to a further extension of the notion of alignment – aligning *information*.

The alignment of information has been made possible, to a great extent, by the leaps and bounds in the development of information and communication technologies. It is now possible to connect every process and every machine, within and across firms, seamlessly: this has made the Extended Enterprise Model workable. The enormous availability of information, and the ease with which it can be exchanged, has modified profoundly the way companies are managed and operated.

The exchange of information is not only aligning people, resources, and processes across the organisation – it is also a way for individuals to uncover their position, as well as that of others, in the pecking order of the organisation, and what are they up to. Thus, *transparency* is increased greatly throughout the organisation. It becomes evident rapidly when somebody is off-track, or outside the loop. As a consequence, it is increasingly difficult for anyone to spend his career *unnoticed* and *immune* to the pressure of an organisation. Uncompetitive people are more exposed.

There is indeed greater alignment – and greater need for it – within companies today than ever before. For management, it has become much easier to identify, and suppress, pockets of resistance within the organisation. As we have already seen, corporate strategies rely increasingly on creating and sustaining a shared sense of urgency, the resilience of the organisation and its staff, and in careful timing of implementation throughout the organisation and the value chain. Obtaining alignment is thus essential for competitiveness, since it ensures that large, international companies remain decisive and agile organisations.

As a consequence of the drive to achieve alignment, companies today are more centralised in their strategy and culture. Alignment serves as a centripetal force, creating a unified core of corporate strategy and culture, and ensuring that there is compliance throughout the organisation. Because implementation of strategy is increasingly left in the hands of those at the periphery, alignment becomes ever more important as a tool of corporate control – the periphery's actions are shaped and guided by the corporate culture, and must comply with the overall strategy emanating from the core of the organisation.

Greater reliance on alignment with core values and strategies can, at times, make an organisation quite vulnerable to committing strategic errors. If there is too much alignment – to the point when there is no opportunity for disagreement to be voiced – top management becomes cut-off from the organisation and feedback mechanisms. The mistakes of a few at the top of an organisation can cascade downward very quickly, and there is no safety net to catch them – a system of checks and balances can be short-circuited. Therefore, top management needs to be more balanced than ever in an aligned organisation, and avoid situations in which its thinking becomes self-reinforcing. To avoid these pitfalls, alignment depends strongly on the strength and transparency of the corporate culture.

7.7 A higher degree of confidence, but not of arrogance

> *"Success is dangerous; one begins to copy oneself. It is more dangerous than to copy others; it leads to sterility!"*
>
> Pablo Picasso, 1881–1973

Arrogance has killed more companies than any strategic mistake. To be confident in oneself, and in the company one works for, is essential for success. Yet, an excess of confidence won't work. Customers and employees want to deal with, and work for, enterprises that know their way, and with people who have a sense of purpose and success, as described earlier. There is, however, a fine line between confidence and arrogance: a line that should never be crossed. High self-confidence and self-worth are important to being a competent individual – such individuals know very well their strengths, as well as their weaknesses.

Problems arise when such self-evaluations turn into arrogance; because there is no sense of self-criticism or, indeed, humility. This sentiment is well captured by a comment once made to me – "we became victims of our own reputation when we started to believe what we were telling others . . .".

Once an organisation starts to take itself overly seriously, it can quickly turn into a dinosaur – the organisation becomes incapable of adjusting its business model to new conditions in its operating environment. Such arrogance in organisations fosters "know-it-all" and "seen-it-all-before" mentalities. "I have been in the car business for 30 years; I know that Americans will never buy small cars . . ." was the common response of automotive industry representatives during the early 1970s, when the Japanese car industry started to compete fiercely with US companies.

Why was the Japanese automotive industry so competitive? Of course, it had a strong business model; it produced smaller, energy-efficient cars, with a focus on excellent manufacturing quality, aggressive pricing, and plenty of exciting options for paying customers. In addition, however, the Japanese manufacturers realised that they built cars to please customers *outside* the company, not for the engineers *inside* the company, forcing a customer-centred marketing approach with plenty of *customisation*. They were selling a driving experience for customers, not a technological experience for engineers. Such an approach made the company outward-oriented, and more immune to the development of arrogance. Regularly spending time on the production line and with customers are good antidotes to arrogance.

However, to be successful, these visits need to be honest efforts to obtain the *truth*, rather than *reaffirmation*. CEOs and senior executives of large companies perform field visits regularly. Executives are usually keen to meet customers, yet, most of these visits are carefully orchestrated affairs. Which customers are the CEO's handlers more likely to choose – the disgruntled ones, who will raise issues and help the company to improve, or carefully selected admirers, who believe that a friendly relationship with the top could be helpful one day? A visit is deemed successful if it is one that doesn't create any problems or raise any issues. The CEO returns home, confident that all is calm on the front, and that the situation is under control. In reality, the firm has cut itself, and the CEO, off from reality. The priority has been to reinforce one's own feeling of superiority and excellence. That is the making of a complacent organisation.

7.8   An enduring passion for reinvention, and against complacency

Success can boost morale and build justifiable pride in one's achievements. However, success can, as we have seen, lead to arrogance. It can also breed complacency: a stage at which one becomes satisfied and absorbed in oneself. In general, a complacent firm or individual becomes indifferent to competitive factors in the environment: customer needs, and customer sensitivities. The consequence of complacency is a failure to adapt and to innovate. Inaction becomes the *modus operandi* of such firms and individuals.

Complacency is self-serving. Once successful, there is a real danger for companies and individuals to become more interested in validating themselves and the business model that brought them to such heights, than in understanding and responding to the market conditions and future challenges. Executives who reach the top of an organisation are, in all likelihood, the product of a successful business model that they themselves have implemented well. Both firms and individuals are, thus, reluctant to question those very same management principles that brought them to the top.

As we have seen earlier, in tightly aligned companies, top management can be cut off from reality, and the rest of the firm, by their handlers: the yes-men, whose primary role is to carefully control access to the chiefs, and filter the information, criticism, and problems they receive. These structures exacerbate a feeling of superiority, but also build isolationism. In many cases, top management is the first culprit for developing complacency, simply because it has allowed the hierarchy to cut it off from the rest of the world. Indeed, it can be surprisingly quiet at the top.

Listening is an art in management. Very few leaders know how to listen. They are much more used to communicating *to* others, to describing the world as they see it, and giving instructions on how to do things, rather than *receiving* information and feedback. Further, being always on the *emitting* side does not allow the mind to be nourished and replenished with fresh and novel ideas.

Many years ago, I asked Ken Olsen, the founder of Digital Equipment Corporation: "what advice would you give to your colleagues, the CEOs of today?" He was at the top of his career, having founded the second largest computer company on the market at the time. He had become a "management philosopher." He paused a moment, and answered: "Go to church more often." I was puzzled. I knew that he was a very religious man, but why this strange advice? He noticed my disarray and pursued: "Yes, they should go to church more often, because that is the only place left in their lives where they have to sit down, be quiet, and listen!"

It takes a lot of energy and stamina to fight oneself out of a cosy and secure environment, and thereby avoid falling victim to complacency. Top managers are generally tempted to favour established strategies, which they have implemented successfully in the past. As a result, in a complacent company, anyone who wishes to depart from the "party line" is risking his career. It takes a lot of courage, will, and energy to lead the way and to continue to innovate at the top, because at that level, the prospective of a promotion is less of an incentive than personal accomplishment and satisfaction.

One of the best ways to avoid complacency is permanently to seek the *truth*. Being in touch with customers, and not necessarily the biggest, or the friendliest, customers, helps to avoid losing touch with reality. Executives must also identify those employees who are most likely to speak out and tell the whole story. In return, of course, they have to accept that they may not like what they hear (Figure 7.8). Young employees, who have just joined the corporation, generally have a pretty good idea of the key issues confronting the company. They can be an invaluable source of information, as they are not yet immersed in corporate politics, and are probably willing to speak their minds.

Finally, corporate boards have an enormous role to play in preventing the onset of management complacency. But boards themselves can

*"We are never more
than 2 years away
from failure!"*

Figure 7.8 – How secure are we? Bill Gates, the chairman of Microsoft, displayed remarkable lucidity when he made this statement a few years ago. Microsoft was already one of the most valuable companies in the world, at least in terms of market capitalisation. His statement shows that he recognised that the IT industry is a very volatile sector that can be changed quickly by technological innovation. Even large companies can enter oblivion – Enron, Andersen, Swissair, and Vivendi – nobody is protected by past success. (Reprinted with the permission of Microsoft Corporation.)

succumb to complacency; instead of being a counterbalance, they can become part of the problem. Complacency can become pervasive in board structures because of the way boards are elected, formed, and how they operate. It is often considered an honour to be elected to the board of a large, public company. In many instances, one is co-opted by peers, who themselves manage other institutions. To complicate the matter further, in some countries, such as Germany, the practice of cross membership of boards is widely accepted – "I am on your board, you are on my board, I do not ask you the tough questions, and you don't either."

Therefore, the way boards are elected, and how they operate, as well as their independence vis-à-vis management, are key safeguards against corporate complacency. Boards have an important role to play in competitiveness, precisely because they are there to make sure management does not lose touch with the reality of business. Boards are the last resort to force a firm to reinvent itself.

> *"The real difficulty lies, not in developing new ideas, but in escaping from old ones!"*
>
> John Maynard Keynes, 1883–1946

Moving away from the past is always a traumatising experience. For example, companies excel in *launching* new products and new services. However, what about *killing* old products? All companies are confronted with underperforming, ageing products that are not generating the same margin as before. In addition, such old products diffuse and crowd out new product offerings, confusing customers. There comes a time when a product has to go.

It is surprising how little management literature and theory exists on the subject of retiring products – it seems that, in many companies, the subject is taboo. One should never touch an old product. Although no one can remember why, there must be a good reason why it is still there. Sometimes, there is an emotional attachment to a product because it is part of the history of the company, or because it has been associated closely with a founder, or a past CEO. Rather than invent completely new products, companies reproduce old, successful models "ad æternam," gradually building upon them until they become obsolete. As a result, many companies are packed with dying products, which kill profitability and prevent new ones from emerging.

Reacting to change

Isambard Kingdom Brunel (Figure 7.9) was probably one of the most formidable engineers of all time, epitomising the Industrial Revolution in Great Britain. He designed and built bridges, railway stations, railways, tunnels, and three ships. These ships, the Great Western, the Great Britain, and the Great Eastern, were to revolutionise shipbuilding. They were, for the first time, built with an iron hull, powered with a steam engine, and driven by a screw propeller. The Great Eastern could sail non-stop to Australia with 4000 passengers on board!

Confronted with such a competitive breakthrough, what did the competition do? To counterbalance the technology of the new vessels, they added one more mast, then another one, and then another one. In 1902, the Baltimore shipyards launched the Thomas Lawson, with 7 masts and 25 sails. She did not last long. The world had changed.

THE NEW PARADIGM:

STEAM ENGINE – IRON HULL – SCREW PROPELLER-DRIVEN

HOW COMPETITORS
REACTED:

MORE OF THE
SAME OLD MODEL...

ISAMBARD K. BRUNEL
1806–1859

Figure 7.9 – Doing more of the same.

But when the world changes, how do most companies react? They do more of the same! If an advertising campaign does not succeed, more money will be poured into the next one. If a catalogue mailing does not work, more, bigger catalogues will be sent the next time. Companies are often "linear" and traditional in their reactions: they seldom do more, *differently* [12].

A permanent process of reinvention is probably better than a brutal attempt to change everything radically in one major corporate revolution. The fact remains that a reinvention process is always, potentially, destabilising for an organisation and its employees. Furthermore, it is probably more difficult to reinvent a company from within, than to create one from scratch. Reinventing a company means dealing with the cultural baggage of the company, its history, and the vested interests that resist any form of change. Even when firms want to reinvent themselves, they are confronted immediately with two key challenges:

1. *The introduction of a new business model probably implies cannibalising at least part of the existing business.*

    The revenue generated by a new business model will generally follow a U curve. Revenues drop during the first stage, when the new model is introduced, and also because of the cannibalisation

---

A major shake-up!

The Heinz tomato ketchup bottle has undergone a major revolution (Figure 7.10). The company realised that the old bottle was not used or stored the way it was marketed. Indeed, most households stored and used it upside-down. So, after a lot of reflection, they decided to undertake a major revolution: change the design of the bottle, and turn the label upside-down. Obvious? The old bottle was launched in 1872, the new one in 2002: 130 years! One can never be too careful.

Figure 7.10 – The world upside-down. (Reproduced by permission of H.J. Heinz Company.)

---

effect. At a later stage, revenues begin to recover, and hopefully grow, as the new model becomes fully operational at a higher level than when the reinventing took place. However, there is a real risk that partner companies from the old model – such as distributors – will not comply, and may even retaliate if they do not benefit at all from the new operating model.

Consequently, they may stop recommending the company's products to their own customers, and may reduce, or even eliminate, the company's products from their catalogue or shelves. It is, therefore, quite an act of faith to hope that the gains from the new business model will quickly offset the losses incurred during the transition period. In a business world, under the pressure of producing ever-growing quarterly results, very few executives are ready to take such risks.

2. *Changing a business model could mean changing the people who used to run the old business model.*

    The toughest challenge when reinventing a company is whether the new strategy can be executed without having to replace a significant portion of the firm's workforce. For example, sales executives, who have spent most of their lives dealing directly with customers, may not have the skills and attitudes necessary to run a distributorship sales structure. Similarly, managers used to dealing with wholesalers and intermediaries, may be at a loss if they have to deal directly with end-users – they may not know how to deal directly with customers' requests, reactions, and complaints.

The most delicate part of a reinvention process is not changing the business model, but getting the firm's corporate culture to adopt the new identity. Corporate culture plays an important role as a stabiliser – the compass that provides a sense of direction and predictability. Some corporate cultures sustain reinvention as a kind of continuous process. Other cultures may place more emphasis on tradition and continuity with the past. In both cases, whenever a strong reappraisal and reorientation of a company's strategy or structure occurs, the corporate culture is going to have to be somewhat adapted to a new reality. Reinvention alters both the business model and the core values of an enterprise. The issue is thus how to create company structures that do not block the ability of a company to reinvent whenever it is necessary.

Nokia provides an example of attempting to solve what can sometimes be considered as "trying to square the circle" in corporate structures. Nokia was founded in 1865, when engineer Frederik Idestam

---

Leaders and makers

There can be many market leaders, but only a few market makers. Leaders respond relatively better than their competitors to the needs of customers. Market makers, however, anticipate these needs and create new business lines and products to fulfil them – they create their own demand. In Figure 7.11, eBay and Amazon.com are market makers. Mobile telephony serves as another case in point. While some companies, like Motorola, pioneer the technology with their inventions, others, like Nokia, transform the technology into a market, and thus become a market maker. The 140-year-old company, Nokia, was built on an incred-

Figure 7.11 – From market leader to market maker.

ible reinvention process, departing completely from the historical products of the company, and building a totally new core competence in an emerging market: mobile telecommunications.

established a wood-pulp mill in the south of Finland. Later, the firm went into tyres, footwear (notably rubber boots), industrial parts, raincoats, TV sets, and electronics, among others. Most of the business units of Nokia were in traditional businesses. In 1990, Finland went into one of the deepest recessions in its history. Many companies were on the brink of bankruptcy. Nokia too had to reinvent itself. In May 1992, it took the historical decision to divest from all non-core businesses, and to focus on telecommunications. It was a good move. The 2100 phone series was targeted to sell 500 000 units. It sold 20 million! In 2004, Nokia had some 35 % of the world market share in mobile telephones. Perhaps these dramatic events induced Nokia to reflect on how to structuralise constant reinvention as a corporate strategy [13].

Companies find it hard to maintain, under a single roof, divisions that have to carry out the day-to-day profitable operations, with those that have to take an inventive approach and develop what could become the future of the firm. The people operating in product development have a very different personal profile and work style than those working in other business units. To reconcile these two aspects, Nokia has created a structure called the Nokia Ventures Organisation, operating in parallel with established business units.

Within this entity, rewards can be based more on entrepreneurship and risk-taking, than execution and bottom line results, as is the case in existing businesses. Its objective is "to identify and develop new business ideas outside Nokia's current focus, and to contribute to the growth and renewal of existing core businesses." When a business idea reaches a certain level of maturity, existing business units can then take over. Nokia's approach solves both the structural and the cultural obstacles to reinvention and innovation – it is an example of institutionalised reinvention within the context of a firm.

The ability of a company and its people to reinvent themselves and their products are keys to competitiveness. This relies heavily on institutional resilience, as well as individual resilience. Furthermore, in the mindset of competitiveness, reinvention keeps the firm ahead of the pack – it forces competitors to play *catch-me-if-you-can*. However, we cannot underestimate the challenge of achieving constant reinvention as an internal process. Usually, reinvention drives come as the result of external disruption, such as restructuring or mergers. Even acquisitions can provide a business opportunity to inject fresh perspectives and rejuvenate a corporate culture. Nestlé's management took the opportunity provided by the acquisition of Carnation (evaporated milk) in the US, and Rowntree (chocolate confectionery) in the UK as a way to revitalise the traditional culture of the Swiss mother company.

Reinvention can be provoked in one of two ways. First, it can be a *reactive* process, motivated by the necessity to overcome adverse conditions encountered by the firm. Second, reinvention can be a *proactive* process, institutionalised into the overall strategy of a successful company seeking to maximise its competitive advantage. Reinventions undertaken in a position of success are a clear sign of the strength of a company. In such cases, the impelling force of urgency is not there. The greatest successes in reinventing a company and its people have thus occurred in organisations with a robust corporate culture, or with people of solid character and values.

Those firms or individuals who *redefine the rules of the game* constantly – not just for them, but also for competitors – have indeed achieved the ultimate level of competitiveness.

Epilogue: A Beautiful, Competitive Mind

> *"Doubt is not a pleasant condition,*
> *but certainty is absurd."*
>
> Voltaire 1694–1778

Competitive people are always operating in a mindset of competitiveness, striving to make choices and implement decisions that increase competitiveness. These people have "competitive minds." Their competitiveness mindset generates the types of behaviours that have been described in the preceding chapter. *What* competitive minds decide can be described and analysed. *Why* they think in this mindset is more difficult to explain. Some of the most competitive people – including very successful business leaders – find it difficult to explain *why* they act in this particular way. They are just as puzzled as anyone else.

A few years ago, a friend of mine told me: "Business leaders don't think, they act!" This statement shocked me. At the time, I was working in situations that put me in contact with many business leaders; to be told that these leaders do not *think* was to me a crime of *lèse majesté*. Nevertheless, somewhere deep inside of me the remark struck a chord, and it got me thinking about what is so special about the mindset of competitiveness. I knew that finding a business leader capable of generating excitement in a plenary session at a large conference was an organiser's nightmare. There is even a widely held notion that captains of industry are poor communicators! Worse, they often give the impression that they have nothing of importance to say beyond the scope of their company!

I began to realise that business leaders do *think*, but that they are not really conscious of their *thinking* process. What appears to be a lack of intellectual depth, is, in fact, indicative of a different type of intelligence – an unconventional way of approaching problems. For business leaders, their thinking process, or why they take decisions, is less important than the outcome! Scholars, however, are interested in finding out what the secret *is*.

The thought process of a competitive business leader is quite different to that of others. In their thinking, abstract concepts don't exist. Intuition replaces theory. Only the market can validate, or invalidate, their assumptions. Trial and error defines the way ahead. Problems are sought out, not avoided. Action is not a means, but an end in itself.

Marx said all philosophy is *praxis* – philosophy doesn't exist without the possibility of being transformed into action. If so, then all business leaders are unknowingly Marxists, since their main purpose is to take action.

Business leaders trust their gut feelings and intuition when faced with a problem, rather than relying solely on rational analysis. They have an intuitive sense for what will work and what will not; when something is right, or when it is not. Anticipating the market is their priority: the desire to act is stronger than any other. Having such an action-driven, intuitive mindset, it is difficult for business leaders to explain, or conceptualise, the reason for their success.

It is possible to find some elements of explanation in theories like Kant's *a priori*, or Locke's empiricism, or in the English behaviouralists. However, I prefer the ideas suggested by the Austrian philosopher Karl Popper – one of the most important scholars of scientific philosophy in the 20th century (Figure 1) [1, 2]. What follows, is a brief sketch of Popper's ideas.

Competitiveness is not the accumulation of certainties

Scientific advancement occurs when a theory is proved false, and is replaced with a better explanation or interpretation of observed reality. Consider, for example, the following statement: "All swans are white." In Popper's view, the fact that we see only white swans in our countries every day, no matter how numerous, *doesn't* necessarily mean that the statement is correct. If the theory is proven "false" by the discovery of a black swan – which, in fact, did happen for the first time near Perth, Australia – it becomes invalidated, and is replaced by a new theory: one that includes the possibility of black swans. Einstein's general theory of relativity replaced and complemented Newton's gravitational theory, by proving that it was partially incorrect; thereby providing a better approximation of reality. His theory will continue to prevail until someone else advances science by proving that Einstein was, at least partly, wrong, and offering an extension, or replacement, theory.

Business leaders do the same – they operate under a set of assumptions that they hold until proven wrong. Competitiveness is often about attacking the established business model of the market leader until it is

Figure 1 – Sir Karl Popper (1902–1994). Popper's work on the philosophy of science, and his reflection on society and politics, have had a considerable impact on many generations of scientists, politicians, and scholars. His two main books, *The Logic of Scientific Discovery* (1934) and *The Open Society and its Enemies* (1945), are his most influential publications. His principle of "falsifiability," as a criterion for demarking science from non-science, is now a fundamental part of philosophy. (Reproduced by permission of Getty Images.)

proven to be wrong. The secret desire of most IT entrepreneurs is to prove that Bill Gates's paradigm of the computer world has become obsolete, and, of course, to replace it with their own. Deep inside, most companies do not compete with competitors just to outperform them, but to prove that their business model is incorrect and, ultimately, to eliminate them.

Competitiveness is developed through trial and error

In Popper's framework, knowledge progresses through the discovery of breakdowns, or inconsistencies, that invalidate an established theory. Most of the time, it is not the result of a rational and consistent reflection, but rather of trial and error: even random twists of fate have been responsible for some of the biggest scientific breakthroughs! When a piece of the theory crumbles, the entire theory quickly begins to unravel.

If a theory is not completely consistent, if there is one exception, it is, by definition, flawed. The smallest fault is enough to invalidate a theory. Once this happens, the search for a new explanation begins – one which also addresses the discovered flaw.

Business leaders are not markedly different in the way they operate. Competitive businesses are energetic, quick-minded, dedicated to action, and resilient. They just try and try again. When a market leader declines, it is not because it has fallen victim or prey to the carefully devised plan of an individual competitor. In a free market environment, large numbers of entrepreneurs, working independently, are trying constantly to do everything possible to destabilise the leader. The *number* of blows the market leader receives is what dethrones it, not the existence of a sophisticated plan to do so. Here, again, trial and error applies.

Popper's theories, as they relate to the behaviour of business leaders, bear a great deal of similarity with the process of "creative destruction," proposed by Joseph Schumpeter. No matter how successful the business model of a company, the market, which is composed of competitors, partners, consumers, and legislators, never stops testing the model to its limits. Unless a firm reacts and adapts constantly, it will not survive. Actually, most of them don't – the vast majority of companies don't last more than 50 years.

Strong competitiveness models accept internal criticism

For Karl Popper, the strength of the democratic system lies in its capacity for self-criticism, its acceptance of constant internal attacks, and its search for mistakes; thereby allowing it to reform continuously and strengthen itself. In contrast, the fatal weakness of communism, as we now realise, was precisely the refusal of internal criticism and the absence of an opportunity to reassess and adapt to changing conditions (Figure 2). The fundamental criticism of communism is not so much that it was flawed as a theory. Communism failed because it was static and inward looking, rather than because it was, at the origin at least, ill-conceived as a system.

One of the causes of communism's downfall – unquestionable certainties – also exists as a cause of decline in competitiveness for companies. Such certainties are the root of complacency and arrogance within a firm. Companies that do not pay attention to internal criticism are doomed to fail, since they cut themselves off from the prime source of invigoration allowing any organisation to reform or reinvent itself.

**Figure 2 – A world of certainties. Within the Soviet model of
communism, uncertainty did not exist. The party and the leader (here
Stalin) would show the way, and have an answer to every question.
Therefore, the system could never be questioned, or criticised.
Communism declined because it lacked the internal criticism necessary
to reform itself and adapt to a changing world. The same situation can
occur in companies: failure to accept criticism, or to pay attention to
new ideas, can lead to a loss in competitiveness.**

Even the most successful business model, or the most profitable
company, cannot survive in the long term by solely managing the *status
quo*. If it breeds "yes-people," relies on past recipes for future success,
avoids hearing bad news, and shies away from radical ideas, such a
firm will be added to the list of extinct species, just like communist
societies.

Authentic scientists spend their time testing their own theories, seeking
weaknesses in a kind of self-destructive process that helps them to
advance further. Competitive leaders do the same: they seek out and
correct the flaws in their business model constantly, as well as the weaknesses within the company: killing their own obsolete products and out-
dated ideas before the competition kills them.

Competitiveness also thrives on thinking the unthinkable

Like scientists, competitive business leaders advance their knowledge by testing the consequences of their intuition on the market. Einstein made this point: "Progress is not the result of an accumulation of information, but the fruit of daring speculation." While the basic assumptions need not necessarily be rational, the management of an intuitive breakthrough must logically follow: implementation of the strategy must be flawless. One could even argue that the basic assumptions for true breakthroughs, or new theories, might even appear "absurd" at first glance.

All the great business success stories are based on apparently absurd theories. We have highlighted earlier in this book how "absurd" the business model of IKEA, or McDonald's, would have seemed to many at the time they were launched. Would people actually buy furniture they had to build themselves? Would people go to a restaurant where they pay for their food, wait in front of the kitchen to collect it on a small tray, and then carry it themselves to the table? More recently, the same could be said of Amazon.com, easyJet or eBay. The odds are, that in a market economy that allows the proliferation of enterprises, "rational" ideas are exploited fully. As a result, the creation of a new business paradigm remains mostly the exclusive terrain of entrepreneurs, who break the mould intuitively, and think the unthinkable.

At the famous Solvay Congress (Figure 3), which brought together the most important scientists of the world at the beginning of the 20th century, Niels Bohr and Einstein were discussing the future. Bohr became irritated with the turn of the conversation and interrupted Einstein, saying: "Stop trying to be logical, the future is not logical. Try to think instead." All too often we reduce thinking to an exercise in logic. Intuitively, business leaders know that logic alone does not help to go forward. Without being too provocative, these statements help us understand why so many "ignorant and uncultivated" business people can still be successful. Unknowingly, they managed to escape from traditional thinking that would destine them to foreseeable obsolescence. A touch of ignorance is a great asset in business: moderately ignorant business leaders are not hostages of a past of which they are unaware; they are not fearful of risks and consequences they cannot assess. Intellectuals have much more trouble acting this way.

A competitive mind has the ability to be detached from the past, and even to be unemotional about it. Of course, the history of a company makes it easier to understand the present, and the issues that it must confront tomorrow; but having a history does not guarantee having a future!

Figure 3 – The Solvay Congress. Belgian industrialist Ernest Solvay (1838–1922) initiated, in 1911, a series of conferences, gathering the most talented scientists of the day to discuss the latest developments in physics. These conferences were held every three years: first at the Institute of Physiology, then, from 1930 onward, at the Free University of Brussels. This picture, taken in 1927, features an impressive gathering of brilliant individuals such as Einstein, Planck, Mme Curie, Bohr, de Broglie, Schroedinger, Pauli, Heisenberg, and Dirac.

The future is not what it used to be . . .
(Paul Valery)

Our brave new world offers an unprecedented amount of opportunities for nations, firms, and individuals. Never before in history have so many people been able to communicate, interact, and exchange goods and ideas with so many other people. Never before has the world been so open, transparent, and accessible. During the past three decades, many barriers and walls have fallen. There are very few places left in the world that do not want to be part of the world!

Yet, this world is also highly volatile and unpredictable. The multiplication of decision-makers – almost two hundred countries, hundreds of millions of companies, six billion individuals – also entails a multiplication of potential breakdown points. The vulnerability of the system seems to increase in direct proportion with its growth. As the world economic environment expands its horizons, it appears to become more permeable to external disruption. "If only the world would stop interfering with our strategy . . ."; unfortunately, the world will increasingly interfere and change the rules of the game. The *context of business* –

the outside world – becomes as important as the *content of business* – being efficient – to ensuring success.

The theory of competitiveness provides the tools to manage such a complex environment. Competitiveness integrates the various facets of the economy – government policies, management practices, education, value systems, technology, and infrastructure – to create an environment conducive to prosperity. It also integrates the softer drivers of prosperity – some of the fundamental characteristics of a post-industrialised society – into a coherent framework.

Competitiveness thrives on competitive people. Are people naturally competitive, or is it a set of skills that can be taught? The answer is probably somewhere in between. Certain individuals probably have a natural aptitude; perhaps not a given *ability* to compete, but the *desire* to compete. Yet, not everyone aspires for superiority: some people even strongly reject the notion of striving for supremacy – they are much more consensus-oriented. After all, societies set limits on the wild, competitive nature of some of their members to ensure the protection of the weakest, and/or less privileged.

One cannot oblige people to compete – the desire to do so is self-imposed. Many business leaders are mistaken in assuming that all of their employees are as keen to beat the competition as they are, as we have seen in the model illustrating the motivation of the *tigers*, *cats*, and *bears*. A rough and tough corporate culture may not always match the aspirations and values of individuals living in a post-industrial society. The "good old days," when the strategy of a company relied on war examples drawn from Sun Tzu, the legendary Chinese military writer, or from Carl von Clausewitz, the German strategist, are over [3, 4]. Competitiveness, as we have seen in this book, is a bit subtler . . .

However, if someone *has* the desire to compete, and is willing to understand the new rules of competitiveness, and to acquire the competencies required, then competitiveness can indeed turn out to be a formidable enabler of success and prosperity. Competitiveness aims at unleashing energy, expanding horizons, and opening new frontiers. This is an ambitious goal, for a nation, a firm, or an individual. Yet, competitiveness is precisely about *raising the general level of ambition*, an aspiration so well encapsulated by Salvador Dali:

> *"At the age of six I wanted to be a cook. At seven I wanted to be Napoleon. And my ambition has been growing steadily ever since . . ."*

> Salvador Dali (1904–1989)

References

Prologue

1. Brown, L. (1993) *The New Shorter Oxford English Dictionary on Historical Principles*. Oxford: Clarendon Press.
2. IMD (2005) *IMD World Competitiveness Yearbook*. Lausanne, Switzerland: IMD International.

Chapter 1

1. Descartes, R. and Clarke, D.M. (1999) *Discourse on Method and Related Writings*. London: Penguin Books.
2. Krugman, P. (1994) Competitiveness: a dangerous obsession. *Foreign Affairs*, 73(2), 28–44.
3. Berner, R., Kiley, D., Der Hovanesian, M., Rowley, I. and Arndt, M. (2005) Special Report – The Best Global Brands; BusinessWeek/Interbrand rank the companies that best built their images – and made them stick, *Business Week*. p. 86.
4. Drucker, P.F. (1954) *The Practice of Management*. New York: Harper.
5. World Commission on Environment and Development (1987) *Our Common Future*. Oxford: Oxford University Press.
6. Dubai Chamber of Commerce and Industry (2004) *Dubai: The City of Opportunities*. Dubai, UAE.
7. United Nations Department of Economic and Social Affairs Population Division (2003) *World Population Prospects: The 2002 Revision*. New York: United Nations. CD-ROM.
8. Schumacher, E.F. (1973) *Small is Beautiful: A Study of Economics as if People Mattered*. London: Blond and Briggs.
9. HP (2001) *The HP Story – 60 Years of Innovation*. www.hp.com/hpinfo/abouthp/histnfacts/, HP.

Chapter 2

1. Smith, A. and Cannan, E. (1904) *An Inquiry into the Nature and Causes of the Wealth of Nations*. London: Methuen & Co.

2. Hume, D. (1752) *Political Discourses*. Edinburgh: Printed by R. Fleming for A. Kincaid and A. Donaldson.
3. Marshall, A. (1907) *Principles of Economics*, 5th edition. London: Macmillan.
4. Say, J.B., Princep, C.R. and Biddle, C.C. (1964) *A Treatise on Political Economy; or, The Production, Distribution & Consumption of Wealth*. Reprints of economic classics. New York: A. M. Kelley bookseller.
5. Ricardo, D. (1819) *On the Principles of Political Economy and Taxation*, 2nd edition. London: John Murray.
6. Braudel, F., *et al.* (1998) *Les Mémoires de la Méditerranée: Préhistoire et Antiquité*. Paris: Éditions de Fallois.
7. de Vivo, G. (1985) Robert Torrens and Ricardo's "Corn-Ratio" Theory of Profits. *Cambridge Journal of Economics*, **9**(1): 89–92.
8. Marx, K. (1872) *Das Kapital. Kritik der Politischen Oekonomic*. Hamburg: O. Meissner.
9. Polo, M., Yule, H. and Cordier, H. (1993) *The Travels of Marco Polo: The Complete Yule–Cordier Edition, including the unabridged third edition (1903) of Henry Yule's annotated translation, as revised by Henri Cordier, together with Cordier's later volume of notes and addenda (1920)*. New York: Dover Publications.
10. Temple, R.K.G. (1986) *China, Land of Discovery*. Multimedia Publications.
11. Needham, J., *et al.* (1954) *Science and Civilisation in China*. Cambridge: Cambridge University Press.
12. Malthus, T.R. (1798) *An essay on the principle of population, as it affects the future improvement of society microform: with remarks on the speculations of Mr. Godwin, M. Condorcet and other writers*. London: Printed for J. Johnson.
13. Menzies, G. (2002) *1421: The Year China Discovered the World*. London: Bantam.
14. Uglow, J.S. (2002) *The Lunar Men: The Friends who Made the Future, 1730–1810*. London: Faber.
15. Weber, M. and Parsons, T. (1958) *The Protestant Ethic and the Spirit of Capitalism*. New York: Scribner.
16. Peyrefitte, A. (1976) *Le Mal Français*. Paris: Plon.
17. Albert, M. (1991) *Capitalisme Contre Capitalisme: L'Histoire immédiate*. Paris: Editions du Seuil.
18. IMD (2005) *IMD World Competitiveness Yearbook*. Lausanne, Switzerland: IMD International.
19. Schumpeter, J.A. (1947) *Capitalism, Socialism, and Democracy,* 2nd edition. New York: Harper & Brothers.
20. Donahue, P. (1989) *Ray Kroc: The Man behind McDonald's*. Princeton, NJ: Films for the Humanities (distributor).
21. Sloan, A.P., McDonald, J. and Stevens, C. (1964) *My Years with General Motors*. Garden City, NY: Doubleday.
22. Gates, B., Myhrvold, N. and Rinearson, P. (1995) *The Road Ahead*. New York: Viking.
23. Drucker, P.F. (1969) *The Age of Discontinuity: Guidelines to our Changing Society*. New York: Harper & Row.

24. Solow, R. (1988) Growth Theory and After. *American Economic Review,* 78(3), 307–17.

25. Gellner, E. (1983) *Nations and Nationalism.* Oxford: Blackwell.

26. Negroponte, N. (1995) *Being Digital.* New York: Knopf.

27. Porter, M.E. (1998) *The Competitive Advantage of Nations: With a New Introduction.* Basingstoke: Macmillan.

28. Morita, A., Reingold, E.M. and Shimomura, M. (1986) *Made in Japan: Akio Morita and Sony.* New York: Dutton.

29. Porter, M.E., Monitor Group, and Harvard Business School (2001) *Clusters of Innovation Initiative. Atlanta – Columbus.* Washington, DC: Council on Competitiveness.

30. Ge, W. (Ed.) (1999) *Special Economic Zones and the Economic Transition in China: Economic ideas leading to the 21st century;* vol. 5. Singapore: World Scientific.

31. World Bank Group (1995) *World Development Report 1995: Workers in an Integrating World.* Washington, DC: O.U. Press.

Chapter 3

1. Molière and Sahlins, B. (2000) *The Bourgeois Gentleman.* Plays for performance. Chicago: I.R. Dee.

2. Sun, T. and Cleary, T. (1998) *The Illustrated Art of War.* Boston: Shambhala; distributed in the US by Random House.

3. Machiavelli, N. and Bondanella, P.E. (2005) *The Prince.* Oxford: Oxford University Press.

4. Friedman, M. (1991) *Monetarist Economics.* IEA masters of modern economics. Cambridge, USA: Blackwell.

5. IMD (2005) *IMD World Competitiveness Yearbook.* Lausanne, Switzerland: IMD International.

6. OECD (1996) *Benchmark Definition of Foreign Direct Investment,* 3rd edition. Paris: OECD.

7. General Agreement on Tariffs and Trade (1979) *The Tokyo round of multilateral trade negotiations.* Geneva.

8. Julius, D.S. (1990) *Global Companies & Public Policy: The Growing Challenge of Foreign Direct Investment.* London: Thomson Learning.

9. Carnegie, A. (1962) *The Gospel of Wealth and Other Timely Essays,* reprint of 1900 edition. Cambridge, US: Harvard University Press.

10. Hamilton, J. and Trautmann, T. (2002) *Sarbanes–Oxley Act of 2002: Law and Explanation.* Chicago: CCH Inc.

11. Organisation for Economic Co-operation and Development (2000) *Measuring Student Knowledge and Skills: The PISA 2000 Assessment of Reading, Mathematical and Scientific Literacy.* Paris: OECD.

12. World Wildlife Fund (2002) *Living Planet Report.* Gland, Switzerland: World Wildlife Fund.

13. Morlot, J.C. and OECD (1999) *National Climate Policies and the Kyoto Protocol.* Paris: OECD.

14. Wallender, H.W. and Council of the Americas (1973) *The Andean Pact: Definition, Design, and Analysis.* New York: Council of the Americas.
15. US Department of the Treasury, Office of Foreign Assets (1976) *Foreign Assets Control Regulations and Related Documents.* Washington, DC: Supt. of Docs. US GPO.
16. Blair, T. (1998) *The Third Way: New Politics for the New Century.* Fabian pamphlet 588. London: Fabian Society.
17. See the Horatio Alger Society http://www.ihot.com/~has/ for a list of publications.
18. Yew, L.K. (1998) *The Singapore Story: Memoirs of Lee Kuan Yew.* Singapore: Singapore Press Holdings.

Chapter 4

1. Dell, M. and Fredman, C. (1999) *Direct from Dell: Strategies that Revolutionized an Industry.* New York: HarperBusiness.
2. Hamel, G. and Prahalad, C.K. (1989) Strategic Intent. *Harvard Business Review*, 67(3), 63.
3. Hamel, G. and Prahalad, C.K. (1994) *Competing for the Future.* Boston: Harvard Business School Press.
4. Chiu, T. and Perot, H.R. (1992) *Ross Perot in His Own Words.* New York: Warner Books.
5. Deming, W.E. (1986) *Out of the Crisis.* Cambridge, US: Massachusetts Institute of Technology Center for Advanced Engineering Study.
6. Deming, W.E. (2000) *The New Economics: For Industry, Government, Education,* 2nd edition. Cambridge, US: MIT Press.
7. Juran, J.M. (2004) *Architect of Quality.* New York: McGraw-Hill.
8. Feigenbaum, A.V. (1991) *Total Quality Control,* 3rd edition. New York: McGraw-Hill.
9. Crosby, P.B. (1979) *Quality is Free: The Art of Making Quality Certain.* New York: Penguin.
10. Hammer, M. and Champy, J. (1993) *Reengineering the Corporation: A Manifesto for Business Revolution.* New York: HarperBusiness.
11. Deloitte Touche Tohmatsu (2003) *The Macro-Economic Case for Outsourcing.* Deloitte Research.
12. IMD (2005) *IMD World Competitiveness Yearbook.* Lausanne, Switzerland: IMD International.
13. Offshoring: Relocating the Back Office. *The Economist.* 13 December 2003.
14. Peppers, D. and Rogers, M. (1993) *The One to One Future: Building Relationships One Customer at a Time.* New York: Currency/Doubleday.
15. Contact Center (2003) *The Contact Center Benchmarking Report.* www.callcentres.com.au/global_call_centre_benchmarking.htm.
16. Whiteman, J. (2001) Mass Customization: A Long March. *The Economist,* 12 July.

Chapter 5

1. Handy, C.B. (1991) *The Age of Unreason,* 2nd edition. London: Business Books.
2. IMD (2005) *IMD World Competitiveness Yearbook.* Lausanne, Switzerland: IMD International.
3. Foss, N.J. (2005) *Strategy, Economic Organisation, and the Knowledge Economy: The Coordination of Firms and Resources.* Oxford: Oxford University Press.
4. Rifkin, J. (1995) *The End of Work: The Decline of the Global Labor Force and the Dawn of the Post-market Era.* New York: G.P. Putnam.
5. Kanter, R.M. (1989) *When Giants Learn to Dance: Mastering the Challenge of Strategy, Management, and Careers in the 1990s.* New York: Simon and Schuster.

Chapter 6

1. Dentsu Institute for Human Studies (1995) *Human Studies* (Number 15). Dentsu Institute for Human Studies, Japan.
2. IMD (2005) *IMD World Competitiveness Yearbook.* Lausanne, Switzerland: IMD International.
3. Maddison, A. (2003) ARTICLE/BOOK TITLE HERE. Paris: OECD.
4. Perlmutter, H.V. (1969) The Tortuous Evolution of the Multinational Corporation. *Columbia Journal of World Business,* Jan/Feb, 9–18.

Chapter 7

1. Fayol, H. and Gray, I. (1984) *General and Industrial Management,* revised edition. New York: Institute of Electrical and Electronics Engineers.
2. Dell, M. and Fredman, C. (1999) *Direct from Dell: Strategies that Revolutionised an Industry.* New York: HarperBusiness.
3. Gupta, P. (2004) *Six Sigma Business Scorecard: Ensuring Performance for Profit.* New York: McGraw-Hill.
4. Pendergrast, M. (1993) *For God, Country, and Coca-Cola: The Unauthorised History of the Great American Soft Drink and the Company that Makes it.* New York: Scribner's.
5. Mintzberg, H. (2004) *Managers, Not MBAs: A Hard Look at the Soft Practice of Managing and Management Development.* San Francisco: Berrett-Koehler.
6. Roddick, A. (2000) *Business as Unusual.* London: Thorsons.
7. Herzberg, F. (1959) *The Motivation to Work.* New York: John Wiley & Sons, Inc.
8. George, B. (2003) Why is it hard to do it right? *Fortune, Time Inc.* 15 September.

9. Harcourt, G.C., Riach, P.A. and Keynes, J.M. (1997) *A "Second Edition" of The General Theory.* New York: Routledge.
10. Chriss, N. (1996) *Black–Scholes and Beyond: Option Pricing Models.* Chicago: Irwin.
11. Ferry, J., Hayek, N. and BBC (1998) *A Brief History of Swatch: Swiss.* BBC Videos for Education and Training. London: Films for the Humanities & Sciences (distributor).
12. Buchanan, R.A. (2002) *Brunel: The Life and Times of Isambard Kingdom Brunel.* London: Hambledon and London.
13. Steinbock, D. (2001) *The Nokia Revolution: The Story of an Extraordinary Company that Transformed an Industry.* New York: AMACOM.

Epilogue

1. Popper, K.R. (2002) *The Open Society and its Enemies,* 5th edition. London: Routledge.
2. Popper, K.R. (2002) *The Logic of Scientific Discovery.* London: Routledge.
3. Sun, T. and Cleary, T. (1998) *The Illustrated Art of War.* Boston: Shambhala, distributed in the US by Random House.
4. von Clausewitz, C., *et al.* (2001) *Clausewitz on Strategy: Inspiration and Insight from a Master Strategist.* New York: John Wiley & Sons, Inc.

Index